THE LORD WAS AT GLASTONBURY

First Published 2010
Copyright © Paul Ashdown 2010

Published by The Squeeze Press
8A Market Place, Glastonbury, Somerset BA6 9HW

A CIP catalogue record for this book is
available from the British Library
ISBN13: 978-1-906069-08-7

Typeset by Wooden Books Ltd,
Glastonbury, Somerset.

Printed and bound by Replika Press, India

www.woodenbooks.com

the
SQUEEZE
PRESS

THE LORD
was at
GLASTONBURY

SOMERSET AND THE JESUS VOYAGE STORY

PAUL ASHDOWN

Fig 1. *Henry Jenner in 1916. A scholar of 'encyclopaedic mind', he was a father of the Cornish language revival, became Cornwall's first Grand Bard, and was Godfather to the Jesus Voyage story.*

Preface

Introduction   1

THE LORD was at Glastonbury in the body and blessed the thorn.

Christopher Smart, *Jubilate Agno*, c.1760,
Fragment B2, line 232.

NEVER THROW ridicule on tradition, because something has happened, something must have given rise to it. It is not to be trusted; but if used carefully it is often useful, and we ought to ask ourselves 'what does it mean?'

Joseph Armitage Robinson, 1909,
On Westminster Abbey's traditions,
as quoted in T. F. Taylor's *J. Armitage Robinson*,
Cambridge, 1991, p. 38.

AND JESUS was a sailor when he walked upon the waters ... and when he knew for certain only drowning men could see him, he said all men shall be sailors then until the seas shall free them.

Leonard Cohen, *Suzanne*, 1966.

PREFACE

This work began as a paper, the bounds of which were soon exceeded as the array of scarcely credible characters who fill its pages began to assert themselves. It was transmuted from the exploration of an obscure byway in local Glastonbury historiography into something more like a study in English attitudes, not least in those tragic and crucial years surrounding the Great War, which I hope may perhaps be of rather broader interest.

In its fairly long gestation, this study has been aided by discussion with, and suggestions from, many people. My thanks are especially due to the irreplaceable David Bromwich, sadly now retired from the Somerset Studies Library, Taunton, whose knowledge of Somerset historical materials is seemingly inexhaustible; to Prof. Michelle Brown, for help with the bibliography of the 'Rood at the North Door' of Old St Paul's; to Dr Timothy Hopkinson Ball for rediscovering the text of the Pilton play and for much other help with source material; to Joanne Laing of the Cornish Studies Library, Redruth, for much assistance; to Abba Seraphim, Coptic Metropolitan of Glastonbury, for the background to R. W. Morgan; and perhaps most of all to Dr Adam Stout for directing me to the work, hitherto unnoticed by myself and many others, of Christopher Smart, firstly in the pages of his study *The Thorn and the Waters* (2007), in which he first drew attention to Smart's significance for Glastonbury studies, and subsequently in personal discussion and a generous sharing of materials. Thanks are also due the staff of the Wedgwood Museum, Barlaston, to Patrick Benham, Neill Bonham, Trevor Maskery, and not least to Diane Parker, maid of Taunton and muse of its birth.

Paul Ashdown, Candlemas 2010.

THE Son of God
Thy hill hath trod
And its curse is broken.

INTRODUCTION

One of the most widespread of modern historical legends, familiar, however vaguely, to most people in this country, is that Jesus came to Britain as a youth with Joseph of Arimathea, and that this belief inspired the poetic lines of William Blake, *And did those feet in Ancient Time walk upon England's mountains green ..?*, set to music by Sir Hubert Parry in 1916 as the hymn *Jerusalem*. Just as *Flower of Scotland*, first performed by the modern folk-group *The Corries* in 1967,[1] became, by popular acclaim, a national anthem for Scots, so *Jerusalem* has become the unofficial anthem of England, dear to nationalists and leftist radicals alike.[2] In September 2009 the *Daily Telegraph* carried an item headed 'Council drowned out by Jerusalem,' which related how the town council in Beaminster, Dorset, was obliged to move its meetings to avoid 'the "raucous" noise from the local Women's Institute singing *Jerusalem*.'[3] Beyond any institutional context, it is still sometimes sung spontaneously at moments felt to carry a particular communal solemnity. When called upon to suggest hymns for church services, for weddings and the like, even, perhaps especially, for persons of no particular devotional background, *Jerusalem* is among the most popular choices, often

1   Written by Roy Williamson, 1965, music composed by Peter McCormick.
2   Mary Lynn Johnson (2003, '*Milton* and its contexts', in the 'Cambs. Comp. to Wllm. Blake', p. 237) has described it as 'this alternative national anthem for England as a spiritual and eternal state'; Blake himself might have balked at the word 'state'.
3   *Daily Telegraph*, 25.9.09, p. 17.

to the despair of modern clergy who are most unhappy with its apocryphal overtones. More than one has banned it from church. Yet this cultural phenomenon has aroused surprisingly little curiosity among historians and folklorists. The Anglo-Saxonist and broadcaster Michael Wood seemingly takes the antiquity of the legend at face value when he writes:

> There is even an old story that Christ himself came here to Glastonbury, a story William Blake used in creating what is often described as our real national anthem: 'Jerusalem'. So when we sing 'And did those feet in ancient times ...' at the Last Night of the Proms, we are actually celebrating a Glastonbury legend (which Elton John echoed in his song for Diana, Princess of Wales at her funeral service in Westminster Abbey).[4]

The only serious academic study of the 'tradition' to date was offered in 1989 in the journal *Folklore* by A. W. Smith, who had previously written on the legends surrounding St Augustine, leader of the 597 AD Papal mission to convert the Anglo-Saxons, and on that of King Lucius, supposedly Britain's first Christian monarch, reigning in the late second century. Smith expressed the hope that his examination of the subject would 'be seen as the most significant unit in these studies of the folklore of Christian origins in Britain,' and it formed the starting-point of the present study. However, Smith admitted that his 'attempts to probe into its roots' were still incomplete. In particular, more may be said of the reception of the legend at Glastonbury, with which it is now perhaps most often associated; further, Smith seems to have been quite seriously misled about aspects of the medieval background to the belief. In both these respects I hope here to supplement his often valuable work.

The voyage-story may be summarised as follows: Joseph of Arimathea, the wealthy secret follower of Jesus who eventually buried

4 Wood, 1999, p. 44.

Him in his own tomb (as told in the Gospels) was actually a relative of the Holy Family. He had made his money as a metal-merchant dealing in British tin. In Jesus's youth, in some versions after the death of Joseph of Nazareth, who is last heard of in scripture when Jesus is about twelve, Joseph the Arimathean took Him on one of his mercantile voyages to Britain. In some versions of the story they end their journey at Glastonbury. Jesus is sometimes said to return alone to Glastonbury in His late twenties to prepare in seclusion for His public ministry, perhaps by studying the wisdom of the druids, who are held to have maintained a college there. Joseph of Arimathea returns to the hallowed spot after the Crucifixion, bearing the Grail and perhaps other relics of the Passion, to found Britain's first Christian community.

Joseph had already been identified as the founder of the church of Glastonbury in the High Middle Ages, in written accounts dating from the thirteenth century onwards. The Jesus story, thus baldly stated, and slotted, as it were, into the void between the Gospel accounts and the medieval Grail romances in which Joseph figured, appears so unlikely that it may be wondered at that it has found any serious adherents at all beyond an inevitable lunatic fringe. Yet until very recent years, and perhaps still, it has been a quiet cornerstone of faith to devout and otherwise seemingly quite sensible people. For example, in 1991 Prebendary Francis Vere Hodge, a former war-time R.A.F. chaplain and a parish priest of many years experience, a saintly man then Chairman of the Glastonbury Abbey Trustees, compiled with great care a small book, with various prayers and notes on the saints of Glastonbury, as part of his efforts to raise funds for a new visitor's centre. Entitled *Glastonbury Gleanings*, it carried a foreword by the then Bishop of Bath and Wells and Archbishop-designate of Canterbury, George Carey. Vere Hodge summarised the 'Somerset Tradition', adding: 'One cannot prove the truth of this by written evidence, but it has been an oral tradition which many Somerset people - and I am one of them - believe is true.'[5] His belief was that the special atmosphere of Glastonbury Abbey, to which many are sensitive, was a product of Christ having been personally present there.

Although its heyday was from the later 1920s to the early 1950s, the story is far from dead, and most of the popular works on Somerset folklore and on Glastonbury and its legends which have been written since continue to make some reference to it. *The Somerset Book*, published in the county in 1982, illustrated with beautiful drawings by Pauline Clements, and with a text by James Robertson, recorded optimistically:

> [Glastonbury] received several visits from Christ who used to come to Somerset quite regularly during his youth with his uncle Joseph of Arimathea who was a tin merchant. On one of these visits Christ built a little church at Glastonbury and preached the Gospel, antedating St Augustine by more than half a millennium and inspiring William Blake to write 'And did those feet in ancient time walk upon England's mountains green?'[6]

Less parochially, that contemporary Bible of international travellers, the *Lonely Planet* guide, records in its British volume that: 'Myths and legends about Glastonbury abound. One story tells how Jesus came here with his great-uncle Joseph of Arimathea, while another reports Joseph bringing the chalice of the Last Supper with him', thus ensuring world-wide transmission of the story to a new generation of back-packing 'pilgrims.'[7]

For the historian, the problem with the tale is not its inherent unlikeliness - far more unlikely things found belief in former times - but the lateness of its emergence. Despite the existence of a formidable literature on Glastonbury and its traditions by the 1890s, and the appearance of several volumes on the folklore of the western counties

5   Hodge, 1991, p. 1.
6   Clements & Robertson, 1982, p. 11.
7   Lonely Planet Britain, 3rd ed. 1999, p. 371.

during the nineteenth century, no trace of the story as such has so far been discovered, either in manuscript or in print, before 1895. Its origins, then, might seem easy to account for. This, however, proves not to be the case, and its investigation is as exacting and difficult a task, and one as seemingly impossible of final resolution, as that of any historical problem of the Dark Ages.

" SEE," EXCLAIMED LEMONDAY, " THERE IS THE PYXIE METAL "

Fig 3. An illustration by Frank Dadd from Sabine Baring-Gould's novel Guavas the Tinner (1897).

I

A TRADITION IS FOUND

In 1989 A. W. Smith suggested that the story in its modern form derived from the Cornish scholar and philologist Henry Jenner (1848-1934). Jenner picked up the story of Jesus's voyage, at second hand, in London, allegedly as a metal-worker's craft tradition. As Jenner himself recorded in 1933, it passed from him to his friend, A. R. Hope Moncrieff, author of popular retellings of the Arthurian legends, who also edited *Black's Guide to the Duchy of Cornwall* from 1895, in which year the story first appeared in the guide.

Jenner also told it to the renowned novelist, hymn-writer and collector of curious lore, the Rev. Sabine Baring-Gould (1834-1924), who featured it in his novel *Guavas the Tinner* in 1897. Baring-Gould mentioned it again in *A Book of the West, an Introduction to Devon and Cornwall*, in 1899.[8] Although, perhaps significantly, the story was first recorded among London artisans, it at first seemingly focused on

8   Smith, 1989, makes heavy weather of these early references. On p. 69, imply-ing Jenner's senility, he states that the reference 'does not in fact' first appear in the 1895 edition of Black's *Guide*, as Jenner stated in 1933, and as was indeed the case. It is unclear why Smith states, on the same page, that 'I have been unable to establish the connection of Mr. Hope Moncrieff with this series of *Guides*', when his name clearly appears as editor on the title page from the 16th edition of 1895 to the 24th edition of 1923. Smith, on p. 70, also contradicts Jenner's 1933 statement that Baring-Gould (at first) put the story in a novel, having himself missed the reference in *Guavas*. Further, he refers to *A Book of the West*, 1899, as the '*Book of Cornwall*'. The second, Cornish, volume of *A Book of the West* was published as an independent work, *Cornwall*, in 1910, with a pocket edition in 1914.

Fig 4. Rev. Sabine Baring-Gould, 1834-1924, Vicar and Squire of Lew Trenchard, Devon. Folklorist, hagiographer, and novelist, he referred to the Jesus voyage story in a novel in 1897, and in A Book of the West, 1899.

Cornwall. The reference in the 16th edition of *Black's Guide* of 1895 occurred in discussion of traditions of a Jewish presence in Cornwall in the area of Marazion:

> This venerable town is locally known as *Market Jew*, from which it has been supposed an ancient Jewish colony. The connection of the Jews with Cornwall is an old story: a legend among metal workers represents Joseph of Arimathea as engaged in the tin trade, travelling between Phoenicia and the Cassiterides,[9] where it is even said that he brought the boy Jesus. But nowadays there are scholars who doubt if Jews were ever settled in Cornwall and laugh away as a corruption the name *Jews' houses* given here and elsewhere to old smelting places; then the fanciful etymology of *Marah Zion* ("bitter Zion") is brought down to the plain prose of an old Cornish word for market. *St. Michael's Mount* may put in a very probable claim to be the *Ictis* of the ancient tin trade.[10]

9   The 'tin-islands' of the classical geographers, identified with the Scillys and the Cornish and Armorican littoral.
10 Moncrieff, ed., 1895, p. 154.

This passage occurred until the last edition for which Moncrieff was responsible, the 24th of 1923. In 1927 the editorship was taken over by J. E. Morris and the *Guide* was completely revised. Here, as Smith records, the Jesus voyage-story disappears. The entry for Marazion or Market Jew now guardedly says 'The odd alternatives have given rise to odder stories of primitive Jewish tin traders: but the first, according to Mr. Salmon, is merely the Cornish plural "marasion", and the second a corruption of the plural "morghaiion", both meaning markets.'[11]

In 1897 the Rev. Sabine Baring-Gould (1834-1924), Squire and Vicar of Lew Trenchard in Devon, and now best remembered for his hymn *Onward Christian Soldiers*, published *Guavas the Tinner*, an everyday story of tinning folk in the Cornwall of the sixteenth century. In this colourful novel, illustrated by Frank Dadd, Guavas has for a pet the last native wolf of England,[12] pyxies play their part, and, at one point, a group of tinners are attempting to test the quality of some ore from a mysterious and uncanny source:

"Mates!" shouted Eldad, who had been un-noticed whilst the discussion proceeded relative to the ore and whence it came. "Mates," said he, I will tap the furnace!"

Then he took an iron rod, and with a loud cry of "Joseph to the tinners' aid!"* he drove it into the clay plug that closed the mouth of the kiln. At once a brilliant silver stream gushed forth, poured through the runnel, and rapidly filled the mould, overflowed, and ran on into a second that communicated with the first by a channel.

The men, looking on, exclaimed: "By the Lord! that's old Elias's tin and no doubt. There is none other like it on the Moor."[13]

11 Morris, ed., 1927, p. 88; see Smith, 1989, p.69 and note 25 (p.82) for refs. regarding the tradition of the Cornish Jews.
12 Baring-Gould, who had visited Iceland and studied the sagas, seems to have had a fondness for wolves. One of his early works was *The Book of Werewolves*, 1865.
13 Baring-Gould, 1897, pp. 197-8.

In his footnote Baring-Gould explained: '*Now corrupted to "Joseph was in the tin trade!" One Cornish tale is that this Joseph was he of Arimathea, that he made his fortune out of tin, and that on one occasion he brought the Child Saviour with him in his boat to Cornwall.'

In *A Book of the West*, 1899, in the second volume, devoted to Cornwall, Baring-Gould returned to the story, which, as Jenner later recorded, had been 'quite new' to him:

> On Dartmoor the stream tin can thus be run out of a peat fire. And the Dartmoor stream tin has this merit: it is absolutely pure, whereas tin elsewhere is mingled with wolfram, that makes it brittle as glass; and to separate wolfram from tin requires a second roasting and is a delicate process.
>
> Another Cornish story is to the effect that Joseph of Arimathea came in a boat to Cornwall, and brought the Child Jesus with him, and the latter taught him how to extract the tin and purge it from its wolfram. This story possibly grew out of the fact that the Jews under the Angevin kings farmed the tin of Cornwall. When tin is flashed, then the tinner shouts, "Joseph was in the tin trade," which is probably a corruption of "'S. Joseph to the tinners aid!"[14]

He went on, in times unconcerned with 'political correctness,' to give an account of the later history of Cornish tin mining:

> In King John's time the tin mines were farmed by the Jews. The right to it was claimed by the king as Earl of Cornwall.
>
> Old smelting-houses in the peninsula are still called "Jews' houses," and, judging by certain noses and lips that one comes across occasionally in the Duchy, they left their half-breeds behind them.
>
> During the time of Richard, Earl of Cornwall and King of the Romans, the produce of the tin mines was considerable, and it

14 Baring-Gould, 1899, vol. ii, p. 57.

was in fact largely due to his reputed wealth from this source that
he was elected (1257).[15]

Baring-Gould's account is not without its problems. Smith records
that enquiry at the Library of the Camborne School of Mines in 1985
produced no reference to the term 'flashing',[16] although Baring-Gould
was well versed in contemporary dialect and folkways. The *Oxford
English Dictionary* records the verb 'flash' as to emit light suddenly,
to gleam; of water, *etc.*, to rush along a surface; and as a glass-maker's
term meaning 'to expand into a sheet.' Any of these meanings would
fit the context.

The detail of Christ teaching Joseph to purge the tin of wolfram
is unique to Baring-Gould. If it was not an imaginative addition of
his own, as there seems no reason to suppose, it suggests that he had
made enquiries, and found a current version of the story in Cornwall
for himself; but the tale had, by 1899, enjoyed the authority of print
in the form of *Black's Guide* for four years, long enough, probably,
for local story-tellers to have seized upon and elaborated it, initially
doubtless in response to visitors' questions. Catering for holiday-makers
was already becoming economically important for the impoverished
South-West. The names of Jesus and Joseph may here have replaced
those of earlier culture-heroes of the tinning trade. As Robert Hunt,
F.R.S., had recorded in his *Popular Romances of the West of England,
or, The Drolls, Traditions, and Superstitions of Old Cornwall*, in 1865,
a work which Baring-Gould used, the tin miners had many similar
traditions. St Pirran or Perran was the miners traditional patron, his
feast on the 5th March being celebrated with much inebriation. His
black flag with its white cross is the standard of Cornwall, and is held
to represent the black ore and the silvery molten tin. He and another
even more obscure saint, St Chiwidden, were reputed to have together

15 Baring-Gould, 1899, vol. ii, p. 59.
16 Smith, 1989, p. 71, and note 32, p. 82

Fig 5. Gwennap Pit, near Redruth, Cornwall. A depression caused by subsidence due to copper mining, John Wesley preached there many times. It was subsequently re-shaped as an open air preaching pit. In the 19th century it was said that St. Paul had also preached at Gwennap.

discovered tin and the secrets of tinning.[17]

The ancient miners, the 'old men', were variously identified with the 'Finician' (Phoenician), the Jew, or the Saracen, those Barbary slavers who were such a threat to Britain's south-western coasts in the earlier seventeenth century,[18] Easterners who, in popular thought, shaded one into the other. Most of the lore of the Jewish miners or 'farmers' of tin, in the guides and in Baring-Gould, derives from Hunt, who also heard stranger tales:

> That the Phoenicians came to Cornwall to buy tin has been so often told, that there is little to be added to the story. It was certainly new, however, to be informed by the miners in Gwennap - that there could be no shade of a doubt but that St Paul himself came to

17 Hunt, 1865, 2nd Series, pp. 20-22; 288.
18 One of whose gold-laden wrecks was discovered off of the cost of Devon in 2002.

Cornwall to buy tin, and that Creegbraws - a mine still in existence - supplied the saint largely with that valuable mineral. Gwennap is regarded by Gwennap men as the centre of Christianity. This feeling has been kept alive by the annual meeting of the Wesleyan body in Gwennap Pit - an old mine-working - on Whit-monday. This high estate and privilege is due, says tradition, to the fact that St Paul himself preached in the parish.*

I have also been told that St Paul preached to the tinners on Dartmoor, and a certain cross on the road from Plympton to Princes-Town has been indicated as the spot upon which the saint stood to enlighten the benighted miners of this wild region.

[footnote] *Is this supported by the statement of Dr Stillingfleet, Bishop of Worcester, who says, "The Christian religion was planted in the Island of Great Britain during the time of the apostles, and probably by St Paul"?[19]

Gwennap Pit is located just to the south of Redruth on the eastern slopes of Carn Marth, made famous through the preaching of John Wesley, who used the pit on 18 occasions from 1776-89. Although sometimes erroneously described as a Roman amphitheatre, the pit was actually a hollow caused by mining subsidence in the mid-eighteenth century. In memory of Wesley, local people in 1806 excavated the pit into a regular oval, some 100 ft. (37m) across and 25 ft. (8m) deep, adding 13 rows of turf seats. A Whit-Monday service has been held there since 1807. The Chartists met there in 1839, and theatrical performance are now occasionally held there.

Edward Stillingfleet (1635-1699), the Bishop of Worcester to whom Hunt refers in his note, was an influential Restoration divine and antiquary, known as 'the beauty of holiness' for his good looks, who wrote his *Orignes Brtannicae, or the Antiquities of the British Churches* in 1685 while still Dean of St Paul's, London. His views there expressed[20] on St Paul in Britain were not original. They

19 Hunt, 1865, 2nd. Series, pp. 112-3.
20 Stillingfleet, 1685, p. 34.

were based on speculations by certain ancient, but here hardly authoritative, ecclesiastical historians which had been taken up by various sixteenth-century Protestant writers, notably William Camden (1551-1623), who mentioned them non-committally in his ground-breaking and popular survey of early history and topography, *Britannia*, first published in Latin in 1586 and translated into English in 1610.[21] Stillingfleet's endorsement of the theory, none the less, lent it continuing respectability with a number of writers in the eighteenth and early nineteenth centuries. They included the Rev. Richard Warner, who in *An History of the Abbey of Glaston; and of the Town of Glastonbury*, 1826, probably following Stillingfleet, went so far as to speculate that 'it is highly probable' that St Paul 'actually unfolded, to the Gentile inhabitants of the vicinity of Glaston, the saving truths of [the Christian] religion.'[22]

The popularisation of these antiquarian speculations about St Paul, which in 1865 Hunt found novel and seems to link with Nonconformity, may have owed something, however, to the unconventional Welsh Anglican curate the Rev R. W. Morgan, who had published *St Paul in Britain* in 1861, a book which was to enjoy a long history in print. We shall meet him again. The role of the pulpit in the dissemination, with a quite spurious air of authority, of the most idiosyncratic historical notions to the non-reading public, and so into local belief, has probably been underestimated by folklorists. Before this role was usurped by the broadcast media, the parson or minister was often the only educated man whose opinions on any serious matter were ever heard by the 'humbler sort.' This, also, is a phenomenon which we shall meet again.

It seems likely, then, that in this instance, somewhere and at some time, the names of Joseph of Arimathea and Jesus, and that of St Paul, have exchanged places, and the former perhaps taken on the lore of Saints Pirran and Chiwidden at the same time. It might be premature, however, to conclude that the version recorded earliest

21 Camden, *Britannia* (1610), Romans in Britaine, 65.
22 Warner, 1826, pp. 157-8.

(by Hunt) was necessarily the more 'authoritative.' It might equally represent the euhemerism of an older tale which the ministers thought too startling or sacrilegious. Local variations may have existed, and there is a possibility that genuinely old traditions concerning Joseph of Arimathea may have lingered in Cornwall, at least at Talland, once a priory of Glastonbury in the Middle Ages.

Hunt also found much to record concerning the Knockers, or *buccas*, who haunted the mines. 'These are the sprites of the mines ... They are said to be the souls of the Jews who formerly worked the tin-mines of Cornwall. They are not allowed to rest because of their wicked practices as tinners, and they share in the general curse which ignorant people believe still hangs on this race.'[23] Later, he quotes the author and Christian socialist Charles Kingsley, now remembered mainly for his novel *The Water Babies* (1863), who had written in an earlier novel, *Yeast*, (1849): 'They are *the ghosts, the miners hold, of the old Jews that crucified our Lord, and were sent for slaves by the Roman emperors to work the mines:* and we find their old smelting-houses, which we call *Jews' houses*, and their blocks at the bottom of the great bogs, which we call *Jews' tin*: and then a town among us too, which we call *Market Jew*, but the old name was Marazion, that means the bitterness of Zion, they tell me; and bitter work it was for them, no doubt, poor souls!'[24]

Perhaps Joseph of Arimathea with his staff became confused in some Cornish minds with the *motiv* of the Wandering Jew, of whom sightings were reported in England as recently as the late

23 Hunt, 1865, 1st Series, p. 67.
24 Hunt, 1865, 2nd Series, p.118, citing Kingsley's novel, *Yeast, a Problem*, 1849. Kingsley, perhaps, knew of those Latin texts which testify that in the fourth century, and perhaps earlier, 'Britain was certainly chosen as a place of exile for a number of individuals, ... some of them prominent. ... The last cases recorded belong to the reign of Magnus Maximus, and they were religious offenders, two supporters of the heretic Priscillianus. Both men, Instantius, a bishop, and a high ranking Spanish laymen named Tiberianus, were sent to the Scilly Isles, where opportunities to propagate their views must have been limited' (Birley, 1979, p. 158, citing Sulpicius Severus, *Chron.* 2. 51. 4; Jerome, *de viris illustribus* 123). Maximus achieved great prominence in Welsh tradition as the emperor Macsen.

eighteenth and early nineteenth centuries; the confusion is already present in the *Flores Historiarum* of Roger of Wendover (d. 1236), one of the earliest versions. In the Grail romances, the Arimathean travels with his company from the city of Sarras, imagined home of the Saracens, a name which also seems to have been applied to the Jews of Cornish imaginings.

In assessing the folklore of the Cornish miners, however, it should be born in mind that, although Cornish tin working is indeed an industry of great antiquity, 'It is also certain that true vein (lode) mining did not commence until the Middle Ages, for the first tin was obtained entirely by streaming, that is by washing it out from alluvial deposits.'[25] The early tin mine at Godolphin, by Mounts Bay, perhaps dates from the sixteenth century. Mining on a significant economic scale began in Cornwall only in the eighteenth century, and this was for copper, the main product of Gwennap. The 1860s saw a commercial decline in Cornish copper production, and copper mining had all but collapsed by 1880. It was in this period that exploitation of the deeper tin deposits began, sometimes beneath the no longer commercial copper workings. A brief tin 'boom' was followed by a slump in the mid-1870s and fluctuating fortunes until the final demise of the tin industry in the early 1920s. It was these economically uncertain times for the miners that formed the background to the data recorded by the would-be folklorists of the late nineteenth and early twentieth centuries.

25 H. V. Williams, n.d., *Cornwall's Old Mines*, p. 7.

Fig 6. Cornish miners deep underground at
Blue Hills Mine, at St. Agnes, c. 1890.

Fig 7. A romantic late nineteenth-century view of Glastonbury's fabled 'Old Church' of wattle boughs, supposedly blessed by Christ's own presence.

2

A MYSTERIOUS LETTER

It was believed by Smith that the 1895 reference in *Black's Guide to the Duchy of Cornwall* was the first appearance of the story in print, and this may well have been the case. However, that same year, 1895, saw another reference to the 'tradition' in the more learned pages of *Somerset & Dorset Notes & Queries*, Vol. IV, Sherborne, 1895, edited by F. W. Weaver & C. H. Mayo. It read as follows:

> 256. GLASTONBURY TRADITION.- Is the following tradition known to any reader of *s. & d. n. & q.*, as existing at the present day in Somerset? It is said that Joseph of Arimathea derived his great riches from trading in tin with Britain, that he made several voyages to this country, and on one occasion brought Our Lord, then a boy, with him, and the place where they sojourned near Glastonbury is called "Paradise" to this day: and even now when the miners of Mendip* (who by the way are recently extinct) arrive at a critical and dangerous moment in the process, they all repeat "Joseph was a tinman," as a charm to avert disaster.
> *[The Mendip mines were *lead mines*.]-EDITOR FOR SOMERSET.
> {footnote}[26]
>
> Σ

This modest item, tucked between a note, with a photograph on the opposite page, about the finding of a medieval copper crucifix in a ditch

26 *SDNQ*, Vol. IV, Sherborne, 1895, ed. F. W. Weaver & C. H. Mayo, pp. 312-313.

at Puxton, Somerset, and a list of 'Dorset Clergy and the Protestations of 1641-2 *Concluded*', escaped the attention of many more than just Mr A. W. Smith. It drew no published response from the readers of *SDNQ* and seemingly vanished from sight thereafter until the end of the 1920s, when it finally achieved brief notice. None of those who were, with increasing vitriol, to defend the veracity and even the genuine existence of the tradition in the first half of the next century, and for whom it would have offered valuable evidence, ever refer to it.

Who, then, was Σ (*sigma*)? In early volumes of *SDNQ*, Σ and Δ (*delta*), S and D, are used to signify Somerset or Dorset contributions from correspondents who preferred to remain anonymous. Unfortunately, the surviving records of *SDNQ* do not go back far enough to allow an identification. Unless some chance discovery should come to light, we can only guess from internal evidence whether Σ may perhaps be one of the people who subsequently concerned themselves with the story. It would be easy to assume, on a casual reading, that the enigmatic Σ had merely read the reference in the new *Black's Guide* to Cornwall and, knowing the medieval tradition linking Joseph of Arimathea to Glastonbury, was curious as to whether the new-found story of the boy Jesus in Cornwall had ever been heard there also. The references to tin trading and mining might seen to indicate that Σ was entirely dependent on *Black's Guide*. This cannot have been the case, however; the reference to the use of a refrain or charm naming Joseph did not, as we have seen, appear in *Black's Guide*. Neither, seemingly, was it mentioned elsewhere in print until Baring-Gould used it in *Guavas the Tinner* in 1897. In juxtaposing the voyage of Jesus and Joseph with a miner's charm, Σ indicates that he had private access to the story which Moncrieff and Baring-Gould derived from Jenner (which we will examine in detail later), anticipating the use made of the second element by Baring-Gould, which was ignored by or unknown to Moncrieff. The coincidence of dates is too close to allow us to suppose that the appearance of the query in *SDNQ* was unrelated to the mention of the same story in the Cornish guide which appeared in the same year. And yet 'Sigma' is unlikely to mask the identity of Moncrieff, Baring-Gould or Jenner, for he knows details which seemingly they do not. Material which he incorporates into the story is not to reappear for many years. The form of the 'charm to avert disaster' is given as 'Joseph was a tinman', not, as given by Baring-Gould in 1897, and subsequently by Jenner himself, 'Joseph was in the tin-trade'. We will hear the form 'Joseph was a tinman' again, but not, seemingly, from sources dependent on Σ. Similarly, we will not hear of Joseph and Jesus at Glastonbury or on Mendip again for a quarter of a century, and the detail concerning a place called Paradise is not mentioned in print again until 1929, and then it is quoted, but without acknowledgement, from Σ.

This is the most puzzling feature of his short query. There were indeed two places on the then outskirts of Glastonbury called Paradise, one an area of orchards to the west of Northload Street, marked as such on the larger scale ordnance maps, the other Paradise Lane north of the Tor. Such fanciful names are not uncommon among English field-names, like 'God's Garden', 'Mount Pleasant' or the more derogatory 'Purgatory', and represent little more than 'sporadic examples of rustic humour'.[27] Many are no older than the eighteenth or nineteenth centuries. The Glastonbury examples are more likely to have been cited in support of an idea or 'tradition' than to have given rise to it.

Perhaps they were first noticed in a quasi-mystical context after a locally influential paper on Glastonbury's Chalice Well, or Blood Spring, was read before the newly formed Glastonbury Antiquarian Society by a Mr. G. W. Wright in 1886. This brought into the public domain, perhaps for the first time, the idea that the russet, iron-rich waters, which had achieved short-lived national celebrity in a therapeutic fad of the mid-eighteenth century, flowed from the Holy Grail, hidden by Joseph of Arimathea under the Chalice Hill which rises above the Well, and were thus imbued with the blood of Christ:

> That it is known as Chalice Hill seems to point to the spot as the one in which the Holy Grael was for a time deposited, but whether

27 Reaney, 1960, p. 207.

hidden, or placed in a building specially prepared for it even legend sayeth not, although legend points to the idea that it was never out of the keeping of the purest in the island.

In his following discussion of the Grail legend, Wright, a native of Glastonbury who had returned after many years in London and founded a lending library there, was probably influenced, directly or indirectly, by Wagner's opera *Parsifal*, first performed in 1882. Wright noted that:

> From France the legend may be traced to Germany, and now a temple is said to have been built in which the cup was preserved. It was called "The Grael Temple," [*sic*] and was considered to be the true representation of paradise on earth.[28]

The Grail, which in the original French poem *Perceval* by Chretien de Troyes, of *c.* 1190, the earliest surviving version of the story, was a dish, and which in the later French poem *Joseph d'Arimathie* by Robert de Boron, of *c.*1200, was a cup, became in the Middle High German poem *Parzival* by Wolfram von Eschenbach, also of *c.* 1200, a stone on which every Easter a dove placed a single consecrated wafer. These transmutations are not so surprising as they appear at first sight. In the medieval Church, antique cups, vessels, and dishes of onyx and similar types of semi-precious stone, and of Greco-Roman or even Egyptian manufacture, were not infrequently put to liturgical use. A great Byzantine onyx dish in Vienna, said to have been obtained by the Hapsburgs from the Dukes of Burgundy, has been one of the claimants to be the 'real' Holy Grail. Wagner used Wolfram as the main source for his opera, setting the story not in Britain but in Gothic Spain, although once more making the Grail a cup. Wolfram wrote that his *Gral* was guarded by 'templars' - knights of a celibate military order - but the idea of a Grail 'temple' reflects Wagner's lavish and

28 Wright, 1887, pp. 22-23.

influential stage-production at Bayreuth, his set based in part on the cathedral of Sienna.

Awareness of either of the obscure Glastonbury 'Paradise' place-names suggests some local knowledge; and yet, as the Somerset editor of *SDNQ*, F. W. Weaver,[29] was quick to point out in his footnote, the Mendip mines yielded lead, not tin. Neither was Σ quite correct in stating that the Mendip metal miners were 'recently extinct'. The last lead-works on Mendip, located at Priddy, was not to close until 1908. It was at Priddy itself, however, that early and persistent witness to the story was indeed subsequently to be reported.

Σ's apparent confusion regarding the mining of tin on Mendip may perhaps be derived from a misinterpretation of matter included in the Rev. W. Phelps's *History and Antiquities of Somersetshire*, published in 1836. In his general introduction, Phelps wrote that the Phoenicians had developed their knowledge of navigation 'at a very early period of the world' and had planted colonies, not only in the Mediterranean but:

> on the distant shores of *Spain* and *Gaul*, and most probably on the western coast of *Britain*. This opinion seems to be corroborated by the history, mythology, superstitions, and language, recorded of the inhabitants of Cornwall; which could not have arisen unless some of these people had resided among them. ... the Phoenicians had an established trade with Britain for *tin* before the Trojan war, 1100 B.C.; and Mr. Whitaker refers the peopling of Britain to nearly the same time; a period coeval with the reigns of David and Solomon.[30]

He went on to note that 'Tin is mentioned by Moses in the Bible; and also by the prophet Ezekiel (chap. xxii verses 10 and 12 [*recte* 18 & 20]).' These verses couple 'brass and iron, and lead, and tin.' Phelps continued: 'The metals of Britain, particularly tin, lead, and iron, were

29 'Frederic William Weaver, M.A. (ed. of the "Visitations of the Counties of Somerset & Herefordshire," "Somerset Incumbents" *etc.*)'.
30 Phelps, 1836, vol. 1, p. 4.

the staple produce of the island.' He noted correctly that 'the former was easily obtained (before the art of mining was introduced), in the beds of rivers'.

In Phelps' Book Two, 'Ecclesiastical History', he referred back to these passages when he asserted that Druidism 'is supposed to have been introduced into this country, at a very early period, from the East, by the Phoenicians, who held a commercial intercourse with Cornwall and the Scilly Islands, many centuries before the Christian aera.' Phelps held a high view of Druids, whom he regarded (following Camden) as having 'acknowledged the being of a God, the Governor of the universe', and went on to observe that the 'Christian missionaries would naturally resort to the sacred circles [of the druids] as the most eligible place to exhort the people …'.

After citing Dugdale's *Monasticon Anglicanum* and Holinshed's *Chronicles* on the coming of St Philip to Gaul and Joseph of Arimathea to Britain, Phelps goes on to present an argument linking the evangelisation

Fig 8. Glastonbury's 'Old Church'
as illustrated in Phelps' History and
Antiquities of Somersetshire, 1836
(Vol. I, p. 38).

of Britain with the trade in metals with the Mediterranean:

> From the observations of the latter writer, we have a clue to the probability of the fact stated [concerning the priority of Glastonbury as the first church in Britain]; and we may be able to show, that the western part of Britain was the country to which the zealous missionaries directed their course. We have already, in the preceding pages, stated that the Phoenicians had established an intercourse with the British isles, long previous to the Christian aera; and had founded colonies on the coasts of Spain and Gaul. Thus a communication was opened between the Holy Land and these distant countries, and kept up by the vessels of the Phoenicians, and afterwards by the Carthaginians, in a direct manner. St. Philip most probably came into the west by one of these means, and landed, we may presume, at *Venetia* in Celtic Gaul, the chief city of that country; and from whence the intercourse with Britain was most frequent, in carrying on the trade with the Britons for the tin and other metals of that country. The Apostle [Philip], in pursuance of his divine commission, to preach the Gospel to the distant nations, availed himself, no doubt, of the opportunity thus offered to extend his labours; and despatched his friend and companion Joseph with eleven other missionaries to Britain. The ports to which these vessels traded were in the neighbourhood of the mining districts; and we may fairly infer that the river *Axe* or *Parret*, was the harbour, whence this holy band landed in Britain, and soon after settled themselves in the country at Glastonbury, then called *Ynisytrin* [*sic*], where they first preached the Gospel to the inhabitants of the district. Here they built a small chapel of rude materials, (wicker-work covered with clay,) which they dedicated to the service of God, and it became the first Christian church, and Joseph and his companions the *origines* of Christian teachers in Britain. Spelman in his *Concilia* gives a wood-cut of this primitive ecclesiastical edifice, which is copied on the other side.[31]

31 Phelps, 1836, vol. 1, p. 39.

Phelps' illustration is not, in fact, a direct reproduction of Spelman's much imitated wood-cut of 1636, but an interpretation of it showing a small building of split tree-trunks, apparently inspired by the Saxon nave of the church of Greensted-juxta-Ongar in Essex. Like Hunt in Cornwall somewhat later, Phelps noted the writings of Bishop Stillingfleet, who had attributed the evangelisation of Britain rather to St Paul, an opinion which, as we have seen, had also been echoed by Rev. Richard Warner, in *An History of the Abbey of Glaston…* of 1826, who also speculated that 'it is highly probable' that St Paul 'actually unfolded, to the Gentile inhabitants of the vicinity of Glaston, the saving truths of religion.'[32]

In his detailed account of the histories of Somerset's individual parishes, Phelps wrote of Priddy and its famous fair. He went on to write that 'There is also a tradition, that a market was formerly held in this place; and the upper part of the village is called *Town*, where it is said to have been kept. There can be no doubt but this village was the head quarters of the miners on Mendip, when the mines were in full activity and work.'[33]

Was Σ confused in attempting to research his 'tradition' not only by reference to the Cornish tin trade, but by Phelps' location of the entreports of that trade at the estuaries of the Parret and the Axe, 'in the neighbourhood of the mining districts'? What influence, if any, did Phelps have on the evolution of the voyage tradition? His account was certainly to be noted at Glastonbury itself.

For the present, the enigma concerning Σ's identity, and the precise nature of the beliefs to which he refers, must remain unresolved. The significance of his unassuming and unregarded query will only become apparent as we examine the controversy which was to enfold the story. It testifies that alongside the main-stream of the 'tradition,' as it developed at first in Cornwall and later among the educated classes of Glastonbury, there was indeed 'something else.'

32 Warner, 1826, pp. 157-8.
33 Phelps, 1836, vol. 1, p. 187.

3

THE GYNAECOLOGIST'S TALE

Baring-Gould's 1899 version of the voyage story, complete with its reference to Joseph bringing the 'child Jesus', was noted by John William Taylor, M.Sc., F.R.C.S., in 1906 in his *The Coming of the Saints*, sub-titled *Imaginations and Studies in Early Church History and Tradition*. Taylor was by profession a gynaecologist, 'A surgeon in busy practice, whose work was strenuous and exacting'. He also wrote poetry of a mostly devotional nature, some of which was published posthumously, with an 'Introductory Memoir' of him, by his wife Pauline, as *The Doorkeeper and Other Poems*, in 1910. One poem was entitled *The Spiritual Surgeon*, which might serve as a not unfitting description of its author. Born in 1851 at Melksham, Wiltshire, 'into a home of simple evangelical piety', the son of the Rev. James Taylor, he was the youngest of five children. According to his wife, he was 'a delicate dreamy boy, very like his mother, with large lustrous eyes of quite remarkable beauty'. He seems to have developed early esoteric interests. 'In an interesting paper on "Psychical Research" he wrote " I think as a boy I rather revelled in the so-called supernatural"'. He was also inspired by the poetry of Swinburne, and by the *Morte d'Arthur* and the Quest of the Holy Grail. As his wife observed, 'Glastonbury, its history and traditions, form not the least interesting part of his book, "The Coming of the Saints"'. He attended Kingswood school in Bath for a time, and, aged seventeen, entered as a student at Charring Cross Medical School. He was subsequently a resident surgeon and medical officer at Charring Cross hospital and moved to Birmingham in 1877 where, familiarly known as Dr Taylor, he was a surgeon in the Birmingham and Midland Hospital for Women at the in-patient department at Sparkhill, where he was a consultant and specialist in gynaecology. He was an active churchman in Birmingham, and also published text books on gynaecology and obstetrics. In 1889 'he married a lady whom he had known as a child, the eldest daughter of the doctor to whom he had been articled in London'. In 1899 he was appointed Professor of Gynaecology in Mason College, shortly afterwards incorporated into the University of Birmingham, which post he held until a few months before his death. In 1904 he was elected President of the British Gynaecological Society, and died aged fifty-eight in 1910.

Despite his early interests, it is still unclear precisely what caused this rather attractive medical man to lay aside his speculum to chronicle *The Coming of the Saints*, 'perhaps the flower of his literary work'. Pauline, his wife, merely records:

> To him it was simply a labour of love, written during the course of many years - in the intervals of his professional work. It involved a considerable amount of hard reading, and patient investigation, but this was always a joy to him. He visited the shrines and other places of interest, about which he writes, during his summer holidays, and his chapter 'On Pilgrimage' will be found not the least attractive in the book.[34]

She tells us that its Introduction 'disarms hostile criticism, and the book has certainly the rare quality of appealing to readers of many different types and of different phases of belief - to devout Churchmen, Dissenters and Roman Catholics alike. It was favourably reviewed both by the *Athenaeum* and the *Academy*.' His poetry, in

34 Taylor, 1910, p.xxv.

which the names of Jesus and Mary are prominent,[35] betrays Catholic sympathies (although he remained an Anglican), and in this, his only published foray into the field of history, he devotes much space to the twelfth-century Provençal legends of the voyage of Joseph of Arimathea to Marseilles with Lazarus and the biblical women, Martha and the 'Three Marys': Mary Magdalene; Mary the wife of Clopas/Alphaeus, mother of James the Less (called the 'brother of the Lord', possibly a cousin, and leader of the Christian community in Jerusalem after his death); and Mary Salome, the mother of the New Testament's 'sons of thunder,' James the Great and John the Evangelist. It was James the Great who was said to have preached in Spain, or had his relics brought there, to Compostella.

After noting traditions of Joseph in Brittany, Taylor turns to Britain: 'Again, we find faint legendary traces of the presence of St. Joseph of Arimathea in Cornwall. He is represented as coming in a boat, as bringing the infant Jesus with him and as teaching the Cornish miners how to purify their tin. But here, too, St. Joseph has no settled resting-place.'[36] He goes on to quote Tertullian (c. 200 AD) who recorded that places in Britain inaccessible to the Romans[37] had already been won for Christ. 'But by what route', he quite legitimately asks, 'leading to a district "inaccessible to the Romans" could the early Christians of the first or second century have brought the news of the Gospel? A complete answer to this question is found in the writings of Diodorus Siculus, who lived in the time of Augustus: It was the route of the tin traders. ... So that, before Christ was born, we find the very route exactly described by Diodorus that was afterwards traditionally chosen by St. Joseph of Arimathea.' Aided by a map, Taylor traced the route from Marseilles up the Rhone, to Limoges and Brittany and

35 In his poem *Minehead*, 1909, he notes of the 'old grey Church' above the harbour: For on the outer wall is carved 'Pray Jesus and Marie' / Home to the sheltering harbour 'send / Oure neyghboures safelie'. An inscription paralleled at Glastonbury, which later inspired the Rev. H. A. Lewis.

36 Taylor, 1906, p. 175.

37 Meaning, probably, beyond the civil zone, as all Britain had been subjugated militarily by AD 80.

across the sea to Cornwall, 'and it is only the journey beyond it - the inland journey from Cornwall to Glastonbury - that would call for the courage and determination of the explorer of an unknown land. The recognition of this route as almost certainly the route of the early missionaries, gives special force to the Cornish tradition.' He asserts that Cornwall was not really Christianised before the sixth century, 'Yet here is the tradition of the actual coming of St. Joseph preserved through all the centuries, and not only so, but the coming is specially associated with the old industry of the tin workers.' He went on to quote Baring-Gould's passage of 1899 in support of the idea of Joseph coming as a tin merchant. Taylor also quotes Ward Lock's *Guide to Penzance, Land's End, and Scilly*, 5th ed.: 'There is a traditional story that Joseph of Arimathea was connected with Marazion when he and other Jews traded with the ancient tin-miners of Cornwall'. This evidently echoes *Black's Guide*, following Jenner. In an after-thought concerning the difficulty of a journey from Cornwall to Glastonbury, Taylor added a footnote:

> On closer study of the probable route it even appears that the last part of the journey was by no means dangerous or through unknown country. There is an old tradition that a trading route existed from pre-Roman times between the tin mines of Cornwall and the lead mines of the Mendips. Traces of this "way" may perhaps still be found in the "Here path" over the Quantocks'.[38]

Taylor himself was acquainted with West Somerset, one of his poems being on Minehead church. However he seems to have borrowed the idea of a prehistoric tin route from a paper in the *Wiltshire Archaeological Magazine* of 1905 by one J. U. Powell,[39] who wrote of

38 Taylor, 1906, p. 180 and note 1.
39 Powell, J.U., *South Wilts in Romano-British Times*, Wilts. Arch. Mag. xxxiv, 1905-6 at pp. 281-8; noted also by Sherlock, 1930, p.18, who writes 'There is said to have been a road connecting the lead mines of Mendip with the tin area of Devon and Cornwall. Her footnote gives *Wilts. Arch. Mag.* xxxiv and vii.

a 'Tin road', known for parts of its Wiltshire course as the Harepath and the Hardway, and of a 'Lead road' from Charterhouse, near Priddy, to Wiltshire, in a context unconnected with the Arimathean. In Powell's scheme they were separate, and the 'Tin road' did not run over the Quantocks but joined the Fosse Way at Ilchester. Anglo-Saxon *here path*, 'army way', variously modernised, is a not uncommon name of old track-ways. It was Taylor's version, however, which was to become pregnant with significance for later writers.

It is clear that Baring-Gould held no personal credence in the Jesus voyage 'tradition', and neither does Taylor. Although he writes of Joseph's route from Cornwall to Glastonbury as following a prehistoric route which ran from there to the Mendip mines, and later says 'In Cornwall we find a tradition that St. Joseph of Arimathea came in a boat and brought the infant Christ with him. He [Joseph] passes on (Tradition)',[40] he does not himself record any account that takes Jesus beyond Cornwall. Taylor's work is, in his own words, one of 'imaginations and studies', and is uncritical by modern scholarly standards, but he shares none of the credulity of the later clerical writers on the theme. However, the chapter in which the story is introduced, 'St. Joseph and Glastonbury', is subtitled 'The Bible of Glastonbury',[41] and a careless reading of it might suggest that Taylor is implying that Christ accompanied Joseph there. He nowhere says this, however, nor does he give any hint of knowledge of the specific Glastonbury and Mendip traditions referred to by Σ in *SDNQ* in 1895.

It is worth posing the question of whether Taylor himself may have been Σ? We know that he worked on *The Coming of the Saints* for many years. His status as a professional man and a churchman might have made him reticent to declare too openly an interest in a 'legend' which might appear eccentric at the very least when its only appearance in print had been in *Black's Guide*. The failure of Σ's query to draw any confirmatory response could explain why its matter

40 Taylor, 1906, p. 224.
41 Taylor, 1906, p. 174.

was not used, and the final step of bringing Jesus to Glastonbury not taken, in the eventual book. This can only be one of several possible guesses, however.

It is unclear whether Taylor's deductions from the story which he did tell, concerning the supposed tin route as that of early missionaries, were entirely his own, or whether he had had contact with Jenner, who certainly followed some of the same reasoning ten years later, perhaps himself influenced by Taylor; and although he does not cite him, and the itinerary which he suggests is a different one, we may also feel that Taylor may have been influenced by the tin-trading theories of Phelps who had written seventy years earlier.

4

THE GRAND BARD OF CORNWALL

In order to gain perspective on the original background to the voyage story, it is necessary to know something of the interesting career of Henry Jenner, who gave it its first impetus. Jenner himself contributed a summary of his life to date to the *Annual Report of the Royal Cornwall Polytechnic Society* on the occasion of his election as President in 1916, which gives us an attractive view of the character of the man.[42] He wrote:

As the President on this occasion happens to be also the Editor, he finds himself in the embarrassing position of having to write his own biographical notice. He has tried to be as little egotistical as is possible in an autobiography. He thinks that a list of his writings relating to Cornwall may possibly be of some slight interest, so he has added one, with a short mention of his other works.

As he recorded, he was born in Cornwall at St Columb Major on August 8th, 1848. 'He was the son of the Rev. Henry Lascelles Jenner, LL.B., of Trinity Hall, Cambridge, then curate of St. Columb, but afterwards first Bishop of Dunedin, New Zealand, and Mary Isabel his wife, daughter of Captain William Finlaison, R.N., formerly of Thurso, in Caithness, and sometime Governor of the Island of

42 *The 83rd Annual Report of the Royal Cornwall Polytechnic Society*, New Series Vol. 3, Pt. II, 1916, Plymouth, pp. 165-173. A portrait of Jenner appears as the frontispiece, and is reproduced as the frontispiece here.

Ascension.' He confessed that 'The family of the President is not of
Cornish origin', and lovingly recorded something of the distinguished
history of his paternal family, which had originated in Sussex. As his
obituary in the *West Briton* recalled:

> Though Mr. Jenner had no Cornish blood in his veins, he was
> a native of the county, ... The Jenners are an ancient English
> family and have been remarkable for the firmness of their "High
> Church-Tory" principles ever since those party names came into
> being. Mr. Jenner was known to many Cornish people as a keen
> conversationalist on religious and political subjects, but the
> firmness with which he stuck to his opinions was tempered by
> the kindness, courtesy and intelligence with which he combated
> his opponents.[43]

Not long after his birth, Jenner's father accepted the living of a
parish near Canterbury, and there 'he spent his boyhood days'.[44] He
was educated at St. Mary's College, Harlow, in Essex. 'Mr. Jenner
was bred in an atmosphere of scholarship and learning, with a strong
bias towards ecclesiastical subjects. At first it was intended that he
should follow in the footsteps of his grandfather, Sir Herbert Jenner,
Dean of the Arches, by taking up the career of an ecclesiastical
lawyer.'[45] He himself recalled in 1916 how 'after a short period of
stop-gap schoolmastering', he 'was appointed in January, 1869, to
a clerkship in the Principal Registry of H.M. Court of Probate, then
situated in its old quarters in Doctors' Commons. In July, 1870,
he was appointed, on the nomination of Archbishop Tait, to the
Department of Manuscripts in the British Museum.'
    Set against the encomia which later gathered about his name,
a jarring note is found in P. R. Harris's 'A History of the British

---

43 *West Briton*, 10 May 1934, 'Cornish Grand Bard - Mr. Henry Jenner Dies at
Hayle - Outstanding Figure in County'.
44 *Annual Report of the Royal Cornwall Polytechnic Society*, Vol. 8, 1934, p. 58.
45 *West Briton*, 10 May, 1934.

Museum Library, 1753-1973.' He records that Jenner, 'who joined the staff of the Department of Manuscripts in 1870 as a junior assistant, incurred the displeasure of Maude Thompson, the newly appointed Keeper of Manuscripts, in 1879. [She] refused to sign Jenner's diary for October because of the poor quality and quantity of his work.' The Trustees decided that Jenner should be transferred to the Department of Printed Books, where his work was monitored for three months, but found to be entirely satisfactory. In 1884 he acceded to the 'responsible' post of 'Placer,' helping arrange for the installation of movable presses in the library and was promoted to the first class of Assistants in 1890. He was praised for his special knowledge of liturgiology and ecclesiology, assisting with book selection, and with the compilation of the heading 'Liturgies' in the general catalogue.[46]

Jenner himself continued to reminisce that 'for forty years he laboured at congenial tasks. The care of invaluable manuscripts of all ages and condition was his first chief work, one result of which was his discovery in 1877 of some fragmentary lines from an otherwise unknown Cornish play of about 1400, written on the back of a charter dated 1340.'[47] These forty-two lines of verse, in Middle Cornish, were an important addition to the sparse surviving literature in that language, and in 1916 Jenner described them as 'probably the earliest extant piece of Cornish literature.'[48]

The Celtic languages became for him another abiding interest. In 1871, at the age of twenty-three, he joined the Philological Society, and was for some years a member of the council of that society. He read a paper on *The Cornish Language* before the Society in 1873. This was followed in 1875 by a paper on *The Manx Language: its Grammar, Literature and Present State*, and the next year, 1876, by

46 Harris, 1998, pp. 368-9; Jenner appears in plate 68, in a group photograph of the senior staff of the Dept. of Printed Books of *c.* 1885, with thick dark hair and an 'Assyrian' beard.
47 *Annual Report of the Royal Cornwall Polytechnic Society*, Vol. 8, 1934, p. 58.
48 *Annual Report of the Royal Cornwall Polytechnic Society*, Vol. 3, Pt. II, 1916, p. 167.

his paper on *Traditional Relics of the Cornish Language in Mounts'
Bay in 1875*.

In 1877 his ties to Cornwall were strengthened by his marriage
to Kitty Lee Rawlings, born at Downes, Hayle. An artist and writer,
she produced short stories, articles and poems, as well as six novels,
some set in the West Country. 'Since their marriage Mr. and Mrs.
Jenner made it their practice to spend their holidays abroad each
year. A good many years ago', the *West Briton* recorded in 1934,
'Mrs. Jenner was received into the Church of Rome, and Mr. Jenner
took a very sympathetic view of that great Christian fellowship to
which his historical and liturgiological studies inclined him, and into
which he was received at the end of last year'. There was one child
of the marriage, Cecily Katherine Ysolt Jenner, of whom her father
recorded in 1916 that she was 'now Sister Mary Beatrix Jenner', a
nun of the Order of the Visitation of Our Lady.

As we have seen, in 1879 Jenner, whose marriage and work on
Cornish had perhaps distracted him from his professional duties,
was transferred under something of a cloud to the Department of
Printed Books at the British Museum, where he remained until his
retirement in 1909. His 'particular work', as he as he himself saw
it, 'was the arrangement and classification by subjects of the books
of the Library, a work which was of considerable interest, for it
involved seeing and considering every book, English and foreign
(except those of the separate Oriental Library) which came into the
British Museum.'[49]

> Thus for nearly half a century Mr. Jenner was intimately connected
> with all that went on in the greatest library of modern times. It was
> Mr. Jenner's business as an official of the reading room to assist
> visitors in their researches, and the splendid tradition of public
> service at the museum did not suffer at his hands. Even in his
> retirement he continued to show the same courtesy and patience

49 *Annual Report of the Royal Cornwall Polytechnic Society*, Vol. 3, Pt. II, 1916, p. 166.

in answering the queries of his many visitors and correspondents. There was little wonder that his mind became encyclopaedic. Of the several subjects in which he had a special interest and at which he worked with care, liturgiology, the history of church ceremonial was, perhaps, his chief love. It is a subject which requires infinite patience and delicacy and a great knowledge of languages.[50]

Jenner continued to work on the Cornish language. He was elected a Fellow of the Society of Antiquaries in 1883, serving at times on its council. He recorded how he 'was one of the originators and organisers' of the series of major historical exhibitions held at the New Gallery in Regent Street, London, the Tudor, Stuart, Guelph and Victorian Exhibitions in 1888 to 1892, and the 'Monarchy of Great Britain and Ireland' exhibition of 1902, which coincided with the coronation of Edward VII. For this he wrote the historical introduction to the catalogue, 'dealing with the origin, development, and constitution of the British Monarchy from the sixth century onward'. From 1890 to 1905, in his own words, 'he assisted in the conducting of a sort of amateur magazine entitled *The Royalist*, which was devoted to the history of the Royal House of Stuart and its adherents, and of the Stuart and Jacobite period generally. In this he wrote a number of historical, biographical, genealogical and other articles, and a certain amount of verse, the last including some translations from Scottish Gaelic.' At the end of his life, it was said he 'had known all the leading British archaeologists and antiquaries of the past fifty years'. On his retirement from the Museum in 1909, Jenner, 'who never cared for London, settled in Cornwall, buying a house close to his wife's old home at Hayle, and christening it Bospowes, the "House of Peace".'[51] From there 'for 25 years he has been the leader of the academic circles of Cornwall'.[52] He was elected a member of the Royal Institution of Cornwall, becoming its president

50 *West Briton*, 10 May, 1934.
51 *West Briton*, 10 May, 1934.
52 *Annual Report of the Royal Cornwall Polytechnic Society*, Vol. 8, 1934, p. 59.

in 1921, and was also active in the Royal Cornwall Polytechnic
Society. He was chairman of the Committee of the County Council of
Cornwall for the Preservation of Ancient Monuments, and president
of the county Folk Dance Society and the Wrestling Association. 'He
was elected permanent president of the first Old Cornwall Society,
started at St. Ives in 1920', by himself and Morton Nance, another
figure of the Cornish language revival, 'and in 1924 he accepted the
permanent presidency of the County Federation'. He also became
president of the Cornwall Music Competition in 1917.

It is not, however, as a county notable with a 'patriarchal
personality' that Jenner deserves to be remembered in British history.
His true importance was highlighted in a subheading of his obituary
in the *West Briton*, 'Recognition as a Celtic Nation'. In 1901, as
he recalled in 1916, 'he was one of the promoters of the proposed
Celtic Cornish Society', the *Cowethas Celto-Kernuack*, designedly
the first Cornish language movement, 'which, though apparently
well supported to begin with, came to nothing. His share in this
matter', he wrote modestly, 'did not go much beyond translating the
prospectus of the Society into Cornish'. He became proficient also in
Breton. 'His interest in Brittany and the Bretons was rewarded by his
elevation to Bardic rank in the Gorsedd of the Bards of Brittany',[53]
founded in 1901. As he remembered:

> In 1903 he attended the Congress of the *Union Regionaliste
> Bretonne* (*Kevredigez Broad Breiz*) at Lesneven, in Finisterre, and
> the Gorsedd of the Bards of Brittany (*Gorsez Barzed Gourenez
> Breiz*), held in connection with the Congress at the great dolmen
> of Kerroc'h in Plouneour-Trez, conferred on him the degree of
> Bard, with the "bardic name" of "Gwaz Mikel " (or in Cornish
> form "Gwas Myhel"), which signifies the "Vassal (or subject) of
> St. Michael," the Patron of Cornwall. It was at the concluding
> "banquet" of this Congress that he made a short speech in Cornish

53 *Annual Report of the Royal Cornwall Polytechnic Society*, Vol. 8, 1934, p. 59.

(perhaps the first set speech that has been made in that tongue since Francis Robinson preached in Cornish at Landeewednack in 1678), and much to his astonishment was very fairly understood by Breton-speaking members of the audience. In the same year he joined the Celtic Association, and at the Pan-Celtic Congress at Carnarvon in August, 1904, he succeeded in persuading the Celtic Association to recognise Cornwall as one of the Celtic nations, which it had hitherto declined to do. He was elected a Vice-President of the Association in 1904.[54]

The paper which Jenner read before the Pan-Celtic Congress at Carnarvon on that momentous occasion, *Cornwall a Celtic Nation*, was published in *The Celtic Review* in 1905.

As the *West Briton* observed after his death in 1934:

Merely to enumerate his offices does not sum up all that Mr. Jenner has done for Cornwall. It is not every county has a man of encyclopaedic mind and great generosity ready to give assistance and information all who asked it. He would take infinite pains to answer the queries of even the most superficial and casual enquirers. People who wrote to him for information on Cornish matters were almost overwhelmed when they received his complete and exhaustive replies written in the smallest and neatest of scripts. Mr. Jenner had not many printed books to his credit. His excellent "Cornish Grammar" was published in 1904, and in the opinion of his many admirers this should have been the first and not the last of works on Cornwall from his pen. He had, however, many living books in the shape of disciples whom he inspired and encouraged.[55]

54 *Annual Report of the Royal Cornwall Polytechnic Society*, Vol. 3, Pt. II, 1916, p. 167-8.
55 *West Briton*, 10 May, 1934. He appended a select bibliography of his numerous papers to his autobiographical notes of 1916, *ibid.*, pp. 169-173, and this was updated after his death in the *Annual Report of the Royal Cornwall Polytechnic Society*, Vol. 8, 1934, pp. 62-64.

His *A Handbook of the Cornish Language*, dedicated in that tongue *Dho 'm Gwreg Gernuak*, 'to my Cornish wife', and published by subscription in 1904, was, indeed, the classic of its subject. He was also successful in securing the admission of Cornishmen proficient in Cornish to the Gorsedd of Wales.

At a meeting of the Federation of Old Cornwall Societies, of which he was the first President,

at Boscawen-Un, [near St Buryan] June 25th, 1927, wearing his Breton bardic robe, he gave an address on the Gorsedd, stating the reasons why Cornwall should have one of its own. A little more than a year later, Sept. 21st, 1928, a CORNISH GORSEDD [*Gorsedd Kernow*] was established at the same spot inaugurated by the Archdruid of Wales, who confirmed his appointment as Grand Bard, and a Gorsedd has been held each year since then, at most of which distinguished fellow-bards of Wales or Brittany have been present.'[56]

His 'position of leadership in Cornwall' was recognised at the International Arthurian Congress held at Truro in 1930, where he was elected President and 'filled the office with dignity and with a display of knowledge that charmed and impressed all the visitors', although he remained critical of Arthurian excesses at Tintagel. It also won recognition from the Celtic Congress:

In 1932 THE CELTIC CONGRESS, a descendent of the old CELTIC ASSOCIATION, was for the first time held in Cornwall, Mr. Jenner having been elected President for that year. This was the means of bringing to Cornwall many people whose names are household words in their own Celtic countries. In this, the Gorsedd and the Annual Cornish Service he saw the realisation of things for which he had worked in earlier years, and a growing recognition

56 *Annual Report of the Royal Cornwall Polytechnic Society*, Vol. 8, 1934, p. 60.

in Cornwall of the desirability of reviving its Cornish language and through this its Celtic Spirit.[57]

His position as first Grand Bard of Cornwall was held until his death. The *West Briton* recorded: 'The Grand Bard of the Cornish Gorsedd, who was aged 85, had been for some time keeping illness at bay, and only his great personality and powerful physique enabled him to preside at the Cornish Gorsedd, held in inclement weather, at Roche Rock, in August.' A number of fellow bards were present at the funeral, and, although robes were not felt appropriate, after the Requiem Mass at St Michael's Roman Catholic Church, Hayle, the symbolical sword of the Gorsedd was placed on the coffin. Mourned by his widow, Henry Jenner was buried in Lelant parish churchyard.[58] His 'notable collection' of Breton and other Celtic books was bequeathed to the library of the Royal Institution of Cornwall at Truro.

Called the 'Father of the Cornish Language Revival,'[59] Jenner was also Godfather of the Jesus voyage 'tradition', and to this discovery of his we must now return.

57 *Annual Report of the Royal Cornwall Polytechnic Society*, Vol. 8, 1934, p. 60.
58 *West Briton*, Thurs. 17 May, 1934.
59 Ellis, P. Berresford, n.d. *The Story of the Cornish Language*, Tor Mark Press, Truro, pp. 24-26.

Fig 9. Fifteenth-century stained glass. Joseph holds vials of the Blood and Sweat of Jesus, as in Glastonbury Abbey's version of his legend. Drawn by Honor Howard-Mercer, 1929.

5

THE LONDON FOREMAN'S TALE

In 1916 Jenner included his own account of the origin of the voyage story in *St Joseph of Arimathea as the Apostle of Britain*, a wide-ranging and learned article in the summer issue of *Pax*, the Quarterly Review of the Benedictines of Caldey Island. Jenner commented, as others have done since, on the seeming lack of a good reason for the choice of Joseph as the legendary Apostle of Britain:

but I think a certain not very widely known tradition may supply a good reason why St Joseph should have been thought to have come to Britain, though I do not go so far as to say that he really did come.

There is a curious practice in use among the makers of metal organ-pipes, of which I heard at second hand from an eye-witness, an amateur in such matters, Mr. James Baillie Hamilton, who told the story to Mr. George Hallam, then one of the masters of Harrow School, who told it to me about twenty years ago. Mr. James Baillie Hamilton - I tell the tale as it was told to me - went to the workshop of one of the principal firms of organ-builders to see the process of making metal pipes. It seems that it is the practice, (in order, I suppose, to obtain a perfectly smooth and homogeneous surface, which, as may be imagined, is of importance to the tone,) to throw a shovelfull of molten metal along a table, on which is stretched a linen cloth. It may be well understood that this is a delicate operation, and requires considerable skill and care, not only to produce the desired effect, but also because it would be easy for a serious accident to happen, either to the operator or to the bystanders, through a slight slip of the hand. It was noticed that each workman before he made his cast said in a low tone, "Joseph was in the tin trade." The foreman, who was taking the visitor round, was asked for an explanation of this saying, and after some persuasion gave it in words to this effect: "We workers in metal are a very old fraternity, and like some other handicrafts we have old traditions among us. One of these, the memory of which is preserved in this invocation, is to the effect that St. Joseph of Arimathea, the rich man of the Gospels, made his money in the tin trade between Phoenicia* and Cornwall. We have also a story that he made several voyages to Britain in his own ships, and that on one occasion he brought with him the Child Christ and his Mother as passengers, and landed them at St. Michael's Mount in Cornwall."

When I heard this story, I said at once that I knew the expression, "Joseph was in the tin trade," as a proverb in Cornwall, though I had never thought enough about it to have considered which of the three scriptural Josephs it might refer to, nor did I remember where or when I had heard it. The tradition of the visit of the Child Christ and His Mother to the Mount is also known in Cornwall. It is mentioned in Black's "Guide to Cornwall," but I think it is possible that the editor, who happens to be a friend of mine, may have got it from me after I had been reminded of the tradition by the organ-making story. It is noteworthy that there exists also a whole set of legends of the wanderings of the Holy Mother and Son in the Outer Hebrides, with some very pretty folk-lore and moral teaching mixed up in them; and places where the events happened are pointed out. I think somewhat similar stories are found in Ireland. But St. Joseph and the tin trade do not come into these. They are mostly connected with St. Bridget, in her rather anachronistic character as "Muime Chriosta" (Foster-mother of Christ), as the Scottish Gaels call her.

[footnote] *Probably this should be Alexandria rather than Phoenicia. After the fall of Tyre in B.C. 332 Alexandria, founded in the same year, took its place as the chief trading city in the tin trade as in other commerce.

Jenner went on to mention other late legends concerning a journey of Joseph to Spanish Galicia with St James and, by an emendation of his own, to Brittany, his point being that these were the only other ancient tin-producing districts in Europe. In the conclusion of his long article he writes:

> We do not know how old the tin trade legend may be, or whether it was invented after the Glastonbury and Grail stories in their twelfth and thirteenth century forms had been generally accepted, as a Cornish pendant to them; but taken with the quite independent legend of St. Joseph's connection with St. James and tin-producing Galicia, and with Wolfram's story of the Spanish resting-place of the Grail and the Toledo provenance of the legend, it seems as if it might be the earlier of the two. At any rate it appears to furnish a reason for the choice of St. Joseph as the Apostle of Britain, and at the worst it adds something of "an artistic verisimilitude to an otherwise bald and unconvincing narrative," making the story seem a little less improbable than it would be without it. It may have been the first, but it certainly was not the last time that Christianity has followed trade routes.[60]

This article, by perhaps the last serious scholar to champion the possible historicity of the Joseph legend, became the *locus classicus* of the Jesus voyage 'tradition'. Jenner was clearly rather pleased with his 'discovery'. He repeated the story as given above, almost word for word, in a reply to a letter from a Mr Hony of Fowey, which appeared in the *Western Morning News* of Plymouth in March 1933, enquiring about the story of Joseph and Jesus and their voyage seeking tin in 'the Isles of Scilly and the mainland of Cornwall'. Jenner's second account,

60 Jenner, 1916, pp. 135-7, 140-1.

however, does add some small details. The occasion on which he first heard the tale is now shown to have been a dinner party:

WAS CHRIST IN CORNWALL?
"JOSEPH WAS IN THE TIN TRADE"
VOYAGE BY OWN SHIP TO ST. MICHAEL'S MOUNT
BY HENRY JENNER
of Hayle.

Mr. T.H.L. Hony's letter, which appropriately appeared on Lady Day, suggests an interesting story, and as I think, though I am not quite sure, that I am answerable for the first publication in print of the curious legend, I may as well explain how I got hold of it, and give my authority for it.

About forty years ago I happened to be dinning at the house of one of the masters of Harrow School, the late Mr. George Hallam, when the following story was told of a friend of his by our host, who had just heard it.

Mr. James Baillie Hamilton, an amateur in organ building, went to the workshop of one of the principal firms of organ builders in London ...

The story follows as before to the point where he observes that he had never thought enough about the saying 'Joseph was in the tin trade' to consider which Joseph it referred to.

I found later that it was well known to other Cornish people. When I went to the British Museum the next day, I looked up St. Joseph of Arimathea in the "Acta Sanctorum," and, though I found nothing about the tin trade and most of what I did find was the usual Gospel of Nicodemus, Glastonbury and Grail legend, there was one life which made him accompany St. James the Great to Galicia in Spain, which was the other tin-producing district of his time. ...

I told the story soon after I heard it to my friend Mr. Ascott

Hope Moncrieff, the editor of Black's "Guide to Cornwall," and he put it into his 1895 edition, which, as far as I know, was its first appearance in print. I also told it to Mr. Baring-Gould, to whom it was quite new, and he worked it into one of his novels, and rather spoilt it by a characteristically conjectural emendation into "Joseph to the tinner's aid."

IN THE HEBRIDES

Soon after that I was staying on South Uist, in the Catholic part of the Outer Hebrides, and found there a whole set of legends of the wanderings of the Holy Mother and Son on those islands, with some very pretty folklore and moral teaching associated with them. There was nothing about St. Joseph or the tin trade in them, and some were connected with St. Bridget in her anachronistic character of "Muime Chriosta" (Foster-mother of Christ), as the Scottish Gaels call her.

I wonder where Mr. Hony got his notion that St. Joseph was the uncle of Our Lady. It is not at all improbable, but I do not remember any mention of such a relationship even in the most fanciful of the Grail romances.[61]

As Mr. Hony rightly says, "It is an attractive legend." It is not impossible that it is true, but, though one would like to believe that Those Two really did come to Cornwall, I fear that one can only ask with William Blake, who seems to have known some form of it,

"And did those Feet ...?

and we shall probably never be able to get an answer to those questions.[62]

What are we to make of this tale told, as in an Arthur Machen fantasy story, amid the port and cigars following a late Victorian

61 The idea originates, in this context, with the Rev. Morgan, who says that Joseph 'is by Eastern tradition said to have been the younger brother of the father of the Virgin Mary.' Morgan, 1861; 1922 ed. p. 119, note 15.

62 *The Western Morning News* (Plymouth) 6 April 1933, p.6; Smith, 1989, pp. 68-9.

dinner? Was it, perhaps, a spoof played by the public-school master on his savant guest, or one which had previously been played on him by his friend, Mr James Baillie Hamilton? Certainly, as in Baring-Gould's version, the technological details within the story inspire little confidence, and yet Hamilton had a practical bent, and achieved his moment of fame when he invented a new keyboard instrument, a harmonium or reed-organ, with three manuals and pedal, which he named the vocalion. He published a twenty page prospectus for his instrument, around the year 1883, entitled *The new musical instrument, the vocalion*, which comprised a compilation of press notices and testimonials.[63] An account of it also appeared in the *Proceedings of the Musical Association*, describing a demonstration held for the Association on the 5th February 1883 at which Hamilton himself was unable to be present because of illness. From this account it is apparent that the instrument, which was seemingly first built at Canterbury, had already been some years in development, and had been demonstrated in Westminster Abbey and St. Giles' Cathedral, Edinburgh. It came in more than one size, the larger version having organ pipes. Hamilton had a show-room in Cadogan Terrace, Hackney.[64] His instrument was later exhibited at the International Inventions Exhibition in London in 1885, and manufactured in America. If his visit to the organ-maker's were a part of his research for his invention, then his story might already have been more than a decade old by the time it reached Hallam's ears.

The host, George Hallam, was still very much alive in 1916. He was a classicist who had published an edition of Ovid's *Fasti* in 1881, and also wrote a *Pictorial and descriptive guide to Harrow and Harrow school* which ran to five editions. As the dinner apparently took place in the early 1890s, a model of sorts could have been found in the story of Glastonbury's Chalice Well or Blood Spring as reddened with the blood of Christ from the Grail which Joseph had hidden there which, as we have seen, seemingly appeared in print

63 Hamilton, ?1883.
64 *Proceedings of the Musical Assoc.*Ninth Series, 1882-83, 1883, pp. 59-69.

for the first time in 1887,[65] and may not have been very much older. The change of emphasis to Cornwall might have been tailored to Jenner's interests, but if this *were* the inspiration, then why was the Glastonbury matter not cited in its support from the beginning? And why was the story attributed not to some rustic, or returning traveller from the West Country, but to a London foreman? To dismiss Jenner's account out of hand is to abandon hope of a solution to the question of the origins of the story. While maintaining a certain reserve, let us see where its pursuit may take us.

For Jenner, clearly, the import of the story was that it offered in the Cornish stanneries an economic underpinning for the by then suspect legend of Joseph. He felt that he might have stumbled upon an older and more credible version of the legend than that of the Grail romances or of what he terms, rather dismissively, 'the common Glastonbury story, as related by John of Glastonbury, Capgrave and many more, in its simplest form'.[66] Amidst the store of erudition on Joseph which he amassed, an analysis of the Glastonbury texts themselves is markedly absent. Neither, despite his growing attraction to the Roman Catholic Church, does he seem to have been much impressed by the larger historical and spiritual implications of a possible visit by the Son of God; Blake and his visions are mentioned only incidentally, in the last year of Jenner's long life. For the first Grand Bard of Cornwall, it was the Duchy that mattered.

It was the saying 'Joseph was in the tin trade' which struck a chord with him. He felt he had heard this before in Cornwall, and subsequent inquiries met the same response in others there. Jenner, encouraged by his wife, the Cornish novelist Kitty Lee, was an avid collector of Cornish vocabulary, songs and phrases. Perhaps it was, indeed, once a genuine saying among those who mined, traded or worked in metal. Perhaps, even, it was part of a skipping rhyme or lullaby in mining communities, the *Joseph was a tin-man ...* refrain to

65 In Wright, 1887, p.21; repeated in Barrett, 1894, p.24. On p. 25 Barrett includes a sketch of the 'Blood Spring' dated 1893.
66 Jenner, 1916, p. 137, note 1.

which Σ seemingly referred in *SDNQ* in 1895, and which others later reported, which Jenner remembered. Jenner says 'I had never thought enough about it to have considered which of the three scriptural Josephs it might refer to, nor did I remember where or when I had heard it.' Jenner's remembered tag, then, came if genuine with no very clear story attached. Perhaps different accounts arose at various times and places to 'explain' it, and the London foreman's may have been an idiosyncratic one. The assumption by Jenner (and perhaps by Σ) that it must refer to a scriptural Joseph at all was quite possibly one made with hindsight. Joseph was hardly an uncommon name and, if a more specific identity is required, then it might have referred to the Wandering Jew, or more generically to the Jewish miners of Cornish folklore, those lost souls who, as we have seen, haunted the mines as the Knockers.

The story of Christ's incarnate presence in Britain is paralleled in some respects by that of the Cup of Nanteos in which we see a similar progression from vague local belief, *via* antiquarian speculation, to widely known modern 'literary' myth. Locally known in Cardiganshire from the 1850s as a healing cup, this broken wooden bowl had been drawn to the attention of the learned when exhibited in 1878 at a meeting of the Cambrian Archaeological Society. In a note in that body's journal of 1888, it was romantically suggested that it might be made from wood of the True Cross. In 1905, coincident with the noted nonconformist 'revival' in Wales in which various 'psychic' phenomena were attested, a booklet appeared suggesting that the Cup was made of olive wood, and was, in fact, the Holy Grail, Christ's cup of the Last Supper, secreted away from Glastonbury on the eve of the Dissolution by seven monks who sought refuge at the Welsh (Cistercian) abbey of Strata Florida, *Ystrad Fflur*. When this in turn was despoiled, the Glastonbury monks and the Cup were sheltered by a local gentry family at Nanteos, the house built by the abbey ruins, to whom the Cup was eventually entrusted.[67] By the 1920s the Nanteos story had begun to gain acknowledgement as a genuine 'tradition' in local guides and popular histories. It acquired further details, such as an apocryphal visit by Richard Wagner, who was supposedly inspired by the Cup to write his opera *Parsifal*. The Cup may actually have informed the mystical writer Arthur Machen's short story *The Great Return*, 1915, which told of the reappearance of the Grail in contemporary Wales. Written at about the same time was his more famous story, *The Bowmen* of 1915, which, taken as fact, inspired the widespread 'Legend of the Angels of Mons.' It should be added here that Glastonbury Abbey never claimed to posses the Grail, howsoever understood, that there is no historical evidence for the fugitive monks, and that modern expert examination declares the cup to be a late medieval 'mazer bowl' made of wych elm.[68] However that may be, the 'legend' of *Cwpan Nanteos* has endured, and will doubtless continue to do so.

67 Stephen J. Williams, The Cup of Nanteos, *Archaeologia Cambrensis* 5, 1888, pp, 170-1; Ethelwyn M. Amery, *Sought and Found: A Story of the Holy Graal*, Aberystwyth, 1905.

68 Mazer wood is that from a nodule on a tree, and a mazer-bowl or -cup is one notionaly turned from such a mazer. For the history of the Cup, see Wood, 2001, and references.

Fig 10. Younghusband's troops enter the ceremonial
West Gate of Lhasa, August 4th, 1904.

6

'AFTER ARMAGEDDON ...'

Coincidentally or otherwise, that same year in which Jenner first recorded his story in print, 1916, had earlier seen the setting of Blake's lines *And did those feet ...?* to music as the hymn *Jerusalem*,[69] which drew much attention in *The Times* and elsewhere. This was occasioned by a West Countryman of sorts, the explorer Sir Francis Younghusband (1863-1942), who spent part of his childhood near Bath and who was educated at Clifton College in Bristol. In 1903-4 he achieved fame as the conqueror of Tibet, and his exploits there were rather unkindly compared with those of Cortez and Pizarro. The treaty which he concluded in Lhasa at the end of hostilities went somewhat beyond his brief. Subsequently regarded as a maverick by the authorities of the *Raj*, 'after retiring from frontier life he began to preach free love to shocked Edwardians, and set up a strange patriotic movement during the First World War with *Jerusalem* as its specially composed rallying song'.[70]

'The Fight for Right', as Younghusband's movement was called, began in August 1915. It was envisaged as an alliance of writers, mystics, artists and composers to embody and lead the moral

69 The 16 lines occur in the preface to Blake's prophetic book, *Milton*, written and etched 1804-8, pp. 480-1 in Geoffrey Keynes *Blake, Complete Writings*, OUP 1979 ed.; all quotations from Blake are hereafter given as [K480-1] referring to the page number of this widely accessible edition. The hymn *Jerusalem*, Parry's 1916 setting of the lines from *Milton*, should not be confused with Blake's later book of the same name, of 1804-1820.
70 French, 1994, p.xx.

crusade against Germany and to support the war. John Buchan, Thomas Hardy and many Old Cliftonians gave support. The Poet Laureate, Robert Bridges, agreed to find a song for the movement. On reflection, he felt that the now famous lines from the Preface to Blake's *Milton* might prove a suitable text. An outsider in his own lifetime, Blake's reputation as a visionary genius had grown through the nineteenth century. In his *William Blake: A Critical Essay*, 1868, the poet Algernon Charles Swinburne had singled out the Preface to *Milton* for special attention, quoting it in full and writing that 'this strange and grand prelude, which, though taken in the letter it may read like foolishness, is in the spirit of it certainty and truth for all time.'[71] W. B. Yeats' accessible 1893 pocket edition of the *Poems of William Blake* in the Muses' Library series printed *And did those feet..* as a discrete poem, headed simply 'From Milton,' and this was in all likelihood Bridges' immediate inspiration.[72]

In March 1916 Bridges approached the composer Sir Hubert Parry (1848-1918), asking him to set 'suitable, simple music to Blake's stanzas - music that an audience could take up and join in.'[73] Parry composed

Fig 11. .Sir Francis Younghusband in 1903, before leaving for Tibet. The tough explorer returned with a mystical bent, and caused the recasting of Blake's lines as the hymn Jerusalem.

Fig 12. Sir Hubert Parry, who wrote the music: 'Here's a tune for you, old chap. Do what you like with it.'

71 Swinburne, 1868, p. 259.
72 Yeats, ed., 1897, 'The Prophetic Books,' p. 233.
73 Letter from Bridges, n.d., Graves, Charles, 1926, ii, 92.

the perfect tune on the 10th March, and showed it to Walford Davies, the conductor, the next day at the Royal College of Music, with the words 'Here's a tune for you, old chap. Do what you like with it'.[74] He was particularly pleased with the D note in the second stanza, where the words 'O clouds unfold ..' break the rhythm. The first public performance was at the Queen's Hall:

> The Queen's Hall meeting took place on 28 March 1916 in front of a large audience. Robert Bridges told them that the country's safety depended on the spirit of its people and 'an irresistible front, united in the principles of Order, and Right, and devoted Patriotic Duty'. By using some quirky textual analysis, he showed that the idea of building Jerusalem in England's green and pleasant land was much the same as the principle behind the Fight for Right. William Blake was claimed as a supporter. Whether Blake, with his radical views on imperialism and social revolution, would have agreed is open to question. But Bridges was sure. 'I asked my friend Sir Hubert Parry to compose a setting of Blake's poem for us,' he told the crowd. 'He has done so, and we shall hear it tonight for the first time.'
>
> A choir of 300 Fighters for Right sang *Jerusalem* with gusto, conducted by Walford Davies, and soon they were accompanied by the congregations of Britain's churches. The Land Army joined in, as did the Officer Training Corps, and the Public Schools and the Suffragettes and the Women's Institute, who have not stopped singing since. *Jerusalem* now appears at the Last Night of the Proms.[75]

Parry was no jingo, and was uneasy about the 'Fight for Right', which collapsed in 1917 amid internal squabbles, and on 17 May 1917 Parry wrote to Younghusband withdrawing *Jerusalem* as the movement's rallying tune. Parry had been better pleased when the women's movement, with which he had a long-standing sympathy, adopted it

74 Graves, 1926, ii, p. 174. See also Dibble, 1992, pp. 482-85.
75 French, 1994, pp.302-3 with refs..

Fig 13. General Allenby enters Jerusalem on foot,
December 11th, 1917. 'We have returned.'

in March 1917. After Parry's death, the tune was re-orchestrated by
Elgar for the Leeds Festival of 1922, and this embellished version is
now that most familiar.

Younghusband's accounts of his movement in his later writings
concentrated on the "the one relic of our work", Parry's *Jerusalem*.[76]
He went on to involvement in organising the early Everest expeditions,
wrote on superior beings living on the planet Altair, and founded the
World Congress of Faiths in 1936.

When Younghusband led an Imperial army into the Holy City of

76 French, 1994,. p. 308.

Lhasa in 1904, his action was controversial. The same could not be said of General Edmund Allenby, who in December 1917 led the first Christian army to take Jerusalem since its fall to Islam in 1244. The city surrendered to his troops on the ninth and, two days later, he dismounted from his charger before the Jaffa Gate, and entered the streets of that Holy City on foot, an example followed by all his officers, including Lawrence of Arabia. Lloyd George commended the event to the Commons as a Christmas present for the nation. It inspired world-wide excitement. One Jewish-American artist equated Allenby's action with the triumph of Judas Maccabaeus, who cleansed the Temple from the 'Abomination of Desolation' in 165 BC. It was a kind of symbolic culmination of British Empire.

Allenby's crowning victory was at Megiddo, the biblical Armagedon, in September 1918, and the capitulation of Turkey followed almost at once. Allenby was created a Field-Marshal, and Viscount Allenby of Megiddo

Fig 14. A contemporary Jewish-American view of the British occupation of Jerusalem.

and (rather incongruously) Felixstowe. These events, coupled with the collapse of the second German *Reich* in November 1918, were productive of a strange sensibility in Britain in which genuine horror and awe at the scale of the sacrifice throughout society was mingled with a kind of exaltation that a prophesied New Age was at last dawning. Nowhere was this heightened emotional state more evident than in Glastonbury, as a perusal of the contemporary local press amply demonstrates, and it often took religious or quasi-mystical forms. Allenby's capture of Jerusalem was enthusiastically celebrated by the weekly *Central Somerset Gazette*:

CAPTURE OF JERUSALEM.
BRITISH ARMY'S FORMAL ENTRY.
A WORLD-WIDE HISTORIC EVENT.
GLASTONBURY'S SPECIAL INTEREST.

At last, the holiest and most historic city of the Christian world, Jerusalem, has fallen to British arms and the Union Jack floats over the shrines of Christian faith.

Deeply significant and interesting as this great historic event is to the country at large, it has an added and a special interest for our ancient borough of Glastonbury. As owing its reputed existence [*sic*] to the first Christian mission from Jerusalem; as the site of the world's first Christian church, and as the old centre of the Grail legend and of national rebirth, Glastonbury has been awaiting the news with an eagerness which has been more deep and personal than that possibly of any other place in the English speaking world. The fact that many Glastonians are in the victorious Army in the ranks of the S.L.I. [Somerset Light Infantry] and other units has of course also added to this special local interest from other aspects.

After detailing military aspects of the capture and preparations for the formal entry, the report continued with a summary of the city's history:

In looking back through the cinema of history and life which the record of Jerusalem presents we find no definite starting point of foundation or building initially from which to start a survey of Jerusalem's extraordinary past. The first mention of it in the Bible is in the mysterious incident of Abraham and Melchizedek, "the priest who lived for ever and ever, without beginning and without end." Many have believed with much reason, that this name typified an early church where the knowledge of God and man's true relations with Him were taught, and a foreshadowing of Christianity as it were. ...

... The Christian drama then subsequently unrolled itself to its climax at Jerusalem and, for some thirty-five years after it was the headquarters of Christian teaching by the Apostles. It was during this period that Joseph of Arimathea, if strongly supported legend is to be believed, sailed for Britain and founded the first Christian Church at our town of Glastonbury. ... Now, with [Jerusalem's] passing under British rule a new era sets in. It is a rather curious coincidence that not only David its first captor, as we have stated, but the present heir apparent of Britain has David as one of his names and our present Premier is also called David! Whether the almost universal popular belief will be fulfilled that the capture of Jerusalem means the beginning of a new and better era in the world remains to be seen.

It may be mentioned for those whose views of this are based on the bible prophecies, that there are also very ancient Egyptian prophecies to this effect relating to the end of 1917. A vast subject of interest is certainly opened up by the fall of Jerusalem.[77]

The extraordinary sensibility following the Great War continued to show up in unexpected places. As late as 1927, E. K. Chambers, in his still classic study of the Arthurian legend, *Arthur of Britain*, explaining the myth of the sleeping Arthur, cited the parallel legends of Kaiser Barbarossa in Germany. When he awakes, 'He will hang

77 *CSG*, 14 Dec. 1917, p.5.

Fig 15. Church Militant: clergy process into
Glastonbury Abbey for the reception of the deeds by
the Archbishop of Canterbury in the presence of the
Prince and Princess of Wales, June 22nd, 1909.

his shield on a withered tree, which will break into leaf and a better day will dawn. ... Frederick is in several other caves, notably on the Unter[s]berg near Salzburg. Here too are the details of the beard and the withered tree. It will leaf again before the final battle, which will be Armageddon. Whether it did leaf again, I do not know.'[78]

Glastonbury had already been popularised as the 'English Jerusalem' before the war, in 1909, in *Glastonbury: The Historic Guide to the "English Jerusalem,"* written by Charles L. Marson, perpetual curate of Hambridge, near Taunton, in the aftermath of the acquisition of the Abbey ruins in the interest of the Church of England in 1908, an event which had aroused national interest and royal patronage. The notion was founded on a poem included by the medieval chronicler John of Glastonbury (1342) which referred to

78 Chambers, 1927, p. 226. Ironically, perhaps, Hitler's mountain-retreat, the Berghof, was built to look across the valley to the Untersberg.

Glastonbury as the 'new Jerusalem.'

In the years immediately following the Great War, Glastonbury was hailed in its local newspaper, which, in those days, gave space to the views of many a mystic, as the English Mecca as well as the English Jerusalem. Nor was its outlook singular. In 1918 the architect Frederick Bligh Bond (a friend of Marson) published *The Gate of Remembrance*, an account of his spiritualistic archaeological techniques as 'director of excavations' at the Abbey, by which, as he believed, information from the memories of the medieval monks were conveyed to him through intermediaries in the form of 'automatic' script. He followed this with a second book, of prophecies of similar provenance concerning the course of the war, *The Hill of Vision*, in 1919. In that same year he was commissioned to design the town's war memorial, and wove into it as much mystical symbolism as he decently could. The poet, dramatist, educationalist and Christian socialist Alice Buckton (1867-1944), who since 1913 had run the Chalice Well property as an esoteric guest house and artistic centre, commissioned an ornamental cover for the well, also, apparently, to Bond's symbolic design, and this was dedicated as a thank-offering for Peace on All Saint's Day 1919.

In 1922 Buckton commissioned and wrote the screen-play for a professionally directed cinema film, *Glastonbury Past and Present*.[79] A silent-film pageant with an amateur local cast, this has been called 'the first documentary of an English town's history'.[80] It began with the arrival of Joseph of Arimathea, played by the Venerable Walter Farrer, Archdeacon of Wells (although without the boy Jesus), and ended with scenes offering a quixotic post-war revival of knight-errantry in the modern world, complete with Britannia giving the Roman - soon to become the Fascist - salute.

It was in 1924 that Violet Firth began her reign as Dion Fortune, the head of her magical order of the 'Society of the Inner Light,' at neighbouring Chalice Orchard. The composer Rutland Boughton's

79 Directed by H. O. Martinek and produced by the Steadfast Film Company, London.
80 Ball, 2004, p. 8.

Glastonbury Festivals, which were meant to echo Bayreuth, also recommenced, following the war, at Easter 1919. This rather intoxicated era, hovering on the brink of the apocalyptic, was captured retrospectively by John Cowper Powys in fictional form in 1933 in his massive and locally controversial novel *A Glastonbury Romance*. This was the atmosphere in which the new-found ancient tradition of the Lord's coming was first publicly received at Glastonbury.

7

GLASTONBURY ROMANCE

At first, as we have seen, the story of Christ's visit to Britain as told by Jenner and those who took their lead from him focused on Cornwall. Whatever whispers of Somerset tradition might have prompted Σ to send his anonymous query to *SDNQ* in 1895 had left no other trace in the public domain at Glastonbury itself, and Σ's own attempt to raise interest in the matter apparently went unregarded.

The year 1906, which saw the publication of Taylor's *Coming of the Saints*, also saw the Butleigh Revel, an exercise in communal drama which was locally long remembered. This was held on June 19th and 20th in the grounds of Butleigh Court, four miles from Glastonbury, home of squire Robert Neville Grenville, a philanthropist and Glastonbury magistrate, prominent in the Somerset Archaeological and Natural History Society and the Glastonbury Antiquarian Society, who then owned both the Glastonbury Tribunal and the Tor. Although, as the programme confessed, 'Butleigh itself can boast no stirring historical events', it claimed 'a share in the glories of the famous Abbey', of which it had once been an estate. Scene one illustrated 'The Coming of St. Joseph', with his arrival at Weary-all Hill and the building of the Wattle Church. This was preceded by a Tableau of 'The Phoenician Traders, (after Lord Leighton's picture in the Royal Exchange)', but the programme records, prosaically, that 'All these Scenes, with the exception of the Tableau of the Phoenician Traders, have a distinct local interest: THAT was chosen as indicating the dawn of the history of our land'. For the writers of the Revel, seemingly, the possible 'local interest' provided by the voyage story was yet to come.

As far as I have been able to discover, the story of Christ's visit is first publicly acknowledged at Glastonbury itself only in 1920. At the Patronal Festival of the parish church of St John the Baptist in that year, on the evening of Midsummer's day, 24th June, Bishop Frodsham, late bishop of North Queensland 'and now Canon of Gloucester' preached what the reporter of the *Central Somerset Gazette* of the 2nd July described as an 'excellent, if somewhat long, sermon' on 'Glastonbury the resting-place of saints', beginning his remarks with the observation that 'Glastonbury has been called the English Jerusalem. ...' He spoke of York, Winchester, London: 'One and all of these cities have their origin in time; but Glastonbury, like that strange solitary figure whose name is associated with the Hebrew Jerusalem, is beyond time as history knows it, "having neither beginning of days nor end of life."'.[81] The reporter went on to note that,

'Following close upon the sermon by Bishop Frodsham on Thursday evening, the Vicar's sermon at Evensong on Sunday was what might be called a second chapter of a great romance. The present Renaissance of Glastonbury, for it really has begun - and no-one with eyes to see can be blind to the fact - shows signs of being as illimitable as history itself. We are witnessing a re-incarnation of the immortal spirit of Glastonbury; it is the proverbial repetition of history.'

That Sunday, the 27th June, in his sermon at St John's ('it was the conclusion of the Patronal Festival') the Vicar, the Rev. C. V. P.

---

81 The reference, as in the report on the capture of Jerusalem, is to Melchizedek, king of Salem and priest of the most high God, seen as the archetype of Christ, in *Gen.* 15.18-19; *Heb.* 7. It would be interesting to know if the congregation included Violet Firth, the future Dion Fortune, who at the winter solstice of 1923 had a spiritual encounter with Mechizedek on Glastonbury Tor.

Day, asserted that:

> 'Glastonbury people should be proud to live in a town that claims
> to be the fountain and origin of the Christian religion of the
> Anglican Communion. Be proud of the fact that history related
> that St Joseph of Arimathea came and lived in the place, and that
> his dust lay mingled with Glastonbury soil. Would they cherish
> too, the legend which stated that Christ Himself may have come
> here, and that the Holy Grail (from which He dispensed the first
> Eucharist) buried there on Chalice Hill? [sic] The Vicar saw no
> reason why the legend that Jesus Christ visited the spot should not
> be believed. All the Apostles were travellers. Joseph of Arimathea's
> ships might well have come to Cornwall. The most ancient ruins in
> Zimbwabee [sic], where towers were arranged in such a splendid
> order, the retorts used to hold the gold of Africa - these were
> exactly the same size and shape as those found in Cornwall to
> hold tin. The townspeople might recall with pride that the ground
> on which Glastonbury is built has, from earliest times, been the
> most sacred spot in England. Saints from the old Galilean church,
> before the Anglo-Saxon invasion of the fifth century, made the
> spot - then a few islands in the sea-marshes - the object of their
> pilgrimage. And the memory of that age turns upon that strange
> catalogue of Cornish saints found nowhere else in England; and
> from that time, through the golden mist of legend, has come down
> to us the names of Arthur and Guenevere.'

The Vicar continued in similar vein, recalling the history
of the abbey in the early middle ages. A digression merited the
subheading:

AN EASTERN PATRIARCH'S RESPECT

The preacher introduced a personal anecdote into his illuminative
sermon. "During an interview," he said, "with the old Patriarch of
Damascus, in his palace near to the house of Annanias, it was of
Glastonbury he spoke and reminded me how sacred a spot it must
be. Your feet are upon the dust of the Empire." It was not possible,

it has been said, to turn over a spade of earth in these few acres
without opening up the ground where some saint was buried.[82]

Here, at last, we have the Jesus voyage story ending in Glastonbury
and, for the first time, offered not as a piece of curious folklore but
as an ornament to, if not, indeed, a support of, Faith.

The Rev. Day, clearly, was not unfriendly to the fashionable
Glastonbury mysticism. The previous Michaelmas he had been
present, with the mayor-elect, and given an address on the value of
'commemorations', at a ceremony orchestrated by Alice Buckton
involving the ceremonial lighting of a 'ban-fire (not bon-fire)', with
symbolism of the quarters and the elements and fireworks, at the
Chalice Well. The dedication of the new cover of the Chalice Well,
which, as we have seen, had been commissioned by Buckton to the
design of Bligh Bond, followed on the Feast of All Saint's, and Rev.
Day again played his part. Bond afterwards gave a curious address
which strayed into angel-magic and other esoteric areas. Also taking
part in the ceremony was Prebendary Charles Bennett, Vicar of Pilton,
whom we shall meet again.[83]

Rev. Charles Victor Parkerson Day, C.B.E., was born in 1863 and
educated at the Abbey School, Beckenham, Kent, and at University
College, Durham. He spent some years in Australia, where George
Horsfall Frodsham, who had graduated at Durham three years later
than himself, became Bishop of North Queensland in 1902. Day
served as a chaplain with the Queensland contingent in South Africa
during the Boer War, 1900-2, and became Frodsham's Commissary in
1908. Returning to England he was, for a while, Principal of his old
school, and briefly Vicar of Wookey. He became Priest in Charge at
St John's, Glastonbury, in 1912. In those innocent days, the *Central*

---

82 This anecdote strangely echoes one John of Glastonbury related six centuries
before, concerning the crusader Rainald of Marksbury and the Sultan. It also
foreshadows one later told by Smithett Lewis in his posthumous notes (Lewis,
L.S., 1953).
83 *CSG*, 26 Sept. 1919, p. 2; Oct. 31, 1919, p. 2; Nov. 7, 1919, 1st p. of supp.;
14th Nov. 1919, 1st p. of supp..

Somerset Gazette could record:

> He loved youth. He was never more happy than when he was
> among the boys - his own Gordon Club, which he founded, the
> Baden Powell Scouts, of whom he was Vice chairman, and the
> Choir boys. Can it be wondered at that the boys rallied round him
> with all the enthusiasm of their young spirits and that they well
> nigh idolised him? Those who have heard his 'Come on boys!' and
> seen them crowd around him and almost struggle to get nearest
> him, know something of the strength of this bond of affection.
> Doubtless this love of his for youth, for young men, was a very
> potent factor in his war service in Mesopotamia and, before that,
> in Gallipoli. Possibly it was as strong, while it was certainly as
> characteristic, as his love of Empire. ... One or two traits of his
> character were remarkable. His fondness for boys and young
> men - one might say almost to the point of indulgence. It was a
> marvellous gift ... It was his personality. His influence was always
> for good. Partly for the boy's sake he took over the Abbey House
> ... that he might entertain the people in the grounds and use some
> of the rooms for the good of the parish. He was willing to spend,
> and he spent on behalf of his boys.

On the outbreak of the Great War, convinced initially, with his
native optimism, that it would be all over in six months, 'he felt that
his place was on the field of active service. This led to an absence
of about five years from the parish'. Glastonbury was left in the
charge of his curate, the Rev. Davies. 'His experience of two-and-
a-half years as Chaplain to the Queensland Contingent in the Boer
War was the foundation of his strikingly successful work amongst
all ranks in the four years of the Great War which followed twelve
years afterwards.'

> What was St. John's loss was the soldier's gain. Of the splendid
> work done by the Vicar as Chaplain to the Forces, at first at home
> and then abroad, chiefly in the East, there is abundant evidence.

During his long stay in Mesopotamia he not only was a true friend in need to numberless men stricken down either by the foe or by disease, but his assistance was invaluable in organising the work of the Chaplains' department. Here he earned his promotion and his decoration which he received from the hands of H.M. the King less than a year ago.

Unfortunately, as with so many others, the Vicar's health was seriously affected by his long stay in the East. He suffered from typhoid fever while there and the climate told on him heavily. He returned to this parish to outward appearance the same active man, the same striking personality as he left it, but appearances were deceptive, and his health was not the same as before.

About a month ago he was seized with serious illness, and after partial recovery was removed to a Clifton Nursing Home where he underwent a serious operation, but succumbed on Friday last.[84]

Fig 16. Rev. Charles Day (1863-1921), who first brought the Jesus Voyage story to Glastonbury. From a microfilm copy of his obituary, Central Somerset Gazette.

84 *CSG*, August 26, 1921.

He died in office on the 20th of August, 1921, aged only 58. He was remembered as kind and cheery, 'a master story-teller' and a pulpit orator of some force and skill. It comes as a slight surprise to learn that Day was a married man. His widow seems to have been genuinely touched by the grief of his parish. His photograph is more suggestive of a boxer or a rugby-player than of a parson; an oarsman in youth, his oars were proudly displayed on the wall at Abbey House. A man of action rather than a scholar, it is perhaps not taking psychology too far to suggest that the boy-loving Vicar of Glaston saw in Joseph of Arimathea a New Testament scout-master, showing his young charge the frontiers of Empire.

Day's successor as Vicar of St John's, Glastonbury, was the Rev. Lionel Smithett Lewis, who became the most prominent of a triumvirate of eccentric Anglican clergymen who were instrumental in the further propagation and development of the Jesus voyage tradition, its emphasis shifting from Cornwall to Glastonbury itself. The son of a vicar, he was born in 1867 at Margate, and was educated at Oundle and at Queen's College, Cambridge. Ordained Deacon in Gloucester and Bristol, 1891, he was a curate in Cheltenham, 1891-5, being priested in 1893. He was a curate in Pimlico, 1895-9, at St Paul's, Clifton, 1899-1900 and at All Saint's, Mile End, in East London, 1900-07. He was Vicar of St Mark's, Whitechapel, 1907-21. One of his two brothers, Rupert Edward, was Head Master of Wells Cathedral School and Priest-Vicar of Wells Cathedral, 1910-22 and Vicar of Pucklechurch with Abson, Gloucestershire, 1922-46. In 1911, Lewis married the daughter of a naval captain, Lilian Isolda Vereker. The marriage seems to have been a happy one.

An 'appreciation', by his last church warden at St John's, published following his death in 1953 in the *Central Somerset Gazette* records that:

He served as a slum Priest in the East End of London for a quarter of a century previous to coming to Glastonbury. His earliest work was in a West End of London parish and, while a young Priest there, he contemplated going out to Australia to join the Bush

Brotherhood. One day he lost his pet dog and, believing it to have been stolen, searched through the East End. During this search he was greatly moved by the emptiness of the lives of many of the young boys and their degeneration. By the time he got home he had reached the decision to devote his life to young people and go, not to Australia, but to the East End of London.[85]

He founded one of the earliest youth clubs in London, later used as a model by other organisations. 'He always camped with the boys when he took them to Epping Forest. He was over 70 before he gave up camping with his young charges. ... at the time of his death, Mrs. Lewis has had letters of sympathy from lads he knew 50 years ago. At the Vicarage [in Glastonbury] he and his wife kept open house for the young people of the neighbourhood. ... His spontaneous charity to anyone in distress was amazing'

Nor were his concerns with humanity alone. He preached to his Glastonbury flock on the hope of immortality of the animals.[86] As early as 1910 he was campaigning against vivisection. He was a founder of Our Dumb Friend's League and a vice-president of the Anti-vivisectionist Society and of the Anti-Vivisection Hospital. *The Times*, in its anonymously contributed obituary, concentrated on his charity towards the animal creation:

all his life he crusaded for the welfare of animals. He considered it part of every Christian's duty to do everything possible to relieve the sufferings of animals and to ensure they were not exploited or ill-treated.

He not only preached this from the pulpit but carried it out in practice. He started the Whitechapel Cats' Shelter ... for the thousands of unwanted, starving, and ill-treated cats which abounded in that part of London. It was in the basement of his building that the late Mrs. M. E. Dickin, M.B.E. founded the

85 *CSG*, 27 July, 1953.
86 *CSG*, 14 July, 1922, p. 6.

now famous People's Dispensary for Sick Animals in 1917, at the invitation of Mr. Lewis, who heard she could not find other suitable premises. He was also closely associated with Nina Duchess of Hamilton in starting the Ferne Animal Sanctuary, Dorset, and gave active help to other animal welfare organisations, including the Animal Defence Society.

A scholar and an authority on antiquities, Mr. Lewis added greatly to the store of knowledge of the history, legends and traditions concerning Glastonbury. It was he who revived [*sic*] the Glastonbury pilgrimages [in 1923] and also the very ancient custom of sending a flowering sprig of the Holy Thorn of Glastonbury to the Queen each Christmas. Queen Mary was the first Queen to receive this tribute since the days of Queen Henrietta Maria. She greatly valued the gift, especially since it came from one personally known to her and for whom she had a very high regard. Queen Mary used to visit Mr. Lewis in his Whitechapel parish and take a personal interest in many of the sad cases he brought to her notice. It was a very great grief to Mr. Lewis that, owing to failing health, he was unable to obey Queen Elizabeth's command to be present at Queen Mary's funeral in St. George's Chapel. Mr. Lewis wrote several books on Glastonbury which passed into many editions. He was especially interested in the persistent tradition that Glastonbury had been visited by Our Lord as a Child in company with S. Joseph of Arimathea, and to which Blake refers in "Jerusalem." He was most anxious to make this widely known as, from his researches, he was convinced it was true.[87]

In *Who's Who in Somerset*, 1934, his recreations were listed as 'Motoring, Cycling, Heraldry, Gardening, Antiquarianism, Connoisseur in Art, Furniture, Silver, Glass, Architecture; and a Pioneer in Lads' Camping'. Lewis, 'ever working in his beloved garden and driving his little car', was Vicar of St John's, Glastonbury, for

87 *Times* 4 Aug. 1953, p. 8., col. 8.

28 years, retiring only in 1950. Beautiful wooden screen-work, some designed by Bond, stained glass, the ivory crucifix he thought once to have belonged to the Abbey, the 'Armada' chest, and the last abbot's cope, which he rescued from the lumber,[88] are among the ornaments he bequeathed to his church. From 1938-1940 he took an interest in the Cup of Nanteos, the Welsh 'Holy Grail', and tried unsuccessfully to persuade the then owner, Mrs. Powell, to 'return' it to Glastonbury to be displayed in a specially built repository in St John's Church.[89] He also caused a medieval chest tomb he believed to have been once used to enshrine Joseph of Arimathea's remains in Abbot Bere's fifteenth century undercroft of St Joseph, beneath the Abbey's Lady Chapel, to be moved from the churchyard into the shelter of the church. The annual Anglican Pilgrimage in June, begun in 1923, and the December ceremony of the cutting of the Thorn for presentation to the monarch, are monuments to Smithett Lewis which are still important public events in Glastonbury's year. His opposition to animal experiments may well have influenced Bligh Bond's gifted daughter Mary, who in later life was a tireless crusader against vivisection and all cruelty.

There was, however, a less congenial side to Smithett Lewis. It is notable that the local obituary in the *Central Somerset Gazette* made no reference to the Jesus voyage tradition, and had less to say than *The Times* on Lewis's Glastonbury scholarship, observing merely that his books on the subject 'have been widely read'; it noted also his reputation as a controversialist in letters to the press. Obviously a gentle, kindly, likeable, and also very loyal man in his personal way, Smithett Lewis had a blind spot in his regard for what he considered the ancient foundation legends of the church from which his orders derived. For him these held a sanctity almost exceeding that of holy writ, and in their defence he could become both spiteful and insensitive to all reason.

In 1922 he published a booklet of twenty-eight pages entitled *St Joseph of Arimathea at Glastonbury or The Apostolic Church*

88 Now displayed in the Abbey's museum.
89 Wood, 2001, pp. 227-228 and *passim*.

Fig 17. Rev. Lionel Smithett Lewis (1867-1953), allegedly referred to as 'the silly Vicar of Glastonbury' by respected local antiquary John Morland.

of Britain. From the beginning, there was a combative note in his text. In his introduction, 'A Preface for Critics', the Vicar dared not hope that his work might 'escape being torn by critics. Critics do a considerable amount of good, perhaps even those more extreme ones which have called themselves "higher." The course of "higher criticism" is a recognised thing. They unite in destruction of the quarry. This is their great gift. It is when they come to construction that they fall out, and begin to devour each other.'[90] The reference, of course, was to 'higher criticism' of the Bible. Later he returned to the theme. 'It is fashionable to decry all legends and deny all tradition. And I have heard it stated with an air of great authority that the story of the foundation of the Church at Glastonbury by Joseph of Arimathea, or other contemporaries of Christ, was invented by

90 Lewis, 1922, p.3.

the monks ...'[91] The 'great authority' which he had in mind was likely to have been that of the scholarly Dean of Wells, J. Armitage Robinson, whose *Somerset Historical Essays* had appeared the previous year, and whose expertise, coincidentally, also extended to biblical 'higher criticism'. Of this more below.

Although Lewis referred to Taylor's *The Coming of the Saints* in 1922,[92] he did not mention the story of Jesus's visit to Britain. His publishing enterprise was, however, such a success that he felt obliged to bring out a 'second and much enlarged edition' of forty-eight pages in 1923. Here, in the course of a discussion of Glastonbury Tor as 'once a centre of Druidic worship', he speculates that:

> Perhaps there is some truth in the strange tradition which still lingers, not only among the hill folk of Somerset, but of Gloucestershire, that St. Joseph of Arimathea came to Britain first as a metal merchant seeking tin from the Scillies and Cornwall, and lead, copper, and other metals from the hills of Somerset, and that Our Lord Himself came with him as a boy. The tradition is so startling that the first impulse is summarily to reject it as ridiculous. But certain it is that it is most persistent. And certain it is that amongst the old tin-workers, who have always observed a certain mystery in their rites, there was a moment when they ceased their work and started singing a quaint song beginning "Joseph was a tin merchant." And certain it is that if St. Joseph was a metal merchant he must somehow have got tin for bronze, and that Britain is almost the sole land of tin mines. And if he were a metal merchant it is not inconsistent with his being a rich man. And the strange story of our Lord's coming, which is so very dear to simple Somerset hearts, would be explained by the Eastern tradition that St. Joseph was the uncle of the Blessed Virgin Mary.* So if there be truth in the ancient story, this old hill [the Tor] with its rites

91 Lewis, 1922, p. 10.
92 Lewis, 1922, p. 24, referring to Taylor's observations on the preservation of the Old Church.

may have attracted the mart which first led here St. Joseph and the Redeemer before He began His ministry. And to it, after the wondrous Resurrection and Ascension, St. Joseph, laden with the New Message of the New Religion, would wend his way on his mission from Gaul to Britain, the seat of Druidism. His knowledge of the Druids would account (in part) for his kindly reception by the Druids of France, and he would come to King Arviragus, or at any rate some of his subjects, as a not unknown person, and hence, perhaps, his kindly reception, and the donation of land.

[footnote:* It is curious that King Arthur claimed descent from St. Joseph; and St. David, said to be his uncle, was said to be kin to the Blessed Virgin Mary.][93]

Lewis's account of the Glastonbury legends was locally well received and favourably reviewed in the national press. Constantly increasing in length and gathering appendices, it ran eventually to seven editions, the last, on which he was working at the time of his death, published posthumously in 1955 by his widow. It is still in print, and on sale in the Abbey book shop. In his third edition of 1924, Smithett Lewis added in a footnote to the words '... and that Our Lord Himself came with him as a boy.': 'There is also a tradition in the West of Ireland that Our Lord came to Glastonbury as a boy.' A second footnote follows '... a quaint song beginning "Joseph was a tin merchant."': 'Mr. Henry Jenner, F.S.A., late of the British Museum, narrates that some years back in North London during the making of tin sheets for organ pipes before the molten tin was poured, a man said every time: "Joseph was in the tin trade." (Quarterly Review of the Benedictines of Caldey, 1916, p. 135-6.)'

In 1925, the Vicar of Glaston published a second work, *Glastonbury, "The Mother of Saints." - Her Saints A.D. 37-1539*, of seventy-two pages, observing in his preface that 'It had to be done. So I have done it. As you have not done it, do not be too hard on

93 Lewis, L. S., 1923, pp. 16-17. Arviragus was the legendary king who supposedly donated twelve hides of land for Joseph's church at Glastonbury.

one who has at least tried with the minimum of time at his disposal.'
Here he appended his tentative and rather breathless account of 1923
(and 1924) as the final section, with certain further observations as
to his sources in footnotes:

THE MOST WONDERFUL TRADITION OF ALL CHRIST AT
GLASTONBURY

Did Our Lord ever come to Glastonbury as a lad? The story not
only lingers here, but elsewhere. Briefly, the tradition is this: That
Our Lord accompanied St. Joseph of Arimathea as a lad on one of
the Saint's expeditions to Britain to seek metal. For the possibilities
of this legend, for the other legends and facts that would fit in
with it, I must quote my *"St Joseph of Arimathea at Glastonbury"*
(Third Edition, pp.17-18) …

In a footnote to his earlier statement that the story lingered in
Gloucestershire, he now writes 'The Ven. Walter Farrer, Archdeacon
of Wells, told me that the legend is to be met with in Gloucestershire.'
After the words '… and that Our Lord Himself came with him as a
boy.', he incorporates his 1924 footnote ' There is also a tradition in
the West of Ireland that Our Lord came to Glastonbury as a boy.' into
the text, adding in a new footnote: 'The Rev. Canon A.R.B. Young,
Prebendary of Clogher Cathedral in Ireland, has heard the tradition
all his life.' The tin-worker's 'quaint song' has been silently amended
to 'Joseph was in the tin trade' to bring it into accord with Jenner's
account, and here in the text he breaks from self quotation to add:
'Mr. Henry Jenner, F.S.A., late of the British Museum, narrates that
some years back in North London during the making of tin sheets for
organ pipes, before the molten metal was poured, a man said every
time, "Joseph was in the tin trade." leaving only 'Quarterly Review
of the Benedictines of Caldey of 1916, pp. 135-6.' as a footnote.
He went on to quote from Taylor concerning the supposed Jewish
colony in Cornwall.

The assertion of 1923 that the story was met with in Gloucestershire,
here attributed to Archdeacon Farrer, almost certainly represents

a misunderstanding, perhaps elicited by leading questions, of the saying, recorded from the seventeenth century,[94] '*as sure as God's in Gloucestershire*', which actually referred to the presence of a supposed relic of Christ's blood at Hailes Abbey between 1270 and 1538. As noted above, Farrer had 'stared' as Joseph of Arimathea in Alice Buckton's film *Glastonbury Past and Present* in 1922. Canon Young's memory perhaps confused Glastonbury with Gloucester, the leading questions here being enquiries relating to the Gaelic folk-traditions referred to by Jenner in 1916. The detail that the organ makers were located in *North* London, not stated elsewhere, might reflect private correspondence with Jenner (first referred to in 1927) but it would be unwise to place much reliance on this addition to the story. Smithett Lewis's account from 1923 is clearly derived in all its essentials from Jenner, with a little of Taylor for good measure. It is likely that his predecessor, the Rev. Day, in his sermon of 1920, also depended, directly or indirectly, on the same source.

The Benedictines of Caldey, in whose journal, *Pax*, Jenner's paper appeared, had long-standing connections with the Glastonbury area. The community was founded in 1902 by Benjamin Fearnley Carlyle (1874-1955), Dom Aelred in religion, a former medical student and their first abbot (1902-21). They settled on Caldey Island in 1906. Dom Aelred was a colourful figure who assumed the role of a Prince of the Church and took to travelling in a large chauffeur-driven Daimler. He was instrumental in the transformation of the active Sisterhood of the Holy Comforter at Edmonton into a community of contemplative Benedictine nuns, and in their removal, in 1906, to Baltonsborough, some five miles from Glastonbury and the reputed birthplace, *c.* 909, of its reforming Benedictine abbot, Dunstan. As their spiritual director he visited them once or twice a year. On such a visitation in September 1910, he stayed for a period in Glastonbury, where he had become friends with the architect, archaeologist, and psychic investigator, Frederick Bligh Bond. The Abbot was interested

94 In Fuller, *Church Hist.*, 1655. See Wilson, F.P., 1970, *Oxford Dict. of Eng. Proverbs*, 3rd. ed. p. 789 & refs.

in psychic matters, and so was doubtless privy to Bond's method of excavation with the aid of 'automatic' script, which was not then widely know. These scripts were produced for him, by various 'mediums', ostensibly from the personalities of the medieval monks and other entities. Bond, a Theosophist, theorised that these apparent personalities were a channel to a universal 'great memory,' similar to the cosmic 'akashic record' of Madame Blavatsky. Others, including his estranged wife, saw the matter simply as spiritualism. Although he lectured on them as early as 1916, his methods were first made generally known, as noted above, in *The Gate of Remembrance*, 1918. On this occasion, in 1910, Carlyle:

'accepted as a gift certain human bones which Mr Bond had dug up and which he was convinced were those of the martyred last Abbot - Richard Whyting - who had been hanged, drawn and quartered for high treason in 1539 by the orders of Henry VIII. In 1895 Pope Leo XIII had beatified Richard Whyting ... Feeling that these 'major relics' which had been authenticated by automatic script ought to be treated reverently, and not just exhibited in a museum as human bones, Mr. Bond offered them to Abbot Aelred on September 22, 1910. He had a shrewd idea that Dr. Kennion, the Bishop of Bath and Wells, would not feel inclined to erect a shrine for them in his cathedral, and was even more certain that the nearby [Roman Catholic] Benedictines of Downside would not be prepared to venerate them merely on the evidence of these spiritualist seances. ... A magnificent reliquary, covered with a rich silken veil, was set up in the midst of the choir [at Caldey], after the bones had been placed in it. ... After the reconciliation of the Community with the Roman Church in March 1913, the relics could not be brought out for veneration, and were hidden away in the sacristy'.[95]

95 Anson, 1958, pp. 137-9.

The bones moved to Prinknash with Carlyle in 1928 where, in the sacristy, they still remain. The Baltonsborough nuns did not follow Dom Aelred into the Roman obedience in 1913, and in 1916 moved to join a second community of Anglican nuns whom he had overseen at West Malling, Kent.

Bligh Bond, coincidentally, was also a cousin of the Rev. Sabine Baring-Gould, who, as we have seen, had first referred to the Jesus voyage story in his novel *Guavas the Tinner* in 1897. Bond visited him regularly in Devon in the 1890s and was even, for a time, romantically attracted to one of Baring-Gould's daughters, although her father discouraged an engagement.[96] Bond himself, in his surviving writings, seemingly does not refer to the story until 1938, when in *The Mystery of Glaston*, he mentions a 'strongly planted tradition - that which still lingers on the high Mendip and elsewhere - to the effect that the boy Jesus did actually come with his uncle to Somerset and may have visited the site of His future mission at Glaston.'[97] The passage in which this occurs is mostly a paraphrase of Dr Biggs' account of 1933, but Bond, who was friendly with Smithett Lewis, must certainly have known of the story earlier than that. His disregard need occasion no surprise, as his writings on Glastonbury focused quite narrowly on his own personal investigations. He remains a possible channel by which the *Pax* article of 1916, or its substance, found its way to Glastonbury. However this may be, it is, none the less, likely that it was through Dom Aelred's personal connections that attention was first drawn at Glastonbury to the Jenner version of the story, with its obvious implications for the Glastonian view of the Arimathean traditions.

For although certainty would be unwise, it seems probable that it was the literary tradition, stemming directly and indirectly from Jenner, and not whatever underground beliefs had prompted the long-forgotten questionings of Σ, of which the High Anglican clergy

96 See now Ball, 2007, based on privately held Bond family papers.
97 Bond, 1938, p. 29.

of Glastonbury took note in the heady days after the soldiers of the New Jerusalem had played their part in the liberation of the Old. It may have been the breezy optimism of the Rev. Day which made anew the leap of logic which brought Jesus from the rocky coves of Cornwall to the ancient sanctuary of Glastonbury itself; or perhaps, as both his sermon, and his absence for much of the 1914-18 war implies, he took on the idea ready formed from among Glastonbury's antiquarian mystics. Prebendary Charles Bennett (see below) with whom he took part in Alice Buckton's Chalice Well ceremony of 1919, may also have played a role. In any case the step, which had *almost* been taken by Taylor in 1906, was sooner or later inevitable.

The favourable reception of the legend at Glastonbury was doubtless aided by the instant popularity of the hymn *Jerusalem*. In 1925, Smithett Lewis concluded his Jesus section, and his book *Glastonbury, "The Mother of Saints"*, with the statement that Blake 'had evidently heard the tradition of Glastonbury, and embalmed it in beautiful verses, to which Hubert Parry wedded equally inspired music. With these I will end'. And so he did. By 1927, no longer entitled, as in 1925, *Jerusalem*, but *The Glastonbury Hymn*, Blake's lines are prefaced to yet a fourth edition of *St Joseph of Arimathea at Glastonbury*.[98]

Other writers also were beginning to note the Glastonbury version of story by the mid-twenties; in 1926 F. J. Snell, in his excellently researched *King Arthur's Country*, writes 'When we were at Glastonbury we were made acquainted with a tradition that Joseph of Arimathea was a tin-merchant, and that he brought our Lord in His boyhood to mid-Somerset.' He calls the former Roman port of Combwich the 'traditional landing-place of Joseph of Arimathea,' and records "an old legend of poetry" which says he travelled from

98 The anonymous reviewer for *The Somerset Yearbook*, 1928, pp. 124-5, calls this a 'somewhat provocative brochure', and suspects that the critics 'will also, perhaps, not approve of Blake's "Jerusalem" being labelled "The Glastonbury Hymn."'

Comwich to Glastonbury "o'er the Mendips."[99]

In Smithett Lewis's fourth edition of *Joseph* in 1927, the only significant addition is to the footnote on Jenner, as in 1924, of the words 'and in a MS letter to myself'.[100] This information, that he had become one of those numerous enquirers with whom Jenner dealt with such patience, does not have the appearance of being new, but rather of representing the remedy of an oversight. In the fifth edition of 1931, the voyage story is given as in 1927.

It was the writings of Smithett Lewis which inspired H. Kendra Baker, in 1930, to publish *Glastonbury Traditions Concerning Joseph of Arimathea, Being a translation from the Latin .. of the second chapter of* Britannicarum Ecclesiarum Antiquitates *of James Usher, Archbishop of Armagh & Primate of All Ireland, published at Dublin, 1639, with the original footnotes*. Published by the British Israelite Covenant Publishing Co. Ltd., this little booklet remains a useful translation from one of the more important early antiquaries on whom Smithett Lewis and his ilk relied.

99 Snell, 1926, p.83.
100 Lewis, 1927, p. 24.

JOSEPH OF ARIMATHEA

AS FOUNDER OF

PILTON CHURCH.

The History of "Our Race."

By Preb. C. W. BENNETT, Pilton Vicarage.

(For Pilton Church Fund).

PRICE 6D. POST FREE 8D.

Fig 18. The cover of the Rev. Bennett's play text,
which brought Jesus to Pilton.

8

WHEN CHRIST WENT TO PILTON

The *Central Somerset Gazette*, and the frequent writings of Lionel Smithett Lewis, allow us to view the legend's reception at Glastonbury with at least some clarity. The same cannot be said of Priddy. We must remember once more the neglected query of Σ to the readers of *Somerset and Dorset Notes and Queries*. This had spoken of the traditions of the miners of the High Mendip, of whom the last had been the lead-miners of the lonely village of Priddy. When in 1923 Smithett Lewis wrote of the story lingering 'among the *hill folk* of Somerset' (my emphasis), he was, seemingly, dimly aware that alongside the learned speculations of Taylor and Jenner the story existed in more feral form on the Mendips. This in itself provides a hint that it had arrived there by a different path of transmission from that which had led to its acceptance at Glastonbury, for which, significantly, he does *not* claim a similar currency among the locals.

The belief certainly seems to have been recorded rather earlier of Priddy. At some uncertain date, probably not many years before 1920, Prebendary C. W. Bennett, Vicar of Pilton, wrote a little play, perhaps inspired by the success of the 1906 Butleigh Revel, entitled *Joseph of Arimathea as the Founder of Pilton Church, The History of "Our Race"*. This retailed at sixpence for the Pilton Church Fund. In a note to his play, Bennett identified the visit of the Christ Child to Somerset as a Priddy legend.

Charles William Bennett was a truly local man, born at Sparkford in 1845, the son of the Rev. Henry Bennett, a graduate of Trinity College, Cambridge, who was Rector of that parish from 1846, and also Rector of South Cadbury from 1836-66, where he was succeeded by Charles' elder brother, Rev. James Arthur Bennett. James Arthur was a well respected antiquary, Secretary of the Somerset Archaeological and Natural History Society (from 1887), and a founder (in 1885) of the Somerset Record Society; he was also a Fellow of the Society of Antiquaries, and on the staff of the Historical Manuscripts Commission. His scholarly papers were numerous, notably a study of Glastonbury Abbey's *Magna Tabula*, a medieval 'visitor's information board', now in the Bodleian Library in Oxford. He collected the folklore of Cadbury Castle, the legendary Camelot, and conducted the first excavations there.[101] He died unexpectedly in 1890, aged 55. Our man, his younger brother Charles William, was educated at Ottery St. Mary and Winchester, and at Lichfield College, where he was priested in 1872. He was a curate in Chesterton, Staffordshire, and at Beaminster, Dorset, before becoming Rector of Sparkford in 1874. That year he married Mary Anne Grahame. He moved from Sparkford to become Rector of Pilton in 1899. He was Prebendary of Barton St David at Wells Cathedral from 1903, and Rural Dean of Shepton Mallet from 1917 until 1923. The anonymous collaborative history *A Walk Through Pilton's Past*, published locally in 1988, records that:

> Prebendary Bennett, known as "Uncle Charlie" was vicar from 1899-1935. In his accustomed uniform of baggy britches and stockings he cycled miles researching and recording the history of the village. He practised homeopathy and willingly treated the whole village. Uncle Charlie would put a mud poultice in white cloth onto wounds and they say that the cuts always healed. He lived to nearly ninety and apparently was active until the last, going about his normal Parish duties on the morning of the day

101 *Magna Tabula*, *PSANHS* 34, 1888; Cadbury Castle, *PSANHS* 36, 1890, pp. 1-19; In Memoriam, *ibid.* p. 193-6.

he died. In the 1930s Uncle Charlie wrote 'The History of Our Race' - a play based on the legend of Joseph of Arimathea as founder of Pilton Church. On the path between the Manor and Church is the Mere Stone which, although moved slightly, marks the division between the hundred of Glaston Twelve Hides and the hundred of Whitstone.

The boundary goes on through the centre of the Church from north to south - a feature unusual enough to suggest that there must have been a special reason for building the Church on this site.[102]

Fig 19. Rev. Charles William Bennett (1845-1935), affectionately remembered in his Pilton parish as 'Uncle Charlie.'

102 Anon., 1988, pp. 8-9.

The first scene of Bennett's play opens at 'Pilton harbour, about A.D. 15:

One of the Crowd.

>Why! I do believe 'tis Joseph! He who comes
>To trade in metals from our Mendip mines.
>Our lead and copper; and such other wares
>As he would gain from us. While in his turn,
>From those far eastern lands across the sea,
>Right wondrous wares he brings us passing fair.

* * *

All.

>Right welcome, Joseph! Welcome all the friends
>Who come with you, both old and new alike.

Joseph.

>Aye! welcome too to you, my Pylton friends!
>Right pleased are we to see again once more
>Your friendly faces, and your beauteous coombe.
>Most of our friends you know, and all I'm sure
>Will find true welcome at your friendly port.

Britons.

>Have you come now to trade? We'll pass the word,
>And by to morrow's eve full many a mass
>Of right good metal shall await your eye.

A Woman.

>Say Joseph! Tell us! Who this beauteous lad?
>Is he your son? He seems to love you well.

Joseph.

>Ah no! but one most dear unto my heart;
>Born and brought up in simple poverty.
>Joseph, a carpenter he Father calls,
>Mary his Mother; yet of David's line.

Something most wonderful about his birth,
And also in himself. No trace of ill
Was ever found in him, in word or deed.
Yet just a lad, most loveable and sweet.
He calls me "uncle," pleased and proud I am
To have him with me. When I offered him
To travel with me to these distant shores
Right willingly he came.
When we first landed on the Cornish coast,
And there I told him of the sparkling tin,
Used by King Solomon for God's own House,
Had come from thence, full pleased indeed he seemed.
For all his life he's ever shown his love
For what he oft doth call "His Father's House."
Here then we'll show him other metals, too,
Used by King Solomon in olden days.
Hundreds of years e'er you and I were born,
To deck God's temple in Jerusalem.

Britons.

Where do you spend the night? Wilt honour us
In making welcome to the best we have?

Joseph.

Ah no! with many thanks! for when last night
We reached the port of Ynyswytrin[103] fair,
Arviragus your king, and our old friend,
Bid us a royal welcome; and would have
Us seek no other shelter while our visit stayed.
Indeed the day grows late. We must away
But look for us to-morrow.
   Fare ye well.[104]

---

103 According to William of Malmesbury in the twelfth century, the old British name of Glastonbury.
104 Bennett, 191., pp. 1-2.

The next scene opens, again at 'Pylton Harbour', eighteen years later. Joseph has returned, not to trade for metal but to bring the gospel of salvation. 'Nay some of you did see Him once with us / While still a boy ...' Again, he excuses himself from the hospitality of the Pilton folk for that of Arviragus at Glaston, but leaves companions to minister in the local villages.[105] In a series of notes to his text, the Rev. Bennett indicates his indebtedness to Taylor, and helpfully elucidates some of the antiquarian lore behind his play.

JOSEPH A METAL MERCHANT.
This is a Mendip and Cornish tradition, and is also mentioned among Gallican legends in [Taylor's] the "Coming of the Saints," where it says that "when the tin flashes," the headman says, "Joseph was in the trade." I was talking to a party of gentlemen some years ago about it, and one said that when in Cornwall several years before, he had wanted to see the tin smelting, but was told it was a secret process, and only by liberal payment did he get in, and that at one point in the process they chanted an invocation to Joseph of Arimathai.

Pilton, or the Pwll, or Pool Town, was an important harbour on the south of the Mendip Hills, and Glastonbury a Island just at the mouth of it. So any missionary party coming to the island would certainly begin work at the harbour. Joseph, as a trader, would probably know the place well.

OUR LORD, AS A BOY, COMING WITH JOSEPH.
This is a legend from Priddy, near Wells, where there have been lead mines since the time of the Phoenicians, though now recently closed.

---

105 'The cells of Kenwys, Ivor, Merston [the companions in his text], are all on the old British Road, afterwards made by the Romans into "the Fosseway," from Exeter through Ilminster and Bath to Lincoln Kil-kenny is in the parish of Ditcheat, Kilver in Shepton Mallet, and Kilmersdon a village about five miles further N. E.' Bennett, 191., p.18.

It also says in an Icelandic Saga that our Lord as a child was brought by his nurse Pilhi to Sumerland, and there immersed up to his hips in warm mud. Another local tradition says that where he stopped to pray to His Father Christians afterwards built a church.

JOSEPH AS CHRIST'S 'UNCLE'

This is a somewhat widely diffused Irish legend, and would fit with Joseph not only refusing to join in Christ's condemnation, but giving his own tomb, and still more wonderful going to Pilate and asking for the body, which for a stranger would be a very marked thing to do.[106]

These textual notes derive from a study by Bennett of the history of Pilton village and its church which is set down in the manuscript 'Notes on Pilton Church by Rev. C. W. Bennett Vicar 1899-(1934) born 1845.'[107] Sadly, the date when he first began this study is again unrecorded, but on pages 75-76 is a note with the date 1928, written in a darker ink similar to that of later notes and emendations entered into the earlier sections of the manuscript. Bennett's method is illuminated by his observation, on his first page, that 'Tradition' (by which he means oral history) is actually 'more reliable than written documents.' On page four, in a chapter headed 'Pilton Harbour - Mendip Lead & Copper,' he writes:

we have a strong old tradition (though the schoolmaster is fast killing all these old traditions alas) that Pilton was a harbour of Mendip from which people used to ship lead & copper from the Mendip Mines such as those at Priddy [note inserted at later date in darker ink: ^ of lead] & Greenore [^ of copper] the former

---

106 Bennett, 191., pp. 17-18.
107 Somerset Record Office D\P\pilt/23/18. The MS is hand-written in an exercise book on *recto* pages only (numbered), with some notes added on the *verso* sides.

quite recently closed, indeed slightly worked during the recent war with Germany. [^ 1914-1916] Those who have investigated the matter tell us that the orebeds have been unmistakably worked over at least three times first with rude implements, then with more civilised ones, and lastly with modern ones.

He observes that the lead was of good quality, and that the Roman baths at Bath were made with Mendip lead, which still held water. 'No wonder that people in other lands wanted such lead, as we know that they did Cornish and Devon tin, and almost certainly also gold.' Their ships came at first to Pilton itself, but afterwards, as geological forces raised the land (as he believed they had) the metal was ferried 'from Pilton Harbour to Meare Pool to be transported into sea-going craft there.'

He details an overland route also, 'used by metal merchants & others,' starting from Uphill and eventually joining the 'Pilgrim's Way' to Dover. 'About 50 years ago the remains of what was evidently an old "pig of lead" was found along this route.' He adds amusingly 'NB Solomon's "Apes & Peacocks" were very possibly lumps of metal, the latter iridescent. He did not go in for monkeys.'

In his chapter on 'The Parish Church' we read:

Old traditions of Joseph of Arimathea & Pilton Church are extremely interesting, not only of the present building, but because it stands on the same site, & is the successor (without any break) of the first Pilton Church which there is much reason to believe may have been built by Joseph of Arimathea.

According to the old Irish tradition Joseph was the Uncle of the Blessed Virgin Mary, and therefore great uncle of Our Lord. According to Mendip tradition Joseph was a Metal Merchant, & used to trade with Cornwall for tin, & with Mendip for lead and copper. We know that every Jew was expected to have a trade, & that Joseph was a wealthy man, so there is nothing impossible in this. His coming here is also mentioned in the annals collected by Cardinal Baronius, and quoted in "The Coming of the Saints" [*i.e.* by Taylor]..[108]

Baronius's reference, of course, was to Joseph's coming to Britain rather than specifically to Pilton. In his next chapter, 'Old Traditions of Joseph and our Lord Coming', he writes:

At least four traditions make Our Lord Himself come to England with Joseph.

The writer was told by a visitor from Bath that a Doctor Hitchcock there had told <u>him</u> that he had seen in an Icelandic Saga an account of Our Lord when a boy being brought by his nurse Pilki to the "Summuland", & immersed in warm mud up to his hips. At the time the writer [presumably Bennett here refers to himself] remarked that the warm mud must have been at Bath, but that we became "The Land of the Sumorsaetan" not until the Saxon Conquest some 500 years later on. But after all this <u>was</u> the "Aedes [probably, writing unclear] Aestiva" the Sumuland in those days.

A tradition from the Lead Mines of Priddy, above Wells, tells us that Our Lord, as a young man, came with His Uncle Joseph on one of the latter's mercantile visits.

& another says that wherever Our Lord was seen praying there afterwards the Christians built Churches & that this accounts for the unlikely places where some Churches stand.' [p.22]

[in a later note opposite p, 23] 'As to the coming of Joseph see the Rev. Lionel S. Lewis' book "Glastonbury and her Saints [1925; 1927] & the Coming of St Paul [presumably Morgan]

Joseph then, if these traditions are correct, must often have come on his commercial journeys to Pilton Harbour, & it is pleasant to think that it is within the bounds of possibility that Our Lord's feet may have trodden the very ground where Pilton

108 *ibid.* p. 20.

Church now stands situated as it is just above the Harbour, & the most likely place for people to meet.' [p. 23]

Bennett went on to speculate that Pilton was probably the second church building (after Glastonbury) ever raised in the world '& as Avalon was an island, Pilton Church is the oldest on the mainland of Britain.' [p.24]

A later section on Druidism shows much acquaintance with eighteenth- and nineteenth-century Welsh neo-druidic lore.[109]

Bennett clearly intended these notes for eventual publication, and printer's quotes were obtained in early 1929 (see below) but I have been unable to ascertain whether his village history ever did, in fact, appear in print.

It is equally unclear whether the play, or perhaps, rather, pageant, was ever performed. Although it is undated, the assertion in the village history *A Walk Through Pilton's Past* that Bennett wrote it in 'the 1930s' probably places it too late. The reference to lead mines at Priddy being 'now recently closed' (echoed in the *Notes)* probably places it after 1908, when St Cuthbert's Works at Priddy, the last working Mendip lead-mine, was shut down. The prophecies to Arviragus (spoken by a companion of Joseph and which occupy the later part of the play), with their biblical quotations identified in the margin and in explanatory notes, are eloquent of British Israelitism. Such 'prophecies' were penned from far back in the nineteenth century. However, the focus in the text on Israel bringing his brother Judah to their common land suggests that it was not written all in ignorance of the Balfour Declaration of the second of November 1917, in which the then Foreign Secretary stated that His Majesty's Government 'view with favour' the establishment of a Jewish national home in Palestine. Likewise an emphasis, so reminiscent of the *Central Somerset Gazette*

109 *ibid.* pp. 51-54.

report, on the name of David, that of the Prince of Wales,[110] suggests that it, too, was written soon after the fall of Jerusalem in December 1917. Perhaps it was, or was meant to be, performed to celebrate the Armistice. This is consistent with the catalogue entry of the Somerset Local Studies Library at Taunton, which records the date of the pamphlet as '191.'. As we have noted, Bennett took part in Alice Buckton's ceremony at Chalice Well in November 1919 at which the new well-cover was dedicated, apparently as a thank-offering for Peace.

The theory that Pilton was 'an important harbour', and therefore a probable landing place for Joseph, reflects a contribution to *SDNQ* of December 1893, by one 'H.', entitled *The Abbot of Glastonbury's Waterways*. Examining a 13th century document, this noted that much of the medieval abbey's economic activity was conducted along a system of waterways, including one from 'Glaston to Steanbow on the Pylle stream', and that there was a vineyard at Pilton. Wine was loaded into boats at La Bowe (Steanbow near Pilton) for shipment to the abbey.[111] The village, with its church, stands at the top of the hill slope above where the northern fork of the alluvium (the former morass of marshland which defined the Glastonbury 'island' or, rather, peninsula) makes its most easterly approach to the Mendips. Bennett lectured 'on the old coastline of Glastonbury' at Miss Buckton's 'Chalice Well Summer School' of 1923, at which Lionel Smithet Lewis also spoke on Joseph of Arimathea.[112]

Although Bennett has read Taylor, he seemingly testifies also to his

110 Bennett, 191., pp. 16-17; unfortunately the new David, like his biblical eponym, had an eye for other men's wives, which led to problems when he ascended the throne as Edward VIII.
111 H, 1893, p. 298-299. The name Pilton comes, seemingly, from the Anglo-Saxon *'tun* (small settlement) on the "pill"'. 'Pill' (cognate with 'pool'), from Welsh *pwll*, is in local use on both sides of the Severn Sea for a tidal creek, and sometimes by extension for a harbour (*e.g.* as in 'The Pill' at Newport, Gwent). Near Pilton are Piltown, a hamlet of the village of West Pennard, above the same stretch of alluvium, and Pylle near East Pennard, where the Pylle or Whitelake stream rises. There is today, once more, a vineyard at Pilton.
112 *CSG*, 7th September 1923, p. 5.

knowledge of a pre-existing local 'legend' at Priddy. This is reminiscent of the query by Σ in *SDNQ* of 1895, which does not mention Priddy by name, but identifies it by implication in its reference to the Mendip metal miners. Its inaccurate aside that they were then 'recently extinct' is echoed in Bennett's play-notes - 'This is a legend from Priddy, near Wells, where there have been lead mines since the time of the Phoenicians, though now recently closed,' although if our dating of his play is correct (and Bennett only became Vicar of Pilton in 1899), then by that time Bennett's statement would indeed be correct. The question arises of whether Bennett's knowledge of the Priddy 'legend' actually represents anything more than an optimistic reading of Σ's query in *SDNQ*?

Alternatively, 'Uncle Charlie' might very well himself be considered the best candidate for identification with the enigmatic Σ. He was still Vicar of Sparkford in 1895, which would be consistent with Σ's inexact knowledge of the current state of mining on Mendip. His brother, James Arthur, is quite likely to have been acquainted with Jenner at the British Museum library, and his death in 1890 might *just* have post-dated Jenner's dinner-party. Although his famous antiquarian brother had been dead, in all probability, for nearly thirty years at least when he wrote his play, Charles had, like him, grown up scrambling on the slopes of Cadbury Castle, whose lore also finds mention in his play. His acquaintance with genuine Somerset folklore cannot be entirely dismissed.

One contra-indication is that Bennett, in his *Notes*, does not mention the Paradise names, but 'Sumerland' was later linked to the phrase from Σ that 'the place where they sojourned near Glastonbury is called "Paradise"' (by Webb in 1929, see below). Charles Bennett in his play notes, refers to a second strand of belief when he tells us that '*Another* local tradition says that where he stopped to pray to His Father Christians afterwards built a church'. Unfortunately, he does not tell us whether he thought this, too, was a Priddy tradition, or one from Pilton, or from elsewhere in Somerset.

If his anecdote about the gentleman visitor to Cornwall can be accepted at face value, it demonstrates local success there at 'cashing in' on the 'tradition' as made known to visitors by *Black's Guide* and Baring-Gould's novel.

It is also possible that the Rev. Bennett's play was first written and performed somewhat later, in connection with fund-raising for the restoration of the Lady Chapel at Pilton Church by the Mothers Union. This was first mooted in December 1928 and, by the following April, estimates had been obtained for the publication of Bennett's *Notes on Pilton Church* as a book.[113] This was certainly the context in which Pilton's remarkable Church Banner was created. Smith comments that it is 'possibly the only artefact certainly evidencing belief in the "Holy Legend" that we have'. It is almost certainly the only one within a church.[114]

In an unsourced press-cutting pasted into Bennett's *Notes* we read that at the rededication of the Lady Chapel on 23 September, 1931:

The Church was filled to its capacity, and the service, which commenced at 7 o'clock, opened with the processional hymn "All people that on earth do dwell," led by the choir with the new banner depicting Our Lord as a child landing at Pilton Harbour with St Joseph of Arimathea.

In splendid *Art Nouveau/Art Deco* style, it depicts a small boy of perhaps seven or eight, with a nimbed head of blond curls, kneeling in the bows of a boat approaching a wooded shore. A man, apparently in his thirties, with a dark beard, wearing a russet turban and a dark blue robe and leaning on a walking stick held in his left hand, points with the other towards some small birds hovering over the shore-line. Behind him, a youth in a russet tunic mans an oar. Blue on the horizon is the outline of the Tor as seen from Pilton, its tower, anachronistically, already in place. The upper part of the blue border

---

113 Pilton Vestry Minutes 1928-1937, sub 15.12.1928, 2.4.1929, Somerset Record Office D\P\pilt/9/1/4.
114 Smith, 1989, p. 64. See Fig. 16 and front cover.

Fig 20. *The Pilton Church Mother's Union Banner of 1931. It has been called the only representation of the Voyage Story in a church. See colour detail, front cover (with permission).*

bears the name PILTON between two crosses, with the monogram JHS in the triangular pennant below. It seems, then, to have been the Rev. Charles Bennett's own local patriotism and love of the story which first led his parishioners to perceive Pilton itself as the landing spot of Joseph and the Lord, and to enshrine this belief in its parish church. The Pilton banner is a rather lovely thing.

The Pilton story reappears in 1973 in Berta Lawrence's *Somerset Folklore*. Herself a Somerset author, she records many local variants on the Arimathean tradition, mainly, it would appear, from oral sources, including a landing at Combwich, or near Glastonbury at Wick Farm near the ancient oak trees Gog and Magog.

Writing before the decimation of the elms by Dutch Elm Disease, she tells us that on 'the eastern side of Mendip in a green bower of trees lies Pilton':

When the inhabitants of Pilton learned that missionaries had brought a new religion to Ynyswitrin and that King Arviragus himself had embraced it [*sic*], they begged Joseph to extend his preaching beyond the boundary of the Twelve Hides of Glastonbury so that they might be similarly blessed.

The missionaries therefore carried the gospel to Pilton, where Joseph built a second mud-and-wattle church in a sheltered hollow above the reach of the waters, and baptised the converts by immersion in a creek. The site of this wattle church is covered by the little Lady chapel in the north aisle of the present church at Pilton. The former boundary line of Glastonbury Twelve Hides [Hundred] runs through this church, in at the Norman south door and out at the north. In a decorated recess, with ball-flower ornament on the moulding of one of its arches, an Easter sepulchre of unusual design can be seen. Instead of having an effigy recumbent on it, the flat slab of the stone tomb chest is ornamented by the head of Christ encased within the head of a foliated cross.

Many believe that Joseph, the Christian missionary, came to a country in some degree familiar to him, because during the previous forty years he had made two or three expeditions with other metal-merchants to Cornwall for tin and to Somerset for lead. He made the first of his trade-voyages to the Mendip region when quite a young man, bringing with him his great-nephew, Jesus of Nazareth, a carpenter's son in his early teens who helped him as a shipwright. They tied up their boat at the landing-stage by Pilton creek and bought lead from the miners who came down from Priddy and Charterhouse-on-Mendip. This story is depicted on the banner hanging in the Lady Chapel at Pilton. ... It is said that

Joseph of Arimathea, or one of his disciples, built a reed-thatched oratory - and later Christians their Lady chapel - on the place where the Christ Child knelt to pray after disembarking.[115]

The village of Pilton is now best known as the actual site of the world-famous Glastonbury rock-music festivals, held, more or less yearly at the end of June or early in July, at Worthy Farm, home of founder Michael Eavis, a farmer of Quaker background and deep Somerset roots, who in his youth, for a time, was actually among Mendip's last coal-miners. His infectious love of the area's ancient traditions has helped make the event the success that it is. The largest outdoor festival of its kind in the world, it can attract upwards of 200,000 visitors to the fields around the mystic pyramid stage, with their distant view of the Tor on the western horizon, a fairy city (or, according to taste, a goblin market) of mushroom growth and equally rapid disappearance. To local people, whether they love it or loathe it, the huge event is known simply as 'Pilton.'

115 Lawrence, 1973, pp. 18-20.

9

THE HEART OF MENDIP: PRIDDY

As we have seen from Σ's query, from its very first known appearance in 1895 Priddy seems to have been the focus in Somerset of the story of the coming of Jesus to Britain, well before Glastonbury, already with its super-abundance of legends, took very much notice of it. It may be that Taylor's speculations of 1906 about a peddler's way from Cornwall to the lead-mining region had also been read and taken note of at Priddy itself.

The Vicar of Priddy from 1879-1896 was the Rev. Joseph Palmer, who was succeeded (1896-1904) by the Rev. Philip Chapman Barker, who also edited the Wells *Diocesan Kalendar* from 1888-1900. Neither, however, is known to have had any connection with the Jesus voyage story. The Vicar of Priddy from 1904 to 1919, when he left the parish for that of Yeovilton, was the Rev. William Henry Creaton, an Oxford man who had held curacies in London, and was Head Master of Wells Cathedral School from 1896-1904. In undated notes included as an appendix in the posthumous 1955 edition of *Joseph*, Smithett Lewis stated that he learned from 'the indefatigable Rev. H. A. Lewis that Mrs. Weeks, postmistress of Priddy, told him ... Rev. W. H. Creaton, Vicar in 1904-1919, later Rector of Yeovilton, Yeovil, had spoken of it [the voyage story].'[116] Had Creaton noted the reference in Taylor, drawn the inference that Jesus had accompanied Joseph to Mendip, and passed the assumption on, via the pulpit, to

116 Lewis, L. S., 1955, p. 162.

his parishioners? Or was the former headmaster, too, puzzled as Σ
seems to have been to discover that the miners already held this belief?
Certainty is impossible. Σ's knowledge can hardly have been first
hand, for when he relates that 'even now when the miners of Mendip
… arrive at a critical and dangerous moment in the process, they all
repeat "Joseph was a tinman," as a charm to avert disaster', (see
above) he seemingly betrays his ignorance of the fact that tin is not
to be found on Mendip, as the Somerset editor of *SDNQ* was quick
to point out. The saying or rhyme '*Joseph was a tinman*', of course,
could still have been known in the Mendip mining communities.
Cornish miners took their skills far and wide, making a valuable
contribution to the development of mining in South Africa, Australia
and North America, to which many emigrated as mining in Cornwall
itself began to decline from the middle of the nineteenth century. It
would be unlikely that none had ever worked in the Somerset lead,
calamine and coal mines, and the form '*Joseph was a tinman*' was,
apparently independently, later recorded in Cornwall itself.

By 1939, another alleged saying, '*as sure as Our Lord was at
Priddy*' had been introduced into the discussion. In *Christ in Cornwall?*
H. A. Lewis wrote:

> Some sceptics are quite incorrigible. They would even deny the
> existence of the legend at all. While anyone who really seeks can
> find abundant evidence that it was a household tradition at Priddy
> in the last generation that Christ came there, and while it is certain
> that there is an age-old proverb in parts of the Mendips "As sure
> as Our Lord was at Priddy";[117]

The background to this, too, is elucidated by Smithett Lewis's
notes, published in 1955:

> I may add that the Rev. H. A. Lewis, on sending his little book

117 Lewis, H.A., 1939, p. 5.

Christ in Cornwall to Mrs. Wardell-Yerborough, widow of a former Vicar of Tewkesbury about 1935, received in a letter of thanks from her, an expression of surprise that he had not quoted a proverb still used in the Mendips, "As sure as Our Lord was at Priddy." She wrote from the Mendips.[118]

There is clearly some confusion here. Although H. A. Lewis's *The Christ Child at Lammana* appeared in 1934, and was possibly the pamphlet intended, *Christ in Cornwall?* was not published as a booklet before 1939. 'Mrs. Wardell-Yerborough' may be identified as the wife of the Rev. William Higgin Beauchamp Yerburgh, Rector of Bredon with Bredon's Norton, near Tewkesbury, from 1920. Yerburgh had connections with Bligh Bond, as in 1922 he introduced a lecture at Bredon's Norton 'with lime-light illustrations on the Glastonbury discoveries and excavations' at which 'the distinguished audience listened with breathless interest to the story unfolded' by Bond.[119]

The saying itself echoes the proverb *as sure as God's in Gloucestershire* from the opposing heights to the north of the Bristol Avon. Tewkesbury, we may note, is also in Gloucestershire. As we have seen above, this well-attested saying refers to a situation which was current from 1270-1538. Popular rhymes, phrases and sayings can be quite remarkably persistent, even when apparently almost meaningless. One may cite *'Fee, Fi, Fo, and Fum ...'* If the alleged Mendip simile, sometimes given as *as sure as our Lord came to Priddy*,[120] was not modelled on the Gloucestershire one specifically to 'verify' the post-1895 literary voyage tradition, then it may well reflect an earlier phase of 'county' rivalry when the presence of the Cistercian monks' blood-relic at Hailes was a likely stimulus to the growth of the Joseph of Arimathea legend among the Benedictines of Glastonbury, and perhaps to their claim, also in the thirteenth century,

118 Lewis, L. S., 1955, p. 163.
119 *CSG*, 5 January 1923, p. 2.
120 As, *e.g..*, in Lawrence, 1973, p. 22.

that they too possessed a portion of the Saviour's blood.

As sure as our Lord was at Priddy may be an echo of some obscure local Arimathean tradition now lost, like that of the nail from the crucifixion said in the seventeenth century to have been found at Montacute.[121] Perhaps Our Lord first came to Priddy, also, in the form of a blood relic or the like, rather than as a living boy. Whatever the original Priddy story behind the saying may have been, it is possible that, like certain medieval traditions we shall have cause to notice later, it only seemed to fit the voyage story with hindsight.

Priddy is a place of magic. Of four great henge monuments of the Neolithic, three stand in unique alignment. Two groups of Bronze Age round barrows, the Ashen Hills and the Priddy Nine Barrows, stand on the hills overlooking the village. Nearby, in 2005, a metal-detectorist came upon the 'Priddy Gold Hoard,' some twenty items of gold jewellery bent out of shape as votive offerings, Somerset's largest collection of Bronze Age gold. The village itself is the highest on Mendip, and its main street aligns over an underground cave system known as Swilden's Hole. The Romans began mining for lead, and the silver extracted from it as a by-product, by 49 AD, within a few years of Vespasian's occupation of the West Country. This was known to antiquaries from the sixteenth century from the discovery of inscribed 'pigs' of lead, one of which is mentioned by the antiquary Camden. The Romans are unlikely to have been the first miners. As we have seen, lead-mining on Mendip continued until St Cuthbert's Works, near Priddy, closed as late as 1908.

Beneath the Mendip scarp nearby is witch-haunted Wookey Hole, probably the cavern noted for its strange underground noises like 'the clashing of many cymbals' by Clement of Alexandria in his *Stromateis* (*'Patch-work'*), of c.200 AD,[122] and from whose Romano-British burial chamber skulls were occasionally washed by the emerging river Axe. In legend, a monk of Glastonbury (un-named, but probably to be identified with Dunstan) is said to have turned a troublesome witch

121 See Ashdown, 2003, pp. 189-90.
122 *Stromateis*, Bk. vi, ch. 3.

Fig 21. *Ruins of St. Cuthbert's Lead Works, Priddy,*
c. 1954. (St. Cuthbert's is the parish church Wells).

who dwelt in the cave into stone in the shape of a notable stalagmite.
The skeletons of an old woman and her goats, along with a crystal
ball, were discovered in the cave in the late nineteenth century to add
substance to the pre-existing legend.

Clearly a meeting place since the Stone Age, Priddy's Fair dates in
local tradition from 1348, when the Wells sheep fair was moved to
the cleaner air of the hills during the Black Death. Except for the 'foot
and mouth' year of 2001, it has been held there ever since. A pile of
sheep hurdles stand, thatched, on the village green. They must not be
moved, or the village will loose the fair. From before recollection it
has attracted the Romany, who deal in horses outside the New Inn.
According to another saying, *Winter begins at Priddy Fair*, held on
the Wednesday next after the twenty-first of August,[123] for it began the

123 The medieval date was 10th August, St Lawrence's Day, his being the dedication of the church.

round of autumnal horse-fairs that followed: Glastonbury's ancient Tor Fair, now reduced to a small collection of roundabouts, and Bridgwater Fair (Joseph of Arimathea's supposed route in reverse, in fact). It was considered unlucky to return from the sometimes rowdy Priddy Fair without receiving a 'buffet'. *Hast been to Priddy Fair, an' not had thy buffet?* asks yet another saying. It is the last genuine folk-event in Somerset, where travelling folk of the old breed may still occasionally be seen step-dancing, or telling monologues to a hushed public bar, purely for their own amusement. Such places have long memories.

Towards the end of 1927, the topographical writer and artist Donald Maxwell (born 1877) published *Unknown Somerset, Being a series of unmethodical Explorations of the County illustrated in line and colour by the Author.* This attractive work was part of a series by Maxwell covering the Clyde valley and several English counties. As he wrote in his preface, 'I have approached the subject of Somerset with very little previous knowledge of it and am an explorer come upon a new land. It has not only been a new land to me but a wonderland and had I called this book an Artist in Wonderland the title would have served well.'[124] Maxwell felt compelled by the size and variety of the county to omit the more famous centres, even 'Old Glastonbury', concentrating instead on less well known or accessible parts. Sedgemoor, Athelney and Cadbury Castle were included. Of the Mendips, Maxwell writes that 'along the top runs a prehistoric road, generally known as a Roman road, but it is older than that, though no doubt improved and used by the Romans. The Britons worked the lead mines and sold to the Phoenicians who traded with them. It is probable that metal for the temple of Solomon came from here as also from Cornwall.'[125] Maxwell devoted his fourth chapter entirely to 'The Legend of Priddy'. His lack of preconception and local allegiance makes his account particularly valuable as an insight into the nature of the tradition by the late

124 Maxwell, 1927, p. v.
125 Maxwell, 1927, pp.48-49.

'twenties.[126] He prefaced his chapter with Blake's famous lines and began with an account of the Phoenician harbours of Tyre and Sidon, which he had seen, having been a war artist in Mesopotamia and a traveller in Palestine. He quoted the *Words and Places* (published in revised form 1909) of Isaac Taylor (1829-1901) on the similarity of the topographical features favoured by the Tyrians for their settlements with St Michael's Mount. Maxwell's account of his visit to Priddy, and to the abandoned industrial landscape whose features have now long since vanished, is worth quotation at length:

It is, I think, an established fact that ships from the Mediterranean came to Somerset as well as to Cornwall for metal. The lead mines of the Mendips as well as the tin mines of Cornwall were a source of great wealth to the Phoenician merchants. ... As far as the Mendip mines are concerned, there is a place at Uphill exactly corresponding to the Phoenician ideal harbour and trading settlement. Brean Down was a rocky peninsula and Uphill a harbour which approximates to the type we are looking for. This was afterwards a Roman harbour for the lead mines, so it is likely to have been the Phoenician port also.[127]

Maxwell turned next to 'the old legend of Priddy':

"There was a rich man of Arimathea named Joseph". Some tradition has it that he was a merchant who traded in metals, that he owned a "line" of ships. An old Cornish doggerel, sung by the tin miners at work, begins: "Joseph was a tin-man." This connexion with distant-trading ships gives some plausibility to the story that when the very earliest Christian Jews were scattered by

126 The review by 'W.W.' of Maxwell's work in *The Somerset Year Book*, 1928, p. 128, says 'He gives the pretty legend of Our Lord having visited this place [Priddy]. It is one which is believed in by some to this day: and Mr. Maxwell was fortunate enough to meet one of the believers.'
127 Maxwell, 1927, p. 58-59.

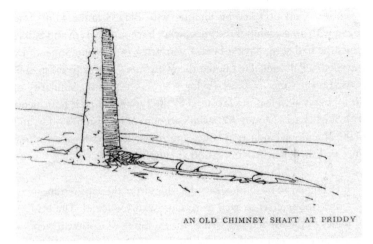

AN OLD CHIMNEY SHAFT AT PRIDDY

Fig 22. An industrial remnant at Priddy, sketched by
Donald Maxwell in 1926 (Maxwell, 1927, p. 58).

persecution St. Joseph escaped by voyaging in one of his own ships.
It was he, as we have seen, who landed at Glastonbury and built
the first Christian church in England. The old and much-loved
tradition still heard among the country people of the Mendips,
although they are very reticent about it, is that Our Lord when
a boy came to England [*sic*] in one of these ships belonging to
Joseph of Arimathea, and there is nothing impossible in a Jewish
lad making such a voyage. Whether or not William Blake had
ever heard of this tradition I do not know, nor whether the black
walls, the chimney shafts and the desolate slag heaps of Priddy
are the "dark Satanic mills" of his *Jerusalem* [*sic*]. They certainly
mark the region of the old Phoenician mines.

I determined on a pilgrimage to find these workings and see
for myself the place from which this tradition came.

One Saturday evening in the height of summer, with a knapsack
and a sketch-book, Maxwell set out from the neighbourhood
of Burrington:

I walked along the crown of the range, a Roman way, I am told, enjoying wide prospects of Somerset, of the Severn, and even of far-off Wales. The distance to Priddy is about nine miles, and I reached the ruined chimney shafts of the old lead mines with their tumbled ground as the sun went down.

A more barren landscape it would be impossible to find. There is a bare rounded hill and upon it a chimney, short, square and almost monumental in its isolation ([illus.] page 58). Towards this runs a green ridge, and other green ridges seem to extend all over the bare ground in different directions. I found out afterwards that these are the ruins of tunnels for conducting the poisonous fumes to the shaft. In many places they are broken through and vaults like catacombs are seen.

About a third of a mile from this isolated shaft and across a reedy lagoon appears the remains of two more chimneys and of buildings ([illus.] page 59). It was dark before I had finished roaming about this strange place and the stars were out, and I might have been in Babylon or in one of the ghostly cities of the East, so deserted and dead was this region of ruins - this place where the Phoenicians had traded, where the Romans had mined and where up till only a few years ago successive generations had toiled for lead. It is some three miles from here to Charterhouse where there are traces of more mines. There is also a depression thought to be an amphitheatre of very small dimensions. The effect of these remains is nowhere so striking as at Priddy, where the ruined masonry of the more recent mining operations heightens the effect.

I was fortunate in finding somewhere to sleep, considering it was the holiday season of the year. A cottage to which a villager directed me let rooms, and some one for the week-end had fallen through. The morrow would be Sunday and I bargained for an early breakfast so that I could get down into Wells by eleven with plenty of time to spend upon the way.

I was fortunate, too, in finding in my hosts such a dear old couple and the old man especially interested in telling me about

RUINS OF LEAD MINES, PRIDDY

Fig 23. The ruins of
St. Cuthbert's Works,
as sketched by Donald
Maxwell in 1926 (Maxwell,
1927, p. 59).

Fig 24. Priddy by night (Donald
Maxwell, 1927, p. 61).

this Priddy tradition concerning which I had asked him questions. From the way he spoke I judged him to be a devout Nonconformist. He evidently regarded with great awe the possibility that Our Lord when a lad might have come to Priddy.

"I always say to the lads in my Bible class," he continued, "that perhaps when He was a lad like one o' them, He walked up the road where they walk. It's one thing, I tell them, to think of the Lord all those years ago, walking on the hills of Palestine, Palestine with its blue sky and palm trees. It's another thing, somehow, if you can tell them that perhaps He walked up the road here at Priddy in the rain with a gusty wind blowing up from Bridgwater Bay."

And so we talked, the old man quoting text after text from Isaiah and Ezekiel to show that the ships of Tyre and Sidon, the very coast of Our Lord's country, traded with the ends of the earth. "Shall not the isles" (perhaps England) "shake at the sound of thy fall [Ez. 26, 15]?" "Now shall the isles tremble in the day of thy fall; yea, the isles that are in the sea shall be troubled at thy departure [Ez. 26, 18]." "Thy rowers have brought thee into great waters [Ez. 27, 26]" - this might mean into the Atlantic - to Britain.

The fact that ships came to Britain from the coast of Palestine is established in history, but the importance of some possible allusion in the pages of the Bible seemed to this earnest advocate of the Somerset tradition to outweigh any other evidence, evidence appealed to on the grounds of possibility or probability for the legend.

"I am a local preacher," he continued, dropping his voice, "and once I preached a sermon at a chapel anniversary. My subject was: 'If Christ still came to Priddy?' You see, I maintained if Jesus was ever a lad in a ship trading from the coast of Palestine He may often have come here. Supposing He came again now? Supposing when a ship put into Bridgwater and a lad from the crew came up here, a young ship's carpenter, and that this were none other than Jesus Christ, how would it affect our lives?

"I wish," he said somewhat wistfully, "that it could be so and that He still came to Priddy." . . . . .

In the morning I was afoot by eight o'clock. The sun streamed over the hill and the grass-covered ruined tunnels and the broken chimney shafts appeared as temple towers wrought in gold and amber, casting shadows of deep blue across the land. The old man, still speaking of his favourite subject, accompanied me to the cross-roads on the hill. As we were about to part the sound of a bell came floating in the wind. It rang three times. I removed my hat until again it rang three times.

"Tell me," he said, "you know the old customs of the Church. Why do they ring that bell? I often hear it. What is it for?"

"That," I replied, "is the Church's way of telling us that Christ still comes to Priddy."[128]

These lengthy discussions between the educated gentleman who knew Palestine and the preacher who knew his Bible so well may have been fruitful for the local development of the tradition. Priddy is a small community, and Maxwell's host is probably to be identified with the elderly man of whom H. A. Lewis was told by the postmistress of Priddy in the mid-1930s, 'Mark Simmons who died aged 90 in 1933, and used to teach in Sunday School and Chapel, [who] would suddenly say to his hearers, "Suppose you saw Jesus coming up the hill again now."' (See below). It is possible that more remains to be discovered about Mark Simmons' contribution to the story. Although in Maxwell's account he seems not particularly well educated, his grounding of the story in the Old Testament prophecies is interesting, and he was doubtless instrumental in keeping it alive in the minds of generations of village youngsters.

It may be some echo of his preaching concerning the ships of Tarshish that we hear in the words of the next writer to refer to the Priddy story, Albert E. Webb, who in 1929 published *Glastonbury Ynyswytryn (Isle of Avalon), Its Story from Celtic Days to the Twentieth Century* from the offices of Glastonbury's *Central Somerset*

128 Maxwell, 1927, pp. 63-66.

Gazette. Webb observed that:

> In Sir Edward Creasy's "History of England" [1869/70] we read: "The British mines mainly supplied the glorious adornment of Solomon's Temple." If the metal traders visited Cornwall for their supply of tin it is not at all improbable that they would visit the Severn Sea for their supply of lead and other metals from Mendip. For Mendip was covered with lead and silver "as with a garment" to adopt an expression used by Pliny. ...
>
> It may very well be true that Joseph of Arimathea was a metal merchant - Cornish, Mendip and Gallican traditions agree in this. It is said that Joseph derived his great riches from trading in metal with Britain, and that he made several voyages to this country. In Ward Lock and Co.'s "Guide to Penzance and West Cornwall" is the following: "There is a traditional story that Joseph of Arimathea himself was connected with Marazion when he and other Jews traded with the ancient tin-miners of Cornwall." Baring-Gould in his "Book of Cornwall" [*sic*] writes: "Another Cornish story is to the effect that Joseph of Arimathea came in a boat to Cornwall and brought the Boy Jesus with him, and the latter taught him how to extract the tin and purge it from its wolfram. When the tin flashed then the tinner shouts: 'Joseph was in the tin trade!'" A tradition still lingers in Somerset of the coming of the Christ and Joseph in a ship of Tarshish; of how they came to the Summerland and "sojourned at the place called Paradise." There is a tradition of our Lord coming as a boy with Joseph at Priddy, in Mendip, where there may have been lead mines since the times of the Phoenicians, though now closed. The truth of these old tales we can neither affirm nor deny; but they are certainly much believed.[129]

---

129 Webb, 1929, pp. 19-21.

He went on to cite Taylor as an authority on the travels of Joseph across Gaul. Webb, we may note, like Taylor, does not himself bring Jesus to Glastonbury. He did, however, go on to tell that 'Joseph of Arimathea is said to have been the younger brother of the father of the Blessed Virgin Mary.' He seems to have read the Rev. Morgan, whose druidical fancies he goes on to echo for several pages, and he repeats a false quotation from Domesday referring to the 'Domus Dei ... called the Secret of the Lord' (see below).

More importantly, he seems to have been the first person since 1895 to have read Σ in the pages of *SDNQ*. Webb's '*It is said that Joseph derived his great riches from trading in* metal *with Britain,* and *that he made several voyages to this country.*' is a direct quotation from Σ's '*It is said that Joseph of Arimathea derived his great riches from trading in* tin *with Britain, that he made several voyages to this country,* and on one occasion...' with the word 'metal' substituted for 'tin' in the original, no doubt taking cognisance of the editorial comment that on Mendip men mined for lead and not tin.

Similarly, Webb's 'of how they came to the Summerland and "*sojourned* at *the place called Paradise.*"' almost exactly quotes Σ's 'and *the place* where they *sojourned* near Glastonbury is *called "Paradise"* to this day.' It is, of course, formally possible that both Σ and Webb are quoting from a common source, but this seems to unnecessarily multiply hypotheses. In his 'Notes' on page 10 he tells us that he gathered information in the library of the Glastonbury Antiquarian Society which certainly had a full run of *SDNQ*. A remaining puzzle is where he found the tradition 'of how they came to the Summerland', which is not to be found in Σ, although something like it is found in the notes to Bennett's play, there attributed to an Icelandic saga. Webb would probably have known, although he nowhere seems to cite the fact, that 'Summerland', *Gwlad-yr-haf*, is the Welsh designation of Somerset.

Webb had Roman Catholic sympathies, and, interestingly, he also tells us in his 'Notes' that the Rev. Fr. Jackson, 'formerly private chaplain at St. Louis Convent', established in Magdalene Street, Glastonbury, in 1926, supplied him with Latin translations. This was his third book on Glastonbury, having been preceded by *Glastonbury Abbey*, a guide to the Abbey ruins, in 1928 and, also in 1928, by his more prosaic *Glastonbury Legend, Tradition, History.*

The Old Testament passages which may have a bearing on the voyage story are worth some examination. Tarshish had earlier been linked to Glastonbury by the Anglican clergyman the Rev. C. L. Marson in his influential *Glastonbury or the English Jerusalem*, published in 1909, just after the acquisition of the Abbey by the Church of England. In his description of the Tor, 'whose very name', he avers, 'is Semitic', he tells us that 'Here they watched for the Phoenician liners - the men of Dido's race - until 146 B.C. Carthage fell, and the great ships of Tarshish sailed no more up the Bristol Channel.'[130] Earlier, he tells us that 'Festus Avienus learnt from a Greek author of about 260 B.C. that the Tartessii were used to come for trade to England [*sic*] for lead and tin. "Tarshish and the isles" really means Cadiz, possibly the Scilly Islands, and certainly Somerset. From the Land's End to the combined mouths of the Parrett, Brue and Axe, there is no safe anchorage for ships, and this then is the key of West Britain.'[131]

Rufius Festus Avienus, a Roman author of the later fourth century, wrote a poem entitled *Ora Maritima*, 'Sea Coasts,' a literary confection which contains borrowings from the early sixth-century BC *Massiolite Periplus*, a navigator's guide from the Greek colony of Marseilles, to which it is our only textual witness. This contains the ancient world's oldest surviving references to Ireland and 'the isle of the Albiones' - Britain.[132]

The biblical Tarshish has been generally identified with Tartessos, a port (and urban centre of a kingdom or region) which from the

---

130 Marson, 1909, pp. 94-95.
131 Marson, 1909, p. 2.
132 Ed. A. Berthelot, *Ora maritima*, Paris 1934. English trans. J. P. Murphy, *Ora maritima or Description of the seacoast.* (Chicago) 1977.

Late Bronze Age stood near the mouth of the Guadalquivir, on the Atlantic coast of Spain. Its exact site is uncertain, but modern opinion favours Huelva. It was once the premier port for the Atlantic tin trade with Greece and the Levant, its role being eventually eclipsed by the nearby Phoenician colony of Gades (Cadiz), itself perhaps founded as early as 1100 BC. Tartessos itself may have been destroyed by the Carthaginians, *c.* 500 BC.[133]

The Bible speaks of Tharshish in the Book of Kings, when describing the riches of Solomon. 'For the king had at sea a navy of Tharshish [or 'ships of Tharshish'] with the navy of Hiram [King of Tyre]: once in three years came the navy of Tharshish, bringing gold and silver, ivory, and apes, and peacocks', (*1 Kings*, 10:22, in King James' version). This can hardly be Spanish Tartessos, as its products are typical of Somaliland and India, and the journey thither began at a Red Sea port. Carpenter[134] suggests that the Hebrew phrase *anyoth t'sis*, translated 'ships (or navy) of Tarshish' originally referred to a type of vessel used by the Phoenician seamen, and perhaps named from Tarsus in Asia Minor, but it was certainly confused in antiquity with the Spanish haven. The Psalmist sang that 'The kings of Tarshish and the isles shall bring presents', seemingly to Solomon, but perhaps later understood as to God (*Psalm* 72:10). The ships of Tarshish became a by-word. *Psalm* 48:7, says of God, 'Thou breakest the ships of Tarshish with an east wind'. Isaiah spoke of 'The burden of Tyre. Howl, ye ships of Tarshish, for it is laid waste... for your strength is laid waste ... Pass over to Tarshish; howl ye inhabitants of the isle.' Isaiah also calls Tyre 'O daughter of Tarshish'. (*Isa.* 23: 1; 6:10' 14). When ordered to Nineveh by God, Jonah instead fled in the opposite direction, to Joppa, 'and he found a ship going to Tarshish: so he paid the fare thereof (*Jo.*1:3)'. The resulting three-day encounter with the whale is too well known for rehearsal here, but it is to

133 For a useful modern archaeological overview of Atlantic trade with the Mediterranean world, see Cunliffe, 2001.
134 Carpenter, 1966, pp. 59-61; 216-19.

be noted that when the Pharisees asked Our Lord for a sign, He replied that no sign should be given 'but the sign of the prophet Jonas', (*Matth.* 13:39), a statement perhaps allowing other parallels to be eventually drawn in addition to that intended.

Jeremiah spoke of 'Silver ... from Tarshish' (*Jer.* 10:9). Ezekiel (27:12) said of Tyre, 'Tarshish was thy merchant by reason of the multitude of all kinds of riches; with silver, iron, tin and lead, they traded in thy fairs' and again (*Ez.* 27:25) 'The ships of Tarshish did sing of thee in thy market'. The reference to lead would seem to have been especially noticed in Priddy; but the ships of Tarshish were not mentioned only in connection with vain riches. They were promised a more spiritual cargo. Through the mouth of Isaiah, God declared 'Who are these that fly as a cloud ...? Surely the isles shall wait for me, and the ships of Tarshish first, to bring thy [Jerusalem's] sons from far, their silver and their gold with them, unto the name of the LORD [Yahweh] thy God, and to the Holy One of Israel, because he hath glorified thee.' (*Is.* 60:8-9). Further, 'And I will set a sign among them, and I will send those that escape [from the judgement on the wicked] of them unto the nations, to Tarshish ... to the isles afar off, that have not heard my fame, neither have seen my glory; and they shall declare my glory among the Gentiles.' (*Is.* 66:19). Of the isles, Isaiah also says that they 'shall wait for his law' (*Is.* 42:4). The 'isles' are a parallelism for the ends of the earth. 'The isles saw it,[135] and feared; the ends of the earth were afraid, drew near and came' (*Is.* 41:5). 'I will also give thee for a light to the Gentiles, that they mayest be my salvation unto the ends of the earth' (*Is.* 49:6); 'the isles shall wait upon me, and on mine arm shall they trust' (*Is.* 51:5). Although for the Jews of Isaiah's day, the isles were those of the Mediterranean, for believers in the voyage story, the prophecies would sing with resonance of the Isles of Albion, and perhaps these very prophecies

135 The advent of God's servant, here Cyrus, but understandable as an archetype of Christ.

had played a part in its genesis.[136]

The Priddy tradition had become sufficiently well known by the early 1930s for casual after-dinner reference. On February 18th 1933 (as the *Somerset Year Book* for that year recorded), at the annual dinner of the Society of Somerset Folk in London, after a repast of *A girt zaddle o' mutton wi' Chitties, zum zider* and other appropriate delicacies, one of several vice-presidents, Mr W. A. Perkins, spoke before the President, Viscount Weymouth, MP for Frome, his Lady wife, and the ladies and gentlemen of the society, of 'Somerset Hospitality':

> Tradition and history recorded the names of many distinguished people who had been received as guests in Somerset. Among them he enumerated the Great Master, who as a youth trod the Mendip Hills, and was entertained by the miners of Priddy; Joseph of Arimathea, when he planted the tree of Christian civilisation at Glastonbury; [*etc. etc.*]

Mr Perkins' observation found confirmation in the same year in *Ictis and Avalon* by Dr C. R. Davey Briggs, who thought the Glastonbury 'island' was Ictis, the island tin-mart of the ancient geographers, and would also seem to have read Maxwell:

> According to local tradition, our Lord visited Priddy in 'the silent years' before he entered his public ministry; and Parry's musical setting has popularised Blake's poem based on this tradition … For the hills would at that period be continually clouded by the smoke from the furnaces, and the conditions of heat and darkness, under which mining and de-silvering were done, might well justify the description 'Satanic mills'.[137]

136 The role of these biblical passages in the evolution of the Grail romances, with their ship of Solomon, is a neglected topic.
137 Biggs, 1933, pp. 15-16.

It is a remarkable thing that Smithett Lewis and his followers apparently remained unaware of the existence of the Rev. Bennett's play, and of the creation of the Pilton Banner in 1931.[138] Pilton first appears in their printed versions of the legend in 1939, when H. A. Lewis writes 'You have to go to Priddy by the old lead mines of the Mendips, or to Pilton, the reputed port from which most of the lead was shipped, to hear the local traditions of the visit of Christ or the Christ Child.'[139] Further on he writes 'In Somerset I have traced the legend definitely at Priddy, in other parts of the Mendips, and at Pilton.'[140] Here again the play is not referred to. However, the connection of the 'legend' with a play does not appear to have been wholly forgotten in other quarters. In a footnote in the 1937 edition of *Joseph*, Smithett Lewis recorded the following anecdote:

> Quite recently a dignitary in Wells is stated to have gone out of his way to tell an antiquarians party who were coming to Glastonbury next day, that the story of Our Lord's coming to Glastonbury and Priddy was entirely invented some 50 years ago by a school teacher at Priddy when writing a play for an entertainment. Unfortunately for the dignitary, there are nonagenerians alive who knew the story in their childhood, not to speak of William Blake's hymn. If one has a zest in destroying beautiful old traditions, it is a pity to invent new myths to do it. There are worthier ways of embalming one-self. The party were not pleased.[141]

In the undated notes incorporated as an appendix in the

138 The more so in that L.S. Lewis and Bennett were acquainted. The latter assisted Lewis at the evening celebration of St Patrick's Day at the Glastonbury women's almshouse chapel in 1922, with a choir selected from the 'Chalice Well Party' (*CSG* 24 March, 1922). As we have seen, they both lectured at at the Chalice Well 'Summer School' of 1923.
139 Lewis, H.A., 1939, p.6.
140 Lewis, H.A., 1939, p. 9.
141 Lewis, L. S., 1937, p.52, note 4.

posthumous 1955 edition, he returned to the theme:

> Some people openly call it a myth. The sad thing is that some of
> them create myths to try to disprove it. I have dealt with such a
> mythical explanation. Unfortunately for the Dignitary and his
> informants, whoever they were, I learn from the indefatigable
> Rev. H. A. Lewis that Mrs. Weeks, postmistress of Priddy, told
> him (a) That Mark Simmons who died aged 90 in 1933, and
> used to teach in Sunday School and Chapel, would suddenly
> say to his hearers, "Suppose you saw Jesus coming up the hill
> again now." (b) Mrs. Barker, widow of a former Vicar, often
> referred to His coming. (c) The Rev. W. H. Creaton, Vicar in
> 1904-1919, later Rector of Yeovilton, Yeovil, had spoken of it.
> (d) Many old folk did so when she was a girl.
>
> So we may feel that the Dignitary and his informant or
> informants have consciously created a myth to disprove what
> they considered one.
>
> True, that Prebendary Palmer, Vicar of East Brent, son of a
> former Vicar of Priddy, when a lad, has said that neither he nor
> his brother ever heard the story. That is not surprising. Young
> men in their holidays think more of cricket, and football, and
> skating, generally.[142]

All this is most interesting. If the Dignitary, as seems almost
certain, is to be identified with J. Armitage Robinson, then, *contra*
Smithett Lewis, he was not a man to invent an historical detail
for no reason; 'some 50 years ago' from Smithett Lewis's present
should take us back to the late 1880s, and Robinson himself
retired in 1932. *If* his remarks were reported correctly, then, the
play of which Robinson had heard would probably have been
staged before Jenner's London dinner party, and before Σ wrote to
SDNQ. The Sunday School and Chapel teacher, Mark Simmons,

142 Lewis, L. S., 1955, pp. 162-3.

who 'would suddenly say to his hearers, "Suppose you saw Jesus coming up the hill again now"', is, as we have seen, probably to be identified with Maxwell's host of 1927. He might, perhaps, have once staged some Sunday-school pageant, although in 1939 H. A. Lewis thought the school-teacher of the Dignitary's account was female. His version relates that 'a dignitary of Wells lately suggested that the "legend of Priddy" was invented quite recently by a schoolmistress, to afford a plot for a children's play!'[143] The Rev. Creaton, also, Vicar of Priddy 1904-1919 and allegedly familiar with the legend, had been Headmaster of Wells Cathedral School from 1896-1904, and so might be described as a teacher. Was there one play, or were there two, the Pilton one perhaps inspired by an earlier one at Priddy?

It seems more economical to suppose that the play referred to by the Dignitary was that of Bennett at Pilton, based, as he averred in his notes, partly on Priddy tradition. The process of 'Chinese whispers' among the un-pleased antiquarians which carried the Dean's words to Smithett Lewis may have stretched fifteen years to fifty. Bennett, as we have seen, was not only a Prebendary of Wells Cathedral from 1903-1934, but Rural Dean of Shepton Mallet from 1917-1923. Armitage Robinson must have known him, although it is perhaps improbable that he studied his play with great attention, and possibly his recollection of its date and authorship, expressed in an 'off the cuff' remark, had indeed become vague. He was known at times to introduce Amy Robinson, whom he married in 1915, as 'my wife, Miss Faithful'.[144] However, if this is the solution to the mystery of the Dignitary of Wells and the play, it does little to clarify the origins of the Priddy tradition as such. The Pilton play can hardly have been its source,

143 Lewis, H. A., 1939, p. 5. He was followed in this by Dobson, who in the Preface to his 5th ed. in 1947 (pp. 6-7) wrote 'if some Priddy School teacher did write a little play for her children, it is far more probable that she based it on an existing tradition well-known in those parts, than that she invented it.'
144 Taylor, 1991, p. 61.

Fig 25. The Very Rev. J. Armitage Robinson D.D., 'An Erudite Dean,' as seen by 'Spy.'

although it is an early testimony to it. Priddy remains the earliest demonstrable localisation of a story which Jenner associated with Cornwall alone.

Smith observes that 'Since the Cornish locations [in which versions of the story were later recorded] are virtually all mining centres - and in Somerset Priddy was also a mining community - there is some ground for seeing this story as a miners' trade tradition, and not a local one at all.'[145] As already mentioned, Cornish miners worked far and wide. Given the prominence of the Romany in tinkering, smithing and farriery, it is also not impossible that gypsy lore provided a link between Cornwall, the Quantocks, Priddy with its renowned horse fair, and the London metal-working shops, providing some basis for Taylor's remarks about a trade route. However it began, at Priddy the legend did take hold, and seem to have developed a life of its own, independent of more literary expressions. Ruth Tongue recorded this version in 1965 in *Somerset Folklore*:

Our Lord in Somerset. Priddy, The Mendip Hills

Somerset has long boasted that its first church was founded by St. Joseph of Arimathea only thirty years after Calvary, but an even more lovely tradition persists on the Quantocks and the Mendips.

Our Lord when a boy came voyaging with a sailor uncle to Britain. Their trading ship put in at Watchet, and from there He walked across the Quantocks to Bridgewater where He boarded a punt and crossed the lakes and marshes to the foot of Mendip, ending his journey high up at Priddy.

Here, say the miners, He walked and talked and worked with them a happy while, and then, loaded with Somerset gear, He went back to Nazareth. *Oral tradition and collection, Crowcombe and Holford, 1901-55*.

---

145 Smith,1989, p. 65.

As a tiny girl I heard the very old grandfather of a visitor direct my brothers how to find 'Our Lord's Path' - at least, I think he called it that - but he was old and toothless and indistinct and my brothers careless. That was in 1901. When in 1908 we explored the Quantocks for it, we could neither find trace of it, nor recall the exact details. I am still hoping to meet some other guide to it if the tradition still lives.* [in a note] * See *Somerset Year Book, 1933,* p. 20.[146]

Ruth Tongue was a folklorist who collected a great deal of material orally, and was also a creative performer at Women's Institutes and the like, retelling stories in Somerset idiom, although she was not, in fact, a dialect-speaker by birth. The reference to the Quantocks, however, raises a suggestion that her memory had been, at least, refreshed by a reading of Taylor. Smith records a version of the legend of 1981 from a Mrs Pat Robinson of Wells, who wrote to him of 'the fables of Joseph of Arimathea (a tin merchant) landing at Paradise Farm near Burnham on Sea with the boy Jesus and walking, via Glastonbury it is said, to Priddy Green'.[147] Indeed, the tradition is far from dead. As dinner-parties figure more than once in this investigation, it is well to record that the hospitality of the Mendip miners may be enlarged upon. Within the last twenty years I have heard, although in true folkloristic fashion I do not remember quite when or how, that Joseph and the young Jesus used to drink with the miners. Some say that this was in the Miner's Arms, near Priddy, now a restaurant where those with sufficiently deep pockets may sample the old miner's snack of 'wall-fish' (snails).[148] Others say that the Lord's first pint was supped in the New Inn on Priddy Green, paradoxically now the older of the two public houses in the

146 Tongue, 1965, p. 187.
147 Smith, 1989, p.63 & 81 note 2.
148 Recorded as a public house only from 1875-1913; on Priddy's pubs see Thomas, 1989, pp. 77-9.

village, although, as an inn, no older than the 1840s.[149]

The most recent history of Priddy, *The Story of Priddy* by Alan Thomas, 1989, strangely omits to mention the supposed visit of Jesus. But it does record that 'lead appears to have been sent vast distances in pre-Roman times. Metallurgists at Massachusetts Institute of Technology have analysed the lead conduits in the remains of the Temple in Jerusalem (built 1014 BC) and concluded that they are made from Mendip lead.'[150] I am unaware of Mr. Thomas's source for this information.

149 As in Mary Caine, 1969, vol. 2, p. 23.
150 Thomas, 1989, p. 23. H. A. Lewis, 1934, p. 7, writes 'there is a legend that Cornish tin was used in Solomon's Temple. (Hamilton Jenkin, "Cornish Mines and Miners," "Old Cornwall," No. 1. p. 9), and that it came from Treveddoe, Warleggan.' Masonic 'lore' may lie behind these ideas.

Fig 26. Dom Ethelbert Horne O.S.B. (1858-
1952), writer, antiquary, and titular Abbot of
Glastonbury.

10

THE MONK'S TALE

The problem of the reliability of dates for what are alleged to be oral sources is also apparent when we turn to another notable creative witness to the 'legend'. In *The Somerset Yearbook* for 1924, Dom Ethelbert Horne published a version of the voyage story as *St. Joseph of Arimathea, A Legend of Glastonbury*.[151] Born Percy Horne in 1858, Dom Ethelbert was a Roman Catholic Benedictine monk of Downside Abbey, professed in 1879. For almost half a century, from 1891 until 1940, he was mission priest at St Benedict's, in the hamlet of Stratton-on-the-Fosse, by the great Abbey's gates. 'He is said to have baptised most of the [village] community, irrespective of creed, and to have blessed their weddings.'[152] He served as Prior of Downside from 1929-34 and was titular Abbot of Glastonbury from 1940 until his death, within a few days of his 94th birthday, in November 1952.

He was a noted antiquary, a member of the Somerset Archaeological and Natural History Society from 1886, Chairman of its Council from 1927-1940, and President 1940-42. He edited the Society's *Proceedings* from 1926-1929 and published many contributions. He was also an active member, and for a time President, of the Glastonbury Antiquarian Society, and was elected a Fellow of the Society of Antiquaries in 1924. He was expert on scratch-dials, on which he published a number of monographs, as well as *Somerset*

---

151 *The Somerset Yearbook*, 1924, pp. 93-95
152 Harding, 1999, p. 179.

Holy Wells for the Somerset Folk Press in 1923.

Horne was a co-director of excavations at Glastonbury Abbey after the disgrace of Frederick Bligh Bond, and as such, like Dean Armitage Robinson, he drew the paranoid ire of Bond, who convinced himself that the whole archaeological programme had fallen 'into the hands of the Roman Catholic Church.' Horne, however, responded with kindness and ensured that a report he had written criticising aspects of Bond's work and interpretation remained private and confidential during Bond's lifetime.[153] His gentleness in this matter confirms the accuracy of his obituary in the *Proceedings*, which recorded that 'Abbot Horne was a pleasant person and friendly companion and enjoyed the everyday things of life. He was an observant man, with a gift for describing what he saw.'[154]

His *St. Joseph* is difficult to assess as although it is, in form, apparently a devotional short story of his own, he writes in a footnote to his title that 'This form of the legend was given by an old Somerset lady about forty-five years ago.'[155] It is unclear whether we are meant to take this seriously. It was written a decade before the attempts of the Rev. H. A. Lewis to record witness to the story in Cornwall from the memories of elderly folk, subsequently used by Smithett Lewis, which might otherwise have provided a model. Here, it is perhaps merely a literary device, familiar, for instance, in the contemporary ghost stories of M. R. James, to assist our suspension of disbelief by reference to a supposed narrator or source, for Horne had literary aspirations. In 1922, also with the Somerset Folk Press, publishers of the *Yearbook*, he had published *Idylls of Mendip*, a small collection of descriptive pieces and short stories of rural life, several of them supposedly told to him by elderly ladies, both those of faded gentility and cottagers, and liberally sprinkled with conversation in dialect, of which he was a master. In 1938 he published *Somerset Folk*, a similar rustic anthology, followed by *West Country Folk* in 1948. If the

153 Ball, 2007, pp. 188; 190-3.
154 *PSANHS* xcvii, 1952, p. 194.
155 Horne, 1924, p. 93.

voyage theme was indeed suggested to him by some elderly lady who had read of it in the newspaper or in Smithett Lewis's booklet of 1923, and took it more or less seriously, he may have projected the telling back to a distant past of 'about forty-five years ago' to protect her anonymity. If we take him at his word, however, then we travel back to *c.* 1879, about the time when he first became a monk, again well before Jenner's dinner party, and our earliest contemporary written witness to the tradition in Somerset, Σ's query of 1895. However, the story as told by Horne contains no trace of anything suggestive of actual folklore, in fact nothing which could not derive from Jenner's account of 1916 in the journal of the Caldey Island Benedictines. It is probably safest to stick with the explanation of literary device.

Horne's story is told with great economy and simplicity. The Boy, or the Child, is sitting outside a house in a Nazareth street, where he lives with his Mother and the Old Man, evidently a carpenter, when the Rich Man arrives. He loved the Boy:

> whose wan, white face filled him with fear for his health. Now the Rich Man did a trade on the great seas, and had ships that went to lands far off and brought back stuff to sell, or things men gave him in exchange for his wares. And his plan was that he would take the Child in one of his ships … and he would reach a land that was green, and where the air blew in soft breaths, and it was cool, and strange birds sang sweet songs, and flowers in the grass and blossoms on the trees were such as were not seen in his own land. And the strong sea wind, and the green land, when they reached there, and the soft breeze, and the birds' songs and the flowers and blossoms, would drive the white from the Boys cheeks, and he would come home once more, so strong and well that his Mother's face would loose its sadness and the Old Man would smile.

Despite the Mother's initial reluctance the plan is agreed upon, and she accompanies the Rich Man and the Boy to the seaside, where a ship awaits, and she sees them off. They sail to the Green Isle, but the Rich Man is disappointed to find no improvement in the Boy's complexion. Shortly before their return, he finds him sat beneath a great tree, with a strange sadness in his eyes. The shadows of the branches form a great black cross on the grass in front of him, 'and in a still, small voice, he told him a dread tale.' The Rich Man seems to freeze with fear.

> And e'er he rose, the Boy bade him come, yes come again some day when all was done and over, back to that same spot, back to the Green Isle, and there build the first House that should be called after his name. There he must tell that story he had heard, there bring men to the House that they might learn all that the Man of Sorrows in after years had done, and so from this holy spot the news of a new life must spread out from end to end of the great land of which this Isle was but so small a part.

They sail back once more to the 'old, old land of the Boys home', and 'his Mother, who is called "Star of the Sea,"' is waiting with the Old Man. The story breaks off to quote from the Gospels of Matthew, and of John, 'And when it was evening, there came a certain Rich Man of Arimathea ...' 'Now there was in the place where He was crucified a garden, and in the garden a new sepulchre ...'

In old age with a band of followers, the Rich Man returns 'on the waves to Avalon', but now 'he leaned upon a staff.' At the place where the shadow had been seen, they cut boughs and laced them together, 'and the shadow of the great cross that fell upon the spot made it the House of God for all time. And it is there now, some of the stones of it, but the roof is gone, and no longer the song of praise and prayer goes up to the great court of heaven where Christ now reigns as the eternal King.' The Rich Man is too old to help with the work, and leans upon his staff to watch. It gets stuck in the ground, and he leaves it there as a token.

> And when the first spring came round, the time of year that he came to the Green Isle with the Child, the staff began to give out

leaves and May-buds, for it had taken root in the ground. And the flowers that grew upon the staff were fair to see, and pearl and pink in hue, just as were the Boy's cheeks when he first felt the soft winds of Avalon upon his face. And when the day of the Boy's Birth came round, once more the staff put forth its pearl and pink blossoms, so that twice each year it told the Rich Man of the Child he had loved so well.

And when at length Joseph of Arimathea died, he was the first of those to be buried in the earth of the Green Isle, where saints have since been laid through well-nigh countless years. And now in the Land where Christ reigns as King, Joseph holds his staff of gold, with leaves and flowers all made in pearls and stones that shine with sun-set hues, and his prayer is joined in that great song the blessed spirits ever sing, for his well-loved Isle of Avalon.

So ends this simple and moving little devotional tale, its conclusion somewhat reminiscent of Tolkien's *Leaf by Niggle*. It is of interest as an early use of the story by a Roman Catholic writer. But a very few years later it could hardly have been written, as denominational attitudes to the inheritance of Glastonbury became more sharply polarised.

GLASTONBURY

Fig 27. Glastonbury Abbey ruins during the excavations.
St. Joseph's Chapel is seen in the background.
Drawn by Honor Howard-Mercer, 1929.

11

CRITICISM AND CONTROVERSY

In *Avalon of the Heart*, 1934, a work which reads almost as a prose poem, and her own personal tribute to Glastonbury, Violet Firth (better known as the occultist Dion Fortune) refers, at first obliquely, to the voyage tradition: 'There was no other spot in these isles that could rival it in length of tradition, for in its first saint it had a link with Our Lord Himself. ... Whether or no God drew near to Glastonbury who shall say? But Glastonbury drew very near to God, and the fragrance of that Presence still lingers.' Later, she writes explicitly:

> Tradition also has a sweet and beautiful story which we must love for its own sake, even if we cannot believe it to be history. It is said that the Christ Child Himself came to Glastonbury as a boy, travelling with the tin-ships, and that He preached the Gospel to the wild miners of Mendip, who heard Him with joy. It is this legend that the great mystic, Blake, refers to in his poem ... But although this story may be a fable when viewed from the standpoint of history, it is a spiritual fact when viewed from the standpoint of the inner life.[156]

Speculation as wild as anything Firth herself wrote elsewhere had already touched upon the story in 1930, in Helen Travers Sherlock's

156 Firth, 1934, pp. 27;49.

St. Joseph and the Saintes-Maries. The legend is introduced, following Smithett Lewis, Taylor and Maxwell:

> there is another version of the story [of Joseph] current in Somerset and in parts of Gloucestershire, a definite belief that when St. Joseph sailed to Britain for his cargo of tin he brought with him in the ship a boy who was none other than Jesus himself. This startling tradition is found in Cornwall as well as in Somerset, and is held all the more devoutly in that it is spoken more rarely and with some reluctance.[157]

Here, Joseph the tin-dealer is held to have taken over the legendary functions of a local tin god (as also, in part, does St Dunstan), as well as of an Ancient Egyptian predecessor, the god Horus, who gives his name to the metal trader's road, the Harroway. 'He had with him in the boat when he came to Somerset the "Son of God"'.[158] It was Ms Sherlock's belief that the Ancient Egyptians had preceded the Phoenicians in voyaging to the westerly 'Islands of the Blessed'. This was among the more coherent of a number of Ancient Egyptian fantasies which Glastonbury attracted to itself between the two world wars.

During the 1930s, Smithett Lewis was joined by two other eccentric Anglican clergymen in the propagation of the voyage 'tradition'. As the pamphlets of all three appeared in numerous rescensions and editions, and each corresponded with and quoted from the others, it becomes very difficult to disentangle precisely who first said what and when. To add to the confusion, the second was also surnamed Lewis. This was the Rev Henry Ardern Lewis, who, when Vicar of Talland in Cornwall, in 1934, published *The Christ Child at Lammana - A Legend of Looe Island*. He followed this around 1936 with *'Ab Antiquo' The Story of Lammana (Looe Island)*, and in 1939 with

157 Sherlock, 1930, p. 4.
158 Sherlock, 1930, pp. 40; 38.

Christ in Cornwall?

In 1936 the Rev. Cyril Comyn Dobson, Vicar of St Mary-in-the-Castle, Hastings, published *Did our Lord visit Britain as they say in Cornwall and Somerset?* at Glastonbury. Dobson, not content with the visit of Christ in childhood, asserted that He had also made a *second* visit to Glastonbury, as a grown man, on the eve of His public ministry. H. A. Lewis, not to be outdone, argued in 1939 that Glastonbury had also been the final home and burial place of the Blessed Virgin Mary, who had accompanied Joseph there after the Crucifixion. We shall examine their individual contributions to the story in greater detail below.

The eccentric trio based their work in part on that of an older clerical writer, the Rev. Richard Williams Morgan (1815-1889), author of *St. Paul in Britain, or, The Origin of British Christianity as opposed to Papal Christianity*, 1861 (see above). Born at Llangyfelyn, Cardiganshire, of a clerical family, Morgan was an enthusiast for his native Welsh tongue. He managed to combine a series of Anglican curacies, in Wales and England, with druidry, and with his consecration as a bishop in a Syrian succession, c.1878, as Mar Pelagius, Heirarch of Caerleon, and Patriarch of the 'Ancient British Church'.[159] His book was later appropriated by the British Israelites, who edited out those sections which did not appeal to them, and, in this form, was still running to a fifth edition as late as 1925. Smithett Lewis avowed his debt to Morgan in his preface to the first edition of *Joseph* of 1922, commending his work 'as a starting point to those who want to begin to look into the matter'. Morgan, significantly, is silent concerning the Jesus voyage 'tradition', for had he known of it he would almost certainly have used it. His work is a store of credulous and misused erudition on druidry, the family of Caratacus

159 Later known as the Orthodox Church of the British Isles, this small independent church survived until 1994 when, re-named the British Orthodox Church, it was received into the canonical Coptic Orthodox Patriarchate of Alexandria as an English-speaking jurisdiction. Its present head, the Metropolitan of Glastonbury, is a senior member of the Coptic Orthodox Synod.

and the origins of Christianity in Britain, in which for him, following the sixteenth-century antiquary Camden and the seventeenth-century divine Stillingfleet, St Paul in person played a part. Most of this was swallowed whole by Messrs. Lewis, Lewis & Dobson, including the fallacious beliefs that a passage in William of Malmesbury's work, relating to Glastonbury's Old Church, was from an epistle of St Augustine, and that *Domesday Book* referred to Glastonbury, in some special sense, as the 'House of God' and the 'Secret of the Lord'; which assertions they now restated in support of the voyage story.

The motivation for Morgan's polemic is quite clear from his title. It was also shared, although it was no longer fashionable to express it quite so plainly, by the other three. As with the historiographical myth of the 'Celtic Church', of which the Glastonbury legends as expounded by Smithett Lewis *et al.* formed a specialised and local branch, behind the gentle legends which they sought to advocate lay a virulent dislike of the Church of Rome. Smithett Lewis deplored its intrusion into his own Glastonbury parish. In 1926 an attractive little temporary Roman Catholic chapel was opened for public worship in a converted stable building beside the Convent in Magdalene Street, and it adopted the parish name of St Mary's Church, Glastonbury 'after the original wattle church of St Joseph of Arimathea'.[160] In 1937 Smithet Lewis wrote of it that 'It is perfectly outrageous, that a little chapel - recently erected by the Italian Mission dares to usurp the name "By their fruits ye shall know them" [*sic*]'.[161]

It is hard now for those without first-hand experience of Ulster, or of those sections of Scottish society where such attitudes linger, to comprehend that Protestant partisanship which was still pronounced

160 *CSG*, 10 Dec. 1926. A Roman Catholic seminary had opened at Tor House (the Chalice Well property) in 1886. 'In 1904 the Sisters of Charity of St Louis, driven from France, had opened a convent and school. ... pilgrimages began again [in the 1920s], chiefly under the inspiration of the Guild of Our Lady of Ransom'; Watkin, 1973, pp. 15-16. The first modern Roman Catholic pilgrimage had occurred in 1895, to mark the beatification by the Pope in that year of Abbot Whiting.

161 Lewis, L.S., *St Joseph of Arimathea at Glastonbury*, 6th ed. 1937, p. 43.

in Somerset in the late nineteenth and early twentieth centuries. The battle of Sedgemoor in 1685, the last major engagement on English soil, had been a tragic dress rehearsal for the legendary Boyne Water of 1690, in which 'Good King William' finally broke James II's Catholic forces in Ireland. The judicial reprisals meted out in Somerset and elsewhere in the West Country by Judge Jeffries in the aftermath of Monmouth's abortive rising cast a long shadow in folklore. The November Somerset carnivals, in which whole communities are still involved, began, like the village bonfire rivalries of Sussex, as very conscious celebrations of the discomfiture of Popery in the failure of the Guy Fawkes' Plot. The end of the nineteenth century saw renewed Protestant unease at Roman Catholic resurgence, symbolised by the building of Westminster Cathedral, which coincided with the beginnings of Irish republican terrorism on the British mainland. In Somerset there was great fear when Glastonbury Abbey, widely seen as a national shrine, came on the market in 1907, that it would become the property of the Roman Church. In the event, it was purchased by private money on behalf of the Church of England, the cost of which was redeemed by public subscription.

Paradoxically, this same period, the later nineteenth and early twentieth century, saw the high tide of Anglo-Catholicism within the Church of England, and it was Anglo-Catholics who were most upset by the result of a Roman investigation into the validity of Anglican orders set up by Leo XIII in 1895, which ended with their declaration by papal bull as null and void in 1896. Dom Francis Aidan Gasquet, sometime Prior of Downside, was a member of the commission of investigation. He became a formidable historian of the dissolution of the monasteries, author of *The Last Abbot of Glastonbury* (1908), and a Cardinal in 1914, the centenary of the arrival in England of what became the Downside Benedictine community.

Just as, at the time of the conciliar movement in the fifteenth century, the English church had used the legend of Joseph of Arimathea to argue for seniority among national churches, and later Henry VIII's apologists had appealed to the heritage of Constantine the Great to justify his independence from the Papacy, so Smithett Lewis, and many who thought like him, sought to 'prove' that the Church of England pre-dated that of Rome by virtue of its foundation by Joseph in 31 or 37AD. Others sought an even older pedigree. In 1938 Bligh Bond wrote: 'The Protestantism of later times is no new thing. It is merely the resurgence of the old spirit of Druidical Britain in another form. Baring-Gould said the same of Welsh Methodism'.[162]

The Glastonbury eccentrics found a foil for themselves in the person of Joseph Armitage Robinson (1858-1933), Dean of Wells, who contrasted with them in almost every respect.[163] Born in Somerset at Keynsham, and by upbringing and temperament an evangelical, he was led by his love of scripture to the serious study of the New Testament, and thence to the early Christian writings of the second century, including those mysterious texts, the apocrypha. He became expert in Armenian. He was led by his love of truth to accept the basic validity of modern textual criticism of the Bible, as pioneered in Germany, and helped to make this acceptable to intelligent Anglican churchmen. Forsaking a purely academic career to serve the wider Church, he became Dean of Westminster in 1899 and Dean of Wells in 1911. These positions, in two ancient churches, turned his attention to English medieval history, and while at Wells he disentangled the textual problems of William of Malmesbury's twelfth century monograph *On the Antiquity of the Church of Glaston* in *Somerset Historical Essays*, 1921. His *The Times of St Dunstan*, 1923, was a pioneering study of Glastonbury's crucial tenth century, and his *Two Glastonbury Legends*, 1926, remains the basis of all serious study of the Arthurian legends at Glastonbury. His medieval studies brought him close to many Roman Catholic scholars, including Dom Ethelbert Horne of Downside Abbey, and to an appreciation of the heritage of the universal Church. From 1921-25, he was a leading Anglican representative in confidential and historic exploratory talks with representatives of the Roman

162 Bond, 1938, p. 18, note. He cites Baring-Gould, *Myths of the Middle Ages*, p.627.
163 For the life of Robinson, see Taylor,T.F., 1991.

Catholic Church in Belgium, the Malines Conversations, which aimed at the eventual re-unification of the two churches, a process which, it was acknowledged, would involve a recognition of the spiritual leadership of the Apostolic See.

Bligh Bond was disgraced in the spring of 1922, when the West-Country press reported a civil court hearing in which both his financial dealings with his estranged wife and his daughter's moral welfare were called into question. His official connection with the Abbey excavations was terminated on the pretext of his failure to work with a co-director. Bond sought to shift the blame for his downfall, and in *The Company of Avalon*, 1924, he suggested that ecclesiastical prejudice against his psychic methods was responsible for his difficulties. Armitage Robinson, who in fact seems to have gone out of his way to ease the blow for Bond, has been presented as his chief antagonist. Smithett Lewis, although himself disapproving of Bond's psychic methods, remained loyal to Bond, and wrote an affectionate obituary after his death in 1945. After a hiatus, excavations at Glastonbury recommenced from 1926, in part under the direction of Robinson's friend, the Roman Catholic Benedictine monk Dom Ethelbert Horne, who in 1940 became titular Abbot of Glastonbury in recognition of his scholarly work.[164]

As we have seen, Smithett Lewis's first essay on the Glastonbury legends in 1922 was seemingly a response to Armitage Robinson's perceived iconoclasm. He appears to have seen *Two Glastonbury Legends* of 1926 as a counter-attack upon his own 'slight work' (T. E. Taylor's description), as assuredly it was not. Taylor records that it 'had begun, most generously, as a talk to a small group of Oxford

---

164 It is only fair to observe that although, by today's archaeological standards, Bond, Horne *et al.* were all amateurs both in excavation technique and in recording and publication, Bond was, in general, no less competent than his immediate successors, but, as with the business of the supposed bones of Abbot Whiting, which he omitted from his published reports, he was prepared to manipulate evidence to accord with his own theories.

undergraduates at a meeting of their archaeological society'.[165]

Smithett Lewis's reaction was to write a ten page foreword to the second edition of his *Glastonbury, "The Mother of Saints"* in 1927, entitled 'Some Answer [*sic*] to the Dean of Well's "Two Glastonbury Legends"'. The intemperance of his personal attack upon the Dean still makes rather shocking reading:

In the 1st Edition of this book I expressed the hope that Dr. Armitage Robinson, Dean of Wells, would have his gifts kindled in defence of early Glastonbury traditions. Since that edition the Dean has written a book. The Dean of Wells was formerly Dean of Westminster, between both of which places and Glastonbury there has been age-long rivalry. The double mantle has proved too much for him. His book is called "Two Glastonbury Legends." In it he tries to destroy the age-long association of St. Joseph of Arimathea and King Arthur with Glastonbury.

Before I say a few words about the Dean's effort I might add that Mr. Christopher Hollis, a recent convert to Rome, has written another book, the religious purpose of which is manifest, called "Glastonbury and England." Mr. Hollis mentally accepts the whole position of the Dean. He is a Wellensian. Having accepted the Dean's findings with his mind as a matter of course, his whole soul revolts from it, and he relieves himself by amusing tirades against "the Dons" and their attitude to Glastonbury. It is not an inspiring sight - a man suffering simultaneously from mental acquiescence and spiritual indigestion. Let us look away to the Dean, who is wrapped in calm without a doubt.

Lest anyone should take these two books too seriously I pen these few lines. It is obviously impossible to deal fully in a foreword with the Dean's attitude. ... It is at the end of our horizon that we reign with an infinite might. In the absence of anything to contradict us we can let ourselves go (and when a new fact comes

165 Taylor, T.F., 1991, p. 105.

in view we can save our faces by posing as discoverers). The Dean simply begs the question and wastes much time and ingenuity. He takes much pains to disjoint that which naturally fits together. *Cui bono*? Even the absence of earlier evidence is no proof that there never was any.

The detail of his arguments, if such they may be called, concern the Joseph legend as such, and therefore need not delay us here. Among them may be found an interesting mention of the Vicar's discovery, in 1923, of a window in St John's Church featuring the fifteenth century arms attributed to Joseph, and of his showing of this window both to Bond, and to the Dean, who had become expert in medieval stained glass. It may be of this window, to which the Dean referred in his 1926 book,[166] that Lewis regarded him (if so, quite groundlessly) as posing as the discoverer. He returned eventually to the attack:

> The Dean is very learned, and his books are always intensely interesting and mines of information. But, after all, the important point is - is he altogether a safe guide? Many gifted people are not. We have said something about his "Two Glastonbury Legends," Let us take two other things: (1) The notices in Glastonbury Abbey, he being Chairman of the Executive Committee of its Trustees; (2) A slab in his own Cathedral. To be a great scholar on any subject one must necessarily have one's limitations. It is very easy to be so occupied in bending over a MS. as to forget all the evidence of the world around. And it is possible to be meticulously careful about dots to i's and extraordinarily oblivious to ordinary every-day facts.

The notices were held to be misleading to visitors, and, in one instance, to do scant justice to the work of the excavator, Bond.

166 Robinson, 1926, pp. 49; 65.

After all, must we take the Dean too seriously? There are interludes when scholars look up from their books and take a glimpse of the world around. "Two Glastonbury Legends," on its last page, has this passage:

"Yet they (the legends) claim respectful treatment on very various grounds. He who rejects them as unworthy trivialities, and will have nothing but the unclothed skeleton of historically attested fact, cuts out the poetry from life and renders himself incapable of understanding the fullness of his inheritance."

This is exactly what the Dean has done. In that sentence the Dean has hanged himself. There he will hang - a man who wrote a book to assassinate two beautiful legends, but does not like to be called an assassin. This is probably the connecting link between him and his humble follower, Mr. Hollis. One commits the crime and the other is an accessory, but their subconscious minds know all the time it is a crime, and they are ashamed of it. It is very pitiful. So much labour! So much ingenuity! I repeat "*Cui bono?*" ... And people write books which their better selves condemn. It is an interesting psychological study.

In this foreword Lewis shows clearly that, if he had not been one earlier, he had by now become a crank on the subject of Glastonbury. Writing when the general tenor of the Malines Conversations had become known, his own 'manifest' religious purpose, expressed with as much subtlety as he could muster, is plain, and in answer to his repeated rhetorical question, '*Cui bono?*', 'who benefits?', we are expected to conclude: 'the Church of Rome'.

It need not be thought that the polemic was all one-sided. Glastonbury's first post-Reformation Roman Catholic parish priest, Fr. Francis Burdett, felt it appropriate to address his congregation at the consecration of the little chapel of St Mary, by the Convent in Magdalene Street, in 1926 with words seemingly calculated as a challenge to the Anglican establishment:

[Historians] might say, some did say, that the church, the Roman

Catholic Church, the Apostolic Roman Catholic Church, descended from St. Peter, the church that alone possess the longest line in Europe, in the world, that great church taught wrong things, perhaps that it teaches wrong things, but they could not deny that the same things it taught at the Reformation it teaches today ... They [the congregation] could not pick and choose. There was only one right faith, though there might be thousands of wrong. ... they had to stand by what they believed and knew to be the truth, though others went on living in blindness, weakness and ignorance. They taught with definite authority and voice, however much other people might dispute and dislike it. That voice came from Rome and had always come from Rome. He [Fr. Burdett] claimed that if Abbot Whiting, martyred and murdered Abbot Whiting, were alive to-day he would come to that place and that alone in Glastonbury to worship ... and to offer up the mass which was the same today as when he lived here in Glastonbury; the words used were identical, the service the same as when given them by St. Peter.[167]

It was the hope of Roman Catholics that the foundation stone for a new, permanent, church at Glastonbury might be laid before the fourth centenary of the judicial murder of the last abbot fell in 1939. After the Roman Catholic Pilgrimage to the slopes of the Tor in 1936, following Benediction in the field behind St Mary's Convent, no less a personage than the Bishop of Clifton, the Irish born Bishop William Lee (1931-1948), could tell the faithful that:

no doubt they had read of, or perhaps seen, other pilgrimages to that place, and the form of service used. It was not for him to go into history; they had sufficient proof for they had the lineal descendants of the Benedictine monks. Others who arranged pilgrimages were perhaps trying to prove continuity because

---

167 *Central Somerset Gazette*, Friday Dec. 10, 1926, p. 5.

they went about in copes in old ruins. Of them Blessed Richard [Whiting] would say: "I know ye not, let me have those who followed my rule." "In vain men vainly boast of the Catholic Church" observed the Bishop.[168]

It had slipped Bishop Lee's mind, as it had not that of the Rev. Lionel Smithett Lewis, that Abbot Whiting had, with whatever inner reservations, signed the Act of Supremacy, and thus died, technically, an Anglican martyr.

Armitage Robinson, 'wrapped in calm without a doubt', was too dignified to respond to the attacks of those who could not hope to match his own deep scholarship, but the Glastonbury eccentrics did not go unchallenged by writers in the Roman interest. In 1931 the Jesuit historian the Rev. Herbert Thurston wrote a withering attack on the 1927 edition of Smithett Lewis's *St Joseph...* in the Roman Catholic periodical *The Month*.[169] He deplored 'the attempt of educated clergymen, who speak to their parishioners with a certain authority and who have the means of knowing better, to persuade the illiterate that St Joseph of Arimathea did in truth end his days in Glastonbury ...'[170] He went on to attack the historical content of Bond's 'automatic' scripts - 'this kind of rubbish, which for many people acquires a quasi-sacred character, because it is believed to be communicated by good spirits who lived as monks ...'

Smithett Lewis's final pre-Second World War edition of *Joseph* ... appeared in 1937. It contained another, equally personal, attack on Robinson, who had by then been in his grave for four years. In his preface, 'A short answer to Dean Armitage Robinson's "Two Glastonbury Legends"', he refers back to the second edition of

168 *Central Somerset Gazette*, Friday July 3, 1936, p. 5.
169 *The English Legend of Joseph of Arimathea*, The Month, Vol. CLVIII, no. 805 - July, pp. 43-54.
170 Thurston stated that 'Mr. Lewis completely ignores Dean Armitage Robinson's refutation ... [of the legend in 1926]', having failed to note his preface to the 2nd. ed. of *Glastonbury, "The Mother of Saints"*. This oversight did not escape Lewis.

Glastonbury, "The Mother of Saints", where 'I answered that attack in some nine pages, and the press supported me. But by many, who had never read that answer' - here he seems to have Thurston in mind - 'the dismissal of the Glastonbury Traditions as unhistorical by so learned a writer, with so much to his credit, has been acquiesced in without any further investigation. It does not occur to them that it was the beginning of the failure of his great power, and his judgement. ... *Dr. Robinson's conclusions were his own*' [underlined in the original]. Dean Robinson's death seems to have removed from him all sense of restraint or fear of criticism. In his 1937 edition he takes on board all the elaborations of H. A. Lewis and of C. C. Dobson. He discussed Dobson's theory that Jesus had 'built a wattle building' somewhat non-committally, but of the Jesus-Maria stone in the present Lady Chapel's south wall he writes

> Did the feet of these holy beings named ever tread this spot? I instinctively take my hat off when I approach it. It is a hallowed spot. Is Mr. Dobson right ...? No one will ever know. But it is a hallowed spot. The very possibility sanctifies beyond all words. One hopes it is true.[171]

He was more confident in, and devoted five pages to the exposition of, a suggestion, personally made to him by H. A. Lewis, which he himself was not to mention in print (and then more tentatively) until 1939, that the Virgin Mary had been buried beneath the Old Church. This was inspired in part by the curious 'Prophecy of Melkin', recorded by John of Glastonbury in 1342, which spoke of the Old Church standing 'above the adorable, venerable Virgin'.[172] 'The simple plain meaning [of Melkin's prophecy]' wrote Smithett Lewis, 'is that she lies buried there.' Smithett Lewis went on to attack the belief in the Assumption - 'perhaps the greatest assumption that ever was conceived'. He implied that Mary might have come to Glaston earlier

171 Lewis, L. S., 1937, p. pp. 33-37.
172 On Melkin, see Carley, 1981, and Ashdown, 2003.

*Fig 28. The 'Jesus-Maria Stone,' Glastonbury
Abbey Lady Chapel (south wall, 13th century) as
engraved by Rev. William Barnes, c. 1833.*

with Jesus, before being brought by Joseph 'to finish her days in the
Britain which tradition claims she had known in earlier days …
possibly to the spot where she had been with Our Lord'.[173]

He tells the voyage story itself as in 1931, but adds:

> As the years go on, and wider knowledge comes, this
> wonderful story of Our Lord's own visit to Somerset and
> Cornwall, immortalised by William Blake … grows more
> and more upon one.[174]

Thurston, strangely, failed in 1931 to condemn the Jesus voyage
story. Possibly he simply overlooked it amongst all of Smithett Lewis's
heterodox gleanings, or perhaps he did not wish to draw attention
to a suggestion which many of his co-religionists might feel was
not merely silly but actually sacrilegious. This was precisely the
ground on which the story was condemned in 1939 by Miss Beatrice

173 Lewis, L. S., 1937, pp. 42-43.
174 Lewis, L. S., 1937, p. 32.

Hamilton Thompson, lecturer in history in the University of Durham, in a 22 page booklet *Glastonbury - Truth and Fiction*, published by Mowbray & Co of London, whose cover enquired 'Did our Lord visit Britain? A competent historian examines the story in the light of the authorities alleged for it, and shows it to be without foundation. Ninepence.' A second impression appeared in 1947. Miss Thompson, 'the not undistinguished daughter of a very distinguished ecclesiastical historian',[175] rejoiced that the 'automatists and spiritualists, who in their endeavours to prove their power have succeeded in putting new stumbling-blocks in the path of the credulous, have been exposed by Father Herbert Thurston in an incisive article in the *Month*.' She went on to applaud Thurston's attack on the 'power of judging historical evidence' of the Rev. Smithett Lewis. She continued:

Let us repeat that it is no part of our purpose to detract from the pleasure that thousands have derived from the legends of S. Joseph and the Holy Grail. ... Unfortunately there have been attempts in recent years to make them, unhistorical as they are, a foundation for other and even less credible stories by connecting S. Joseph's supposed visit to Britain and Glastonbury with certain imaginary doings of our Lord Himself.

DID OUR LORD VISIT BRITAIN?

Before examining these stories we must premise that we do so with great reluctance. With all respect to the good faith and good intentions of those who have disseminated them, we are bound to say that it seems irreverent and almost impious to attempt to peer

175 Review, *SDNQ*, vol. 23, p. 71. Among the works of her father, A. Hamilton Thompson, many be mentioned the still useful *English Monasteries*, Cambridge 1913. Here (p. 5) he wrote 'At this time [that of St Augustine] the chief strength of Celtic monachism was naturally in the north, although it had penetrated southwards to such isolated outposts as Glastonbury.' This suggests he believed Glaston to be an Irish Columban offshoot. He also noted (p. 148) that 'Guide books are not as a rule very trustworthy' but that 'F. Bligh Bond's guide to Glastonbury abbey' was a notable exception. He addressed the *Somerset Arch. & Natural Hist. Soc.* members in an excursion to the Abbey in 1926, when Bond (rather surprisingly) also spoke.

behind the veil which Holy Scripture has drawn over the sacred Boyhood and Manhood between the visit to the Temple and the beginning of the public ministry; to seek to drag into the light that which He Himself and the New Testament writers have always seemed to desire should be kept hid.

The principle agent in the attempt to popularise the stories to which we refer appears to be a pamphlet written by the Rev. C. C. Dobson, author of *The Mystery of the Great Pyramid* and other works. The pamphlet with which we are now concerned is entitled *Did Our Lord Visit Britain?* and, to speak candidly, appears to be a particularly dangerous though doubtless sincere attempt to transform a tangle of very insecurely founded theories into an intelligible story.[176]

As an academic, Miss Thompson naturally found no difficulty in demonstrating the 'incompetence to deal with the subject' of the Rev. Dobson, although her own historical competence was less than she supposed; her summary of that Glastonbury history which she found acceptable was highly uncritical, her reliance on secondary sources almost total, and, as we have seen, she was in error in regarding Dobson as the main cultivator of that nut which she chose to attack with such a large hammer. Surprisingly, she conceded that 'the tradition that Joseph was engaged in the tin-trade is fairly widespread', but she was particularly harsh on the link with Blake. 'Mr. Dobson categorically states, as no serious student of Blake would either dare or wish to do, that ... Blake is "quoting the tradition so dear to every native of Cornwall and Somerset ..."' She pointed out, quite correctly, Blake's lack of interest in Glastonbury or Somerset, and suggested, reasonably, that Parry's popularisation of Blake's 'lyric' was responsible for its becoming 'the principle buttress of ... a story of which there is no reason to suppose that Blake had ever heard.'[177] She began her conclusions with another side-swipe at Smithett Lewis.

176 Thompson, 1939, pp. 5; 8-9.
177 Thompson, 1939, pp. 11-13.

She found that his passage on St George at Glastonbury 'reads like a parody of some of his other arguments, and presumably was not intended to be taken seriously. Perhaps he was trying to see how much his readers could be induced to swallow.' Quickly putting levity aside, she returned to the high seriousness of her theme:

> As we have said, such stories appear to us to involve an unseemly prying into sacred and secret things. And it becomes still more shocking when the argument, as we have shown, is based on paltering with the truth and, in some cases, it would appear, on downright fabrication.[178] ... Glastonbury and its legends have for too long been at the mercy of any well-meaning person who likes to improve upon its traditions. Enough harm has already been done by spiritualists to whom Glastonbury has become a happy hunting-ground, and though Mr. Dobson and Mr. Lewis have no inclinations in this dangerous direction, they have nevertheless laid themselves open (however innocently) to the almost equally serious charge of distorting fact. ... We should have no quarrel with any one who honestly attempted to trace the history of this or any legend simply as a legend, but we must resolutely oppose any attempt to convert fancy into fact, by means or methods which, if not wantonly dishonest, are at any rate slipshod and unsound. ... Such well-meaning and misguided writing may do much mischief, and it is time that these stories were left alone, until they can be viewed in their proper perspective with whatever respect may be due to them as well-meant exercises of imagination.[179]

Let us hope that that time has now arrived. It is hard, with hindsight, however, to see that 'much mischief' ever did actually result from the story, in which many good and gentle souls, whose only fault might be credulity, have found an almost secret well-spring

178 This refers to the spurious quotations from St Augustine and *Domesday Book*.
179 Thompson, 1939, pp. 21-22.

of inner faith. The Rt. Rev. Ethelbert Horne, O.S.B., seems to have kept a low profile during these exchanges, and, for once, Violet Firth seems to have shown more wisdom than the champions of orthodoxy. Michael Wood quotes the modern Roman Catholic monastic historian Dom David Knowles (1896-1974) as demonstrating the power which the Glastonbury mythos can hold even for 'the most sober scholar'. In describing the execution of the last Abbot on the Tor, Knowles imagines the old man's eyes suryeying the '"clouded hills" to the north, once hallowed, so the story ran, by the footsteps of the "beauteous lamb of God". .. On the pleasant pastures of Mendip had shone the countenance of the Child Jesus.'[180]

180 Wood, 1999, pp. 63-4 (quotation unlocated).

12

THE FOLKLORIST: HENRY ARDERN LEWIS

The first of Smithett Lewis's disciples was Henry Ardern Lewis, who graduated from Oxford with a third in 1902, and became a priest in 1904. His early career was varied. He was an assistant chaplain to the South African Railway Mission, 1905-08 He was a naval chaplain 1915-19, and returned to Africa, spending a year in Sierra Leone, 1919-20, and was a college chaplain at Lagos, Nigeria, 1922-29. Returning to Britain, he took a succession of Cornish parishes, becoming Vicar of St Cleer, 1929-33, Talland, 1933-6, and Penwerris, 1936-43. He ended his career at St Martin's in the Isles of Scilly, where he continued to write on local legends and archaeology. It was seemingly while at Talland, the site, in the middle ages, of a small priory of Glastonbury Abbey, that he read Smithett Lewis and became interested in the investigation of the Jesus voyage story, in 'The Quest' for what he would dub the 'Holy Legend'. As he tells us himself in *Glastonbury, The Holy Land of Britain*, 1946,

> In this Supplement to "Christ in Cornwall" I return to the spot whence I started on "The Quest." It had its origin in a short reference to the Holy Legend of Our Lord's visit to Britain in an early edition of Rev. Lionel Lewis' "St Joseph of Arimathea at Glastonbury".[181]

---

181 Lewis, H.A., 1946, *Christ in Cornwall?*, p. 16.

On 20th January 1934 he read a paper, *The Christ Child at Lammana - A Legend of Looe and Talland*, before the Looe Old Cornwall Society. This was reprinted in *The Cornish Times* and issued as a booklet of 20 pages in the same year. In this paper, he ventured 'to take a legend which at first sounds highly improbable, if not impossible, and try to show it to be certainly possible, with even some elements of probability in it. ... I am proposing to tell you first a legend, which never seems to have been very widely published or believed, and which has practically died out today, in the faint hope of reviving it.' He went on to tell how Joseph was a tin-merchant, and uncle of the Blessed Virgin Mary, who 'frequently paid trading visits here, calling at various suitable spots, on or near the coast.' On one occasion he brought the 'Child Jesus', and one of the places where they landed 'was the Island of St. Michael of Lammana, now known as Looe Island.':

> May I say at once that the legend is more frequently associated with St. Michael's Mount, and I am indebted chiefly to Mr. Lightowler for another version linking it with this very part. Perhaps he will be able to tell us how he got his version, but I have already found one of our older inhabitants at Polperro, whose family has long been associated with this part, who tell me that he has heard "something about Joseph of Arimathea and Lemaine" (the later version and spelling of Lammana).

Lewis conceded that 'Of course it could never be PROVED true. But can it ever be proved untrue? It is not a little remarkable, to my mind, that the legend of some visit of Our Lord to Britain should have been known to William Blake at the end of the 18th century, at a time when we regard religious faith as moribund. ... but where did he get the legend? When I asked Mr. Henry Jenner, F.S.A., whom I shall later quote, this question, his reply was, "Where, indeed?"[182] He rehearsed the legend and its supports from Smithett Lewis and Jenner.

182 Lewis, H.A., 1934, p. 6.

*Fig 29. Looe Island, Cornwall, which, with a
chapel at Talland on the mainland opposite,
formed the property of Lammana, held by
Glastonbury Abbey from before 1144 until the
later 13th century.*

He suggested Lammana might be, not an alternative claimant as the site of the *Ictis* of Diodorus Siculus, but a 'most likely ADDITIONAL trading post', stressing its natural advantages as a harbour and proximity to the tin workings of the Looe valley.

> As regards the use of small islands off the coast for trading purposes, we have the exact counterpart in the early trade with West Africa, where there was a chain of such islands off the coast or up the estuaries, from Goree to the Cameroons, some of which I have visited and seen the remains of the fortifications thereon. When there was any doubt as to the reception likely on the mainland, it was obviously safer to land on an island and induce the natives to come out there for barter. I suggest, therefore, that round the S.W. coasts of Britain, nearest to the tin district, there would be Looe Island, St. Michael's Mount, perhaps others, and almost certainly Glastonbury (then an island), near the lead and copper mines of Somerset.[183]

183 Lewis, H.A., 1934, p. 11. There were no copper mines in Somerset.

He discussed the history of the Priory of Lammana, which included a chapel on the mainland and another on the island. He thought the existence of two chapels indicated a particularly holy spot:

> In this connection note the very strong curse appended to the deed by which Hastutus de Solenny (circa 1200), confirmed the grant of Lammana to Glastonbury, given to them by his predecessors "ab antiquo," in which curse he prays that whosoever nullifies this grant may "have his name blotted out of the book of Life, and expiate his sin with the traitor Judas." In view of this curse, one feels a little anxious about the fate of Richard, King of the Romans, who in 1239 gave permission to the Abbot of Glastonbury to alienate it, and of the Abbot Michael, who about that time availed himself of the permission, and "let the manor of Lammana in Cornwall on a perpetual lease."[184]

He thought one or more of the hermits who accompanied Joseph after the Crucifixion might have come from Glastonbury to found the hermitage on St Michael's Island.

In his booklet, he appended part of a long and not uncritical letter from C. K. C. Andrew, sometime Chairman and Recorder of the Looe Old Cornwall Society who stated that ten years spent in Looe 'gave me no first-hand knowledge of [the legend's] existence'. However, he did not entirely dismiss the story, and speculated further on its economic background, noting that the Romans had in 56 BC crushed the Veneti of Armorica, who had monopolised the cross-Channel traffic, and had also developed new sources of tin in Spain. 'Was not this just the opportunity that would appeal to an enterprising Semite: to sail around land in his own ship, buy good tin cheap from the overstocked Britons who had lost their markets, and sell at an enhanced profit in the eastern colonies of the Empire?'[185]

H. A. Lewis had already begun to collect his own material on the

184 Lewis, H.A., 1934, p. 12.
185 Lewis, H.A., 1934, p. 18. Letter dated 10th Feb. 1934.

'legend'. Noting that Jenner's letter to the *Western Morning News* of 1933 was 'followed by a letter signed E.C.G., Plymouth, on April 12th [1933] in which the writer records the songs and carols sung by children and remembered by a Cornishwoman, beginning "Joseph was a tin merchant"', he adds in a footnote 'I have traced memories of these songs in Looe.' 'Joseph was a tin merchant' is a variant of the Jenner charm 'Joseph was in the tin trade', recorded in Baring-Gould's novel, but might represent a simple adaptation of it. Lewis also referred to correspondence with the Benedictines of Caldey.[186]

H. A. Lewis followed his 1934 pamphlet, in *c.* 1936, with another booklet, of 27 pages, entitled *"Ab Antiquo", The Story of Lammana (Looe Island).*[187] Lammana was a priory of Glastonbury by 1144, and continued so until *c.*1250. H. A. Lewis believed that it had been so *ab antiquo*, 'from antiquity', from as early as the pre-Conquest period[188] He began by recapitulating 'The Legend', the Jesus voyage story. 'Since writing "The Child Christ of [*sic*] Lammana" some 18 months ago I have spent much time in research.' He recorded the identities, and some of the words, of certain of the elderly people of whom he had enquired concerning the legend: 'Mrs. George of Polperro, an old lady of over 70 had "always heard that Christ came to Cornwall. And why not?"' We must remember that it was now forty years since the story had first attracted notice from its appearance in *Black's Guide* as a 'legend', and long enough, probably, for it to seem immemorial to those, perhaps not themselves very literate, who had first heard of it in their now distant youth. Material which was suggestive of independent folklore was harder to come by. 'Miss Shapcott has told us that her mother used the song "Joseph was a tin-merchant (or tin-man), and the miners loved him well" as a lullaby. She adds that

---

186 Lewis, H.A., 1934, pp.14-15.
187 The 1930s pamphlet is undated. It was re-issued in 1946, to which edition my page references refer.
188 For a modern study of Lammana Priory, see O. J. Padel, *Glastonbury's Cornish Connections*, in *The Archaeology and History of Glastonbury Abbey*, ed. Lesley Abrams and James P. Carley, Boydell, Woodbridge, pp. 253-6.

Fig 30. Bottalack Tin Mine, St. Just, Cornwall, as seen in the 1920s.

this was a time when the miners were in bad odour at Looe'.[189] Miss Shapcott's reminiscence is interesting. As we have seen, the version of the 'song' known to Σ in 1895, and associated by him with the Mendip miners, was the variant 'Joseph was a tinman'. This argues for the authenticity of Miss Shapcott's lullaby.

H. A. Lewis here makes his first references to a matter to which he later returned, a Breton legend:

> that S. Anne, the mother of the Blessed Virgin, was born in "Cornuaille" of royal stock, and later returned to end her life at La Palue, where she was visited by Our Lord. While "Cornuaille" is now a district of Brittany, it was so called after Cornwall, and the legend might refer to the land from which many of the Bretons emigrated in the days of the Saxon invasion. I leave to others to venture further in the attempt to identify "La Palue" with old Parlooe. It seems fantastic, but it is curious that, in common

189 Lewis, H.A., *Ab Antiquo*, 1946, p. 6.

parlance during the last century, "Parlooe" was undoubtedly used
of the old Lammana, in distinction from the rest of Portlooe.[190]

The bulk of this booklet, however, is devoted to tracing, in an
interesting and reasonably competent manner, the history of the
chapels of the Lammana Priory, which endured as free chapels until
the Reformation.

H. A. Lewis's next contribution to the story appeared in 1939,
when his *Christ in Cornwall? Legends of St. Just-in-Roseland and
Other Parts* was published by J. H. Lake & Co. of Falmouth.[191] He
was by now Vicar of Penwerris. He seems to have been spurred in
part by Thompson's attack on Dobson, for his booklet begins 'Miss
Hamilton Thompson[192] has lately published a booklet, in which she
sets out to disprove most of the holy legends of Glastonbury and
Cornwall, and in particular that of the visit of Our Lord to this land.
... The title alone shows the prejudiced attitude of the writer ...' As
his conviction of the truth of the 'Holy Legend', as he now first calls
it, has grown, so his critical faculties seem to have suffered, and this
work is noticeably less balanced than his previous ones. He has, by
now, been much influenced by Smithett Lewis, and by Dobson, whose
booklet first appeared in 1936.

H. A. Lewis, as we have already seen, was not content with arm-
chair scholarship, but went out to try his hand at collecting the raw
data of folklore in the field. His findings are the basis of the printed
tradition of the legend in Cornwall, continuing in various local and
church guides, for, as in Somerset, it is still kept alive. A current guide
to *St. Just in Roseland Church*, for example, contains a section on

190 Lewis, H.A., *Ab Antiquo*, 1946, pp. 7-8.
191 In its second edition of 1946, and third edition of 1948, it had a supplement
on Glastonbury and was entitled *Christ in Cornwall? and Glastonbury, the Holy
Land of Britain*.
192 Replaced in the 1946 ed. by 'A talented authoress...'

Christ in Roseland, which tells us that

> There is a legend which claims that Christ came to St Just. The
> story goes that Joseph of Arimathea was a tin merchant and that
> when he came on business to the Fal, he brought the boy Jesus with
> him. During his visit, Jesus came into St Just Pool and landed at St
> Just, which, it is said, was a sacred place even then and that Jesus
> talked to the religious leaders there. It is a persistent legend and one
> which crops up in several places along the Cornish coast. All that
> can be said is that it could have happened and that it warms the
> heart to have such a story associated with this lovely place.[193]

Henry Lewis himself tells us, in *Christ in Cornwall?* in 1939,
that he offers:

> ...the various versions of the legend, mostly in the very words
> in which they were given me by my informants, the majority of
> whom are simple folk with no pretension to much "book learning."
> It will be seen at once that it is almost exclusively associated in
> Cornwall with the tin trade, in the mining districts and the adjacent
> ports from which British tin was exported before and during the
> first century A.D. It is *not* usually found in parts where monastic
> influence was most pronounced. Even at Glastonbury the legend
> perpetuated and embellished by the monks of the middle ages
> was about Joseph of Arimathea, rather than about Our Lord, as
> the holy visitor.
>   You have to go to Priddy by the old lead mines of the
> Mendips, or to Pilton, the reputed port from which much of the
> lead was shipped, to hear local traditions of the visit of Christ or
> the Christ Child. In Cornwall it is found at such widely separated
> places as Marazion and Ding Dong in Penwith, St. Day and
> Falmouth in Carnmarth, St. Justin-Roseland, and Lammana

193 *St. Just-in-Roseland Church - the Parish Church of St. Just and St. Mawes*,
anon, n.d., p. 9.

(Looe Island) in Wivelshire. These are all either tin districts or adjacent havens. Only Lammana can claim definite association with any of the big monastic houses* [footnote: *Lammana was a tiny priory of Glastonbury before the Conquest. For its history see my "Ab Antiquo."]: and, what is to me most striking, St Michael's Mount, while expressly mentioned in the tinners' version of the legend, did not itself perpetuate it through the monastery, whose claim to pilgrimage was based on three supposed apparitions of the Archangel.[194]

Lewis cautioned of the difficulties which beset the collector of folklore:

Before I proceed to show that the legend did actually exist in Cornwall, and still survives in parts, I throw out a word of warning to casual searchers. It is no use tackling all and sundry with a bald question "Did you ever hear . . . ?" The probability is that you would get a negative answer in almost every case. The Cornish folk are not fond of talking about their old legends and traditions to us "foreigners." They are very sensitive to ridicule, and ridicule has, alas, nearly killed the Holy Legend. Once suggest that a tradition is "rubbish," and no oyster can ever be closer than the Cornish man or woman. ... For the same reason, the younger generation has not often heard of it, because the parents have feared that their sophisticated children would laugh at them.[195]

This was, and is, undoubtedly true, and has validity well beyond Cornwall; but his own methods of enquiry into the 'Holy Legend' could be heavy-handed to a degree that hardly inspires confidence in his findings. In the passage quoted above, Lewis referred to a man

194 Lewis, H.A., 1939, pp. 2-3.
195 Lewis, H.A., 1939, pp. 5-6.

who initially denied knowledge of the story.[196] He had more to say of him in the second edition of *Christ in Cornwall?* of 1946:

An old man who had lived all his life at Port Looe (the old Lammana), used to deny stoutly that he had ever heard of the tradition. I persisted, because this was the very land mentioned as the scene of the landing. At last I was able to confront him with evidence that his late wife had often spoken of it. A final question elicited the following, "Oh yes, I've 'eared 'er talk of it."[197]

One wonders how many of his informants were as steadfast in resisting the hectoring leading questions of the educated Vicar of their parish, and, with the deference then expected, found it easier to confirm what he wished to hear. But not all of his folklore recording can be so lightly dismissed. In that same, second, edition he went on to cite the case of another elderly couple:

Another old man who was born on Looe Island was as close as can be. He would say he never talked of anything he did not believe, or believe anything he did not see, etc., but he talked vaguely of "all kinds of stories." He remembered an old inscription on stone, now alas, lost. His wife, now nearly a centenarian, who came from Porthallow, spoke mysteriously of a piece of cloth which, they said, "was part of the cloth in which Our Saviour's body was buried," and of other "relics" of the sepulchre. These might have been "relics" from the old Chapel of Lammana, and, whether genuine or not, would then reflect an old Arimathean tradition, in line with that of Glastonbury, the parent Community.[198]

196 'I have even known a man, as I recorded in "The Child Christ at Lammana," who stoutly denied that he had ever heard anything about it, until confronted with positive evidence that his late wife often used to speak of it.' (p.6) There appears, in fact, to be no reference to this anecdote in the pamphlet version of the paper.
197 Lewis, H.A., *Christ in Cornwall*, 1946, p. 8.
198 Lewis, H.A., *Christ in Cornwall*, 1946, p. 8.

Although he omitted mention of her in his first, 1939, edition of *Christ in Cornwall?*, H. A. Lewis had already referred to this old lady in *Ab Antiquo*, of *c.*1936:

Now I am told a startling story by Mrs. Vague of Watergate, aged 85, who spent her young days at Port Looe and Portallow, of a piece of old cloth, treasured by a family at the latter place, which they said was part of the "cloth in which Our Saviour's body was buried." Might this not have been one of the holy "relics" of the old Chapel [of Lammana], which were no doubt dispersed when the King had taken all the articles of realisable value, and the Chapel was closed? Students of Arthurian legends will surely remember Dindrane, sister of Perceval, craving, "sith I am of his (Joseph's) lineage," a portion of the "sovran cloth" from the Holy Sepulchre,* and the final scene of the "disparting of the hallows" at the Chapel of the Grail.** The "sovran cloth" was surely a faint memory of some far legend of Joseph of Arimathea. The same family also speak, with tantalising lack of detail, of "other remains of the sepulchre" and other "strange stories," of which so far they will not speak.[199]

[notes, p. 8] *High History of the Holy Grail XV. 18. **High History of the Holy Grail XXXV. 26

There was, indeed, a very obscure Glastonbury tradition concerning the shroud of Christ. It was mentioned as among the relics brought by Joseph to Britain by a Somerset writer, Thomas Escott, in 1908, referring back to the time of his own childhood in the mid-nineteenth century, when actual pieces of it were alleged to survive at Glastonbury.[200] The tradition seems traceable perhaps as far back as the earlier thirteenth century, when, as H. A. Lewis noted, a shroud of Christ is mentioned in the Old French text *Perlesvaus*, also known

199 Lewis, H.A., 1946, *Ab Antiquo*, p. 7.
200 Escott, 1908, p. 12. See Ashdown, 2003, and refs.

as *The High History of the Holy Graal*.[201] Here it is kept in a chapel in the Graveyard Perilous, probably a fictionalisation of Glastonbury. This identification was suggested by Taylor in an appendix to *The Coming of the Saints*, where he quotes part of the passage.[202] Escott may well have read Taylor, published in 1906, but he came from an old Somerset family, and there seems no reason to believe he based his story on Taylor, or to doubt the genuineness of his childhood recollections. H. A. Lewis had, of course, also read Taylor, who was probably responsible for drawing his attention to the *Perlesvaus*, but neither he nor Smithett Lewis show any indication of ever having heard of Escott's account of fragments of a shroud surviving into modern times at Glastonbury, and his old lady is perhaps unlikely to have read of them independently. It is possible, then, as he believed, that he had indeed found evidence of Arimathean tradition, derived from Glastonbury, surviving at Talland from the thirteenth century, when the Glastonbury connection was lost. Perhaps significantly, however, this tradition was related to Joseph alone, and not to the voyage story. The fate of the relics of the sepulchre, by definition, post-dated the Incarnation.

Other accounts recorded by H. A. Lewis echo the mid-nineteenth century traditions we have already noted, recorded by Hunt, concerning St Paul at Creeg Brawse and Gwennap:

A well-known Falmothian, who was brought up near Chacewater, says he often heard the old people, when he was a boy, say that "Joseph of Arimathea and the Child Christ worked (sic) at Creeg Brawse." This is a very ancient tin mine between Chacewater and St. Day. I wonder if it is only chance that an adjoining hamlet is named "Salem."

Another exceptionally well-informed person tells me that at St. Day the miners always used to say that Christ came to the mines. I always suspect that this was also the original tradition

201 Trans. Evans, S., 1898, Temple Classics.
202 Taylor, 1906, Appendix M, p.317.

about Gwennap Pit, but if so it has been obliterated by the recent connection with John Wesley. It may well have been the reason that drew Wesley to use it as his open-air chapel.[203]

Whatever combination of oral tradition and book-learning lay behind these suggestions, we can be fairly confident that they had some genuine existence independent of Lewis. The detail of Joseph and the Child Christ *working* in the mine has an air of genuine folklore, perhaps, as already suggested, replacing the names of Saints Piran and Chiwidden, although it is impossible to assign a date to this development, which could well have been as late as the 1890s.

Lewis returned in his 1939 booklet to the theme of the Breton legend of St Anne to which he had referred in *Ab Antiquo*. Here he revealed his source as *Sainte Anne de la Palude*, in Anatole le Braz, *Au Pays des Pardons* (1894), who, as he writes,[204] recorded a 'beautiful Breton legend, in equally beautiful language'. Visiting St Anne's church, he remarks to the old sacristan how she resembles the saint in her statue, to be told that 'like me, thank God, she is a Breton'. Le Braz (1859-1926) was a prolific writer on Breton folklore. His book had been translated into English in 1906 by Frances M. Gostling, '*Officier d'Academie*', who had found it on a railway bookstall and fallen in love with it, as *The Land of Pardons*, but Lewis added his own translation of an extract as an appendix at the end of *Christ in Cornwall?*.[205] He made a lot less of this Breton parallel than he might have done, remarking merely that 'If Christ could come as far as Brittany, he could quite well have come on here.' He was correct in thinking that stories, particularly saints legends, might be interchangeable in their location on either side of the Channel. The community of culture between the sea-farers of

203 Lewis, H.A., 1939, p. 8.

204 Lewis, H.A. 1939, p. 9-10.

205 Lewis, H.A. 1939, p. 24-28. Smithett Lewis gives a version of the same story in the 6th ed. of Joseph, 1937, pp. 38-41. He writes that he owed it to Sir Courtenay Bennett, and that it is also found in Hachette's *Guide Bleu, Bretagne*.

Cornwall and Brittany, whose languages were more or less mutually intelligible, endured well beyond the Middle Ages. It faded only with the rapid decline of Cornish in the eighteenth century, its death-knell being sounded by the Revolutionary and Napoleonic wars and the concurrent rise of Nonconformity in Cornwall, which, as in Wales, was highly corrosive to all folk-culture.

The story as retold by Lewis may be summarised as follows. Anne is a Queen at Moellien, in which castle her room may still be seen. Her husband, 'a very hard man', was 'jealous of his wife, and did not want her to bear children. When he discovered that she was with child, he flew into a violent passion, and drove her out like a beggar, in the middle of the night, in the depth of winter, half naked, into the icy storm.' One may suspect some euphemism here; the contrast with Joseph of Nazareth's treatment of the pregnant Mary is clear.[206] Anne wanders pitifully to the bay of Trefentec, where an angel in white awaits her in a barque of light, and the wind, in which is the will of God, bears them to Judea. 'Some days later Anne gave birth to a daughter, destined by God to be the Virgin'. As she grew old, Anne prayed that she might see her home again, at la Palude in Plounevez Porzay. The angel with the barque returns, now dressed in black to signify her widowhood, for her husband is dead. On her homecoming, she lives a life of sainthood, penitence and prayer. 'The light of her eyes radiated far over the waters like a moonbeam. On stormy nights, she was the saviour of the fishers … Jesus, her grandson, undertook for her sake the voyage to Basse-Bretagne. Before he was to climb Calvary, he went to ask her blessing, accompanied by the disciples Peter and John. Their parting was a bitter one. Anne wept tears of blood, and Jesus tried in vain to console her. At last he said to her, 'Think, grand-mere, of your Bretons. Speak, and in thy name I will grant them whatever they ask.'''

In the original account of La Braz, although H. A. Lewis does

206 A parallel might also be found in the Breton legend of St Budoc's mother, unjustly accused of infidelity by her royal husband and cast adrift in a barrel. See Doble, 1937, p. 2.

not note it, Anne asks that a church be built for her on the spot, from which 'So far as its spire can be seen, and so far as its bell can be heard, may all sick bodies, all suffering souls, alive or dead, find peace!'. Jesus, to confirm His promise, 'stuck his walking-staff into the sand, and immediately, from the dry side of the sand-dune, a fountain sprang forth. It has been flowing ever since, inexhaustible.'[207]

Whatever its date, the atmosphere of this moving story is wholly Celtic.[208] One is reminded of Patrick on the mountain of Cruachan Aigli, fasting against God for the salvation of the Irish, and in whose early legends the staff of Jesus also figures, and of Brigit, carried by the angels across the sea, through space and time, to nurse the Christ Child, to whose legend Jenner referred. Something of that same atmosphere may be sensed, perhaps, in certain of the material which Lewis collected. At Falmouth there was:

a marvellous old saint, who has just found rest from long and painful cancer, [who] said once in the dreamy voice with which she brought out all her bright "gems": "Folks say that Jesus passed by here, and blessed these parts. I think it was because it is the end of the world." The latter sentence, of course, referred to Land's End.[209]

Also at Falmouth was 'A dear old lady, but very illiterate, who recently died at the age of over 80, [who] came out with this, when I was talking about the song "Joseph was a tin-man", "Of course, we know Our Saviour preached to the miners. He was very fond of the miners."'[210]

'Folks say that Jesus passed by here and blessed these parts' was

207 La Braz, trans. Gostling, p. 197.
208 A Welsh royal and saintly pedigree in MS Harleian 3859, of the eleventh century, is traced to one Anna, *consobrina*, 'cousin', of the Virgin Mary, cf. Elizabeth, mother of the Baptist.
209 Lewis, H.A., 1939, pp.7-8.
210 Lewis, H.A., 1939, p. 7.

quoted on the cover of *Christ in Cornwall?*, above 'Price 4d.'

'Several informants from Redruth have said they had heard
something about the legend, and one in particular knew the song
"Joseph was a tin-man" very well.'[211] Several of his informants were
thus said to have known the song *Joseph was a tin-man*, possibly
also known in Somerset, well; unfortunately, none so well as to
actually remember the words of it. One elderly lady, whom he met
in Plymouth, and had heard the 'legend' as a child at Minions,
thought 'that it went on about his coming from the sea in a boat.'[212]
One may suspect some leading in these cases, as Lewis was anxious
to complete a 'song' which may, in fact, have been no more than a
two line skipping refrain, as Smith suggests.

> I have already referred several times to the old song beginning
> "Joseph was a tin man." It is known to many, but, unfortunately,
> I have so far failed to find anyone who can remember the rest.
> One informant said it went on "And the miners loved him well."
> Beyond that it still remains a blank, apart from one woman who
> was sure it was about "his coming in a ship."[213]

An investigation of the localisations of the story in Cornwall,
as recorded from the 1890s onwards, is beyond the scope of this
study, the focus of which is on Somerset. A detailed enquiry would
need to be made, individually, in each of those places which Lewis
mentions, through the archives of the local press, old church
guides, *etc.* As a folklorist, Henry Lewis's enthusiasm was his
own undoing. He would have served his 'Holy Legend' better
had he been able to cultivate a greater detachment, and devoted
more care to recording in detail what his old people actually had
to tell him, rather than trying to force their reminiscences into
quixotic attempts to prove that the story might be 'true'. Sadly,

211 Lewis, H.A., 1939, p. 8.
212 Lewis, H.A., 1939, p. 9.
213 Lewis, H.A., 1939, p. 11.

any real chance of discovering what elements of genuine antiquity it contained died with that generation which he buried. From the scraps which he has given us, it seems possible that in Cornwall there were two strands of tradition. The first concerned 'timeless' or non-'historical' visits of Jesus either as Child or Man to bless the poor at the extremity of His world, similar in character to the Hebridean and Breton parallels.

The second concerned Joseph the tin-man, whoever he may, originally, have been. The bare existence, at least, of this strand seems to have been confirmed by Σ in 1895, who also knew of it, apparently in Somerset, independently of the old people to whom Henry Lewis talked in the 1930s. Both strands might be 'old' - at least in the sense of being pre-Victorian. What neither Henry Lewis nor anyone else has demonstrated is that *in Cornwall* these themes were ever combined before the printed versions of the 'London foreman's tale' became available, at first or second hand, after 1895. In a literate or semi-literate society, the relationship between oral and written tradition is always complex, but folk-belief is dynamic and ongoing. One may cite the case of the Loch Ness Monster in the 1930s, in which press reports and well-publicised spoofs cross-fertilised with all-but-extinct Highland lore about water-creatures to produce the modern tradition. Something similar may have happened in Cornwall in the late 1890s. Lewis paints a charmingly rustic picture derived from a man he met in Falmouth,

> who, as a boy, used to be much at St Just, and who later used to visit the farmers in their homes, when acting as a local preacher. He tells me that the older folk often talked about it, and in particular recounts how as a boy he used to sit with the farmers on the beach below the Church, waiting for the tide to bring barges of manure. He tells how, "as often as not," the conversation would come round to the Holy Legend, and he says that "it was as much as your life was

worth" to express any doubt about Christ coming to St. Just.[214]

Lewis adds, significantly, 'The period of which he is speaking cannot be more than forty years ago', *i.e.*, *c*.1899. He meant by this to demonstrate the survival of an old tradition. He may actually have recorded for us the beginnings of a new one among them that awaited the arrival of the manure boats with the tide.

Lewis devotes much space to arguments from Jenner and elsewhere to support the possible truth of the 'legend', and was not above argument from silence. 'It has often been objected that such an adventure would have shown itself in his [Jesus's] parables and discourses. If there is little or no reference to travel abroad, there is equally little to carpentry and Nazareth'. He added ruefully, 'those of us who have lived abroad know that most people are not much interested in hearing about our lives there.'[215]

At some point before 1937, H. A. Lewis visited Glastonbury, discussed the stories with Smithett Lewis, and appears also to have sought popular accounts in Somerset:

> In Somerset I have traced the legend definitely at Priddy, in other parts of the Mendips, and at Pilton, [adding, in the 2nd ed., 'where our Lord and Joseph are said to have landed in the old Harbour.'] At Glastonbury, as I said, it is chiefly concerned with Joseph in popular memory.[216]

He returned to the theme in his supplement on Glastonbury:

> Fireside stories of the Holy visit still linger at Glastonbury, and far more so at Priddy in the Mendips. Why the tradition was not

214 Lewis, H.A., 1939, pp. 6-7.
215 Lewis, H.A., 1939, p. 4.
216 In the 2nd ed. this becomes 'we saw that it was chiefly concerned with Joseph in popular memory, but various Appendices show that the holier version undoubtedly existed once.' p. 8.

more emphasised at Glastonbury has always puzzled me. That it existed is beyond doubt, but the monks of the Middle Ages appear to have elaborated the cult of Our Lady and St. Joseph, almost to the exclusion of the holier tradition of Our Lord. Perhaps even then there were doubters, as today, who would say "Oh! That is going a bit too far." But what of that stone in the South wall of the Lady Chapel, with the two mysterious and isolated names 'IESUS-MARIA'? No explanation.[217]

In 1939, H. A. Lewis incorporated the theorising of Dobson (see below) that Jesus had made more than one visit to Britain into his presentation of the story:

When I wrote "The Child Christ at Lammana," I was going on one aspect of the legend only, that which I traced at Looe, and that which is enshrined in the tinners' tradition, viz., that our Lord came as a Child with Joseph of Arimathea. It will be noticed, however, that in other versions, notably those at Priddy and St Just, I find no suggestion at all that they are about a child. I am indebted to the Rev. C. C. Dobson ("Did Our Lord Visit Britain?") for the suggestion which I am now inclined to accept, that Christ *first* visited our shores as a Child and that later he sojourned here for a longer or shorter time as a Man.[218]

Henry Lewis thought that 'whatever we may think of the suitability or otherwise of Avalon, it could not have been more unsuitable for quiet preparation than Galilee, whose chief claim to fame [*amended in 1946 to* claim to notoriety] at that time appears to have been that it was the breeding-ground of sedition and lawlessness.' Jesus's 'chief friends and acquaintances' in Somerset

217 Lewis, H.A., 1946, p.18.
218 Lewis, H.A., 1939, pp. 14-15. By the 2nd ed. of 1946, (p. 12) his expression of support for Dobson's theory has hardened to 'the suggestion which I now accept.'

would doubtless have been in the Lake Villages, which did not long survive the Roman occupation:

> Small wonder then that such a faint memory should survive of that holy visit. But it did survive more by the mines of Priddy, which continued to be worked without a break for long after the Romans came to Bath. It probably survived also in the deep veneration felt for that building [Glastonbury's wattle Old Church] which men *may* have believed to have been constructed by the very hands of the Carpenter of Nazareth.[219]

H. A. Lewis was himself responsible for a remarkable sequel to the Jesus voyage story. Although his theory had already been discussed by Smithett Lewis in 1937 (see above), he at first introduced it cautiously in the 1939 edition of *Christ in Cornwall?*:

> It will be noted that the tinners' tradition, as given through Mr. Jenner, includes the Blessed Virgin Mary. Even this is not so impossible as appears at first sight, at least if we feel that there is any basis at all for the Breton tradition given above. I have also heard a story from a Falmouth lady, whose childhood was largely spent in Alexandria and France, that she was told sometime that "Our Lady came to England and died here." Before I ever heard this from her, I had myself traced what I took to be signs of some sort of legend in connection with Glastonbury, suggesting the life and passing of the Blessed Virgin there.[220]

In *Glastonbury, the Holy Land of Britain*, the supplement to his second edition of 1946, the story is told in full and doubt is cast aside: 'hardly less wonderful' than Christ's two visits there, Glastonbury became 'another hidden retreat, the final home and grave of his

219 Lewis, H.A., 1939, p. 16.
220 Lewis, H.A., 1939, p. 11. He adds in a footnote (p.28) 'See Rev. L.S. Lewis' "St Joseph of Arimathea at Glastonbury" - 6th Ed'n - pps. 41-46.

blessed Mother.'[221]

The other amazing conclusion I have reached is that Our Lady lived and died at Glastonbury. ... The basis of my "amazing" surmise lies again in striking phrases in old documents more than in folk memories and oral tradition. We shall see that such oral traditions did exist in 1502, and I have traced a dim echo of it in living memory. After I had just returned from Glastonbury, a lady said to me "Did you ever hear that Our Lady came to England and died here?" I was amazed. I had just returned from the spot outside the walls of the Lady Chapel at Glastonbury, where the surmise had first caught and stunned me, but I had said no word of it to her. I then asked where she had heard it, and she said she had been at school in Alexandria with Nuns who were all connected with the old aristocracy of France, and "it might have been they" who told her. A Roman Catholic friend of mine has just pointed out how remarkable it would be for Nuns of the French aristocracy to attribute such a story to England rather than to France, if it were pure invention.[222]

Outside the Lady Chapel at Glastonbury I had been pondering over two passages which I had often read, but perhaps had never sufficiently studied. One day as I sat looking at the "IESUS-MARIA" stone it all came back, and staggered me by the implication. First there was the passage from the old bard Melchinus, where he speaks of the early disciples building the Wattle Church *over* ("super") *the powerful, adorable virgin.* The present vicar of Glastonbury [L. S. Lewis] said afterwards that he believed I was the first person who had dared to translate the simple Latin word literally. Why not? It is at least a simpler translation than Dean Armitage Robinson's

221 Lewis, H.A., 1946, p. 16.
222 George Jowett (see below p.), who had corresponded with Smithett Lewis shortly before the latters' death, identified the 'old English lady', educated at a French convent in Alexandria, as a Mrs. Cottrell, of Penwerris, Cornwall; Jowett, 1961, p. 141.

"for the adoring of a powerful virgin"[223] What Melchinus said, rightly or wrongly, was that the Ealde Chirche was built over the grave of the Blessed Virgin.[224]

His second passage was from the verse *Lyfe of Joseph of Armathia*, a Glastonbury text of 1502, to the words of which he gave an over-literal interpretation. Here, after dealing with Joseph's experiences following the Crucifixion, a new section is introduced with the words *Now here* [hear] *how Ioseph came into englande* ... It then *back-tracks*, as Lewis seems not to notice, to tells how Joseph spent 15 years with Our Lady, until *after hyr assumpcyon*, when he sails with St Philip to France on his way to Britain.[225] While the Melkin prophecy is undoubtedly puzzling in many ways, no sensible person could possibly draw the inference from the *Lyfe* which H. A. Lewis does. The Falmouth lady who had been educated by French nuns, and whose memory of the matter was clearly vague, presumably had some version of the voyage of the Three Marys to Provence in mind and, perhaps having once read Taylor, had confused these with the Virgin.

According to Henry Lewis's 'reconstruction', Mary lived with the Apostle John 'for a comparatively short while. He then transferred his trust to Joseph, who, after seeing the Bethany family safe in the Rhone valley, brought the Blessed Virgin to Avalon. This was to be *her* secret refuge, beside the little building which her Blessed Son had built and

---

223 Robinson, 1926, p. 30: 'Fashioned of wattles / For the adoring of a mighty Virgin ...' Here he attempts a poetic 'free rendering of the untranslatable words of Melkin's prophecy' (p. 60, where he gives the original Latin text). The prophecy is embedded in John of Glastonbury's Chronicle of 1342, and perhaps refers to some image associated with St Mary's Well in its thirteenth century undercroft below the south-west corner of the Lady Chapel.

224 Lewis, H.A., 1946, pp. 19-20.

225 Skeat. p. 40.

already bequeathed to her. Here she died, probably about 48 A.D.'[226]

In 1948 he added in a footnote to 'Why the tradition was not *more* emphasised at Glastonbury has always puzzled me':

> A lady who tells me that her ancestors lived in Somerset, and some time near Glastonbury, but who would rather remain anonymous, says in a letter to me:- "my family (on both sides) have lived in Somerset for many generations, and have always believed that when Joseph of Arimathea came to trade in tin, he brought the boy Jesus with him to "the Summerland" to continue his education on the Isle of Avalon, and that after the Crucifixion Joseph of Arimathea, Mary, and other disciples lived, and died, there." She says also that she was brought up by her grandmother, who "never questioned" these legends. As my correspondent can hardly be less than middle-aged, and as she says that her grandmother had been told the Story by *her* grandmother, we have here no mean link in the long chain of oral tradition round Glastonbury.[227]

This is interesting, in view of Σ's 1895 comments about Paradise, and the still more obscure 'Summerland' strand of tradition, but it is too vague and too late to offer any independent evidential value.

Lewis added the carol *I saw three ships* to his list of possible evidences. 'In the oldest form I can trace, the three ships bring, among others, "Joseph and his fair layde." Of course, this might mean Joseph of Nazareth, but in view of the fact that the rhyme is about ships, I think it is quite probable that it first referred to the legend, and that "his fair layde" was originally "our fair Ladye."[228]

Some may take all this as evidence that the Rev. Henry Lewis had finally lost touch with reality. There are, however, certain waves

226 Lewis, H.A., 1946, p. 21. Joseph's guardianship of Mary is found in a late (perhaps 13th century) Latin apocryphon on the Assumption of the Virgin summarised by M. R. James, 1924, pp. 216-8.
227 Lewis, 1948, p. 19, corresponding to p. 18 of the 2nd ed.
228 Lewis, H.A., 1939, p. 19.

of human thought and spirituality which seem to occur almost at a subconscious level. His inspiration that Glastonbury was the last earthly home and resting-place of the Virgin anticipated, in a way, the post-war shift in Roman Catholic devotion from the cult of the martyrs of 1539 to the renewal of the Shrine of Our Lady of Glastonbury, where a new wooden image of her was blessed by the Apostolic Delegate in 1955, and the restoration of that veneration for the Mother of God which had been in abeyance at Glastonbury since the fifteenth century. This in turn has been to some extent overtaken during the last twenty years by a neo-pagan emphasis which would doubtless have shocked Lewis (associated with the writings of Kathy Jones among others) on Avalon as a pre-eminent shrine of the Great Goddess of many names, whose banners, that of Mary among them, now thread the September streets.

Fig 31. Our Lady of Glastonbury (painted wood, 1955).
The design is taken from a
14th-century Abbey seal.
From a devotional card.

13

THE THEORIST: CYRIL COMYN DOBSON

The last of the chief creative exponents of the voyage story to enter the fray was Cyril Comyn Dobson. Born in 1879, he graduated from Selwyn College, Cambridge, in 1901 and worked in Bristol as Curate in Charge at Clifton, 1903-06, and Shirehampton with Avonmouth, 1906-09. He left Bristol to become Priest in Charge at St Stephen's, Cardiff, 1910-15, and Vicar of St Peter's, Paddington, 1915-24. He was Vicar at St Mary-in-the-Castle, Hastings, from 1924.

He began to write pamphlets on devotional and esoteric subjects, including *The Bible and Spiritualism*, 1920; *The Story of the Empty Tomb as if told by Joseph of Arimathea*, 1920; *The Mystery of the Great Pyramid*, 1926; *The Risen Lord and His Disciples*, 1929; *Torchbearers of Truth Amid Alpine Snows*, 1929; *The Face of Christ: Earliest Likenesses from the Catacombs*, 1933; *The Founding of the Church of Rome*, 1935; *Britain's Place in History*, 1936; and *The Mystery of the Fate of the Ark of the Covenant*, 1939. The Ark had, apparently, ended up at Tara in Ireland. Despite the range of his enthusiasms, Dobson is perhaps the least interesting and attractive of the eccentric clerical trio who wrote on the voyage story. Lacking the antiquarian pretensions of Smithett Lewis, and the ambitions of H. A. Lewis as a collector of folklore 'in the field', he is the most heavily dependent on Morgan's druidical fantasies. He also lacks those touches of unintentional humour which enliven a reading of H. A. Lewis. His main contributions to the Glastonbury *mythos* were threefold. He popularised the notion that places named 'Paradise' marked stages of the Lord's journey, a suggestion which as we have seen was not in origin his own. He suggested that Jesus had stayed for a time not at the abbey site but by Chalice Well. This may have been his own inference from an idea, traceable from the late 1880s, that early hermit-missionaries had dwelt there. His third contribution, a suggestion which does appear to have been his own, was that Christ made not merely one, but two, visits to Britain, the first as a boy with Joseph, and a second, alone, to prepare for His historical ministry.

H. A. Lewis subsequently acknowledged his debt to Dobson 'for the suggestion that Our Lord came to Britain *twice* at least'. The bulk of Dobson's work is given over to attempts, which owe little to logic, to support the veracity of the voyage story from Morgan and other dubious sources, and from the silences of the biblical record. The absence from Scripture of any denial that Christ ever took a West Country holiday in Britain is seen as tacit support for the proposition:

> Negatively, too, probably most will admit that no adequate reason exists why it may not be true. The mere possibility of its truth has in the writer's view been ample warrant for its investigation, and that investigation reveals stronger basis than he, at any rate, believed existed. It is perhaps best that its truth should not be definitely established, lest the place [Glastonbury?] should become the scene of superstitious veneration.
>
> But the very suggestion may at least prove an inspiration to all who love the Lord, and love our Land.[229]

Or, as H. A. Lewis put it, 'what more likely than that he should choose this spot?'[230]

Dobson's *Did Our Lord Visit Britain as they say in Cornwall and Somerset?*, an attractively produced booklet with 36 pages and six photographic plates, first appeared in April 1936, and required a second edition (revised) that same September. It was printed and

229 Dobson, April 1936, p. 36.
230 Lewis, H.A., 1946, p. 17.

published by The Avalon Press, "Central Somerset Gazette" Office, 27, High Street, Glastonbury.[231]

An article based on it, though with some differences of tone, appeared in the *Central Somerset Gazette* in June 1936.[232] entitled 'A Tradition Dear to Somerset and Cornish Hearts'. This began (with even more emphasis than in the April booklet) 'It must have been very pleasing to Somerset and Cornish hearts that, at our late King's special command, Blake's "Jerusalem" was sung at the great Jubilee Concert at the Albert Hall last year, for it enshrines the tradition so dear to them that Our Lord was brought when a boy to Cornwall and Somerset by Joseph of Arimathea.' Thus the unwary reader might draw the unwarranted inference of royal endorsement of the story.

In the first edition of his booklet in April 1936, Dobson introduced the 'tradition' as follows:

'The bare tradition is that given in Baring Gould's "Book of Cornwall," [*sic*] where he writes: "Another Cornish story is to the effect that Joseph of Arimathea came in a boat to Cornwall and brought the boy Jesus with him, and the latter taught him how to extract the tin and purge it from its wolfram. When the tin is flashed then the tinner shouts: 'Joseph was in the trade!'"

A tradition also lingers in Somerset of the coming of Christ and Joseph in a ship of Tarshish, of how they came to Summerland and "sojourned at the place called Paradise."

There is a third tradition of Our Lord coming as a boy with Joseph at Priddy in Mendip, where lead was mined since the times of the Phoenicians'.[233]

---

231 Dobson, C.C., *Did Our Lord Visit Britain as they say in Cornwall and Somerset?* First pub. April 1936; 2nd ed., rev., September 1936; 3rd ed. rev., January 1938; 4th ed., rev., 1940; 5th ed., rev; 1947; 6th ed. slightly rev., 1949; 7th ed., rev. 1954, many eds. with numerous reprints. The last ed. was under the imprint of Covenant Publishing Co. Ltd., 6, Buckingham Gate, London SW.1.
232 *CSG* June 12th 1936.
233 Dobson, April 1936, pp. 10-11.

This whole passage is plagiarised, carelessly and without acknowledgement, from Albert Webb (see above)[234]. Dobson does cite Taylor and Smithett Lewis, but he knows no more of the Cornish versions, being as yet unfamiliar with the work of H. A. Lewis. It is clear that when Dobson began to concern himself with the propagation of the 'tradition' he had no independent sources of information. In this first, April 1936, airing of his views, Dobson's grasp even of Somerset geography was still a trifle unsteady, as he apparently believed that Glastonbury stood on the river Parrett, and that this ran 'along the foot of the Mendips':

> The tradition exists in Cornwall, in Somerset, and locally at Priddy in the heart of the Mendip Hills close to Glastonbury, the centre of the ancient lead-mining industry. There was a close connection between the mining of lead and other metals in the Mendips and in the tin-mining of Cornwall. ... Metals from the Mendips were brought also to the same port of export, Mount St. Michael, and it is not difficult to trace the route. On the Somerset coast lies Burnham at the mouth of the river Parrett, which runs inland to Glastonbury, running along the foot of the Mendips. Round about Glastonbury it expanded into wide and extensive marshes constituting Glastonbury an Island. The two ancient villages of mud and wattle houses which have been excavated from the ancient bog land stood on higher ground which formed islands in the marshes. Ships came right inland from the mouth of the river at Burnham to Glastonbury. Here the metal was shipped in coastal boats, and carried round to Mount St. Michael, ... Joseph of Arimathea would reach [it] on one of his trading voyages bringing the Holy Boy with him, and we have the tradition in Cornwall to this effect. Joseph would next continue his journey to the Mendips in connection with this branch of his business. He would either take a coasting ship to Glastonbury via Burnham accompanied

234 Webb, 1929, p. 20.

by Our Lord, and we have the Somersetshire tradition of His coming in a ship of Tarshish, or he would journey by land. Joseph's business visit would end at Priddy, the centre of the lead mining industry, and here again we find the tradition.[235]

In Dobson's analysis, however, not all the stories related to a childhood visit. 'Our Lord either remained in Britain or returned later as a young man, and stayed in quiet retirement at Glastonbury. Here he erected for himself a small house of mud and wattles. Later Joseph of Arimathea, fleeing from Palestine, settled in the same place and erected a mud and wattle Church there.'[236] He posed the question 'Did Our Lord come to Britain with Joseph, and did He remain in quiet at Glastonbury before his ministry?'[237] He noted the absence of information in the Gospels on 'Our Lords life between the ages of 12 and 30', and deduced that his first subsequent public appearances were as a stranger. He also noted the tradition referred to by Smithett Lewis in his fourth edition of *Joseph*, there attributed, following Morgan, to an 'Epistle to Pope Gregory' of St Augustine. This told that at Glastonbury the First Neophytes of the Catholic Law, 'God beforehand acquainting them, found a Church constructed by no human art, but by the Hands of Christ Himself, for the salvation of his people.' Smithett Lewis had added in a footnote that 'The Saxon Priest B', the actual author of the quotation, 'quotes it in his very early life of St. Dunstan about 1,000 AD'.[238] Dobson therefore suggested a second and later visit:

As a boy He was brought merely for a visit by Joseph of Arimathea on one of his voyages. Later as a young man He returned and settled at Glastonbury for the purpose of quiet study, prayer, and

235 Dobson, April 1936, pp. 25-26.
236 Dobson, April 1936, p. 11.
237 Dobson, April 1936, p. 18.
238 Lewis, L. S., *Joseph*, 4th ed., 1927, p. 29, following Morgan, 1861 p. 123. On this important quotation, see below.

meditation. Here He erected for Himself a small house of mud and wattles. … Subsequent to His passion Joseph of Arimathea sought the same place of retreat, already hallowed by the residence of Our Lord. The small house Our Lord had erected was consecrated by Joseph to serve as a private chapel, for himself and his eleven companions. He then erected the mud and wattles Church [*i.e.* at the Abbey site] for preaching to the people.

A stay at Glastonbury of this description by Our Lord would attract little attention The residents would only look upon Him as a quiet reserved man living somewhat as a hermit. No account of his visit would be written. He would depart as quietly as He came. In after days when Joseph of Arimathea settled in the same place, and told the wonderful story he had brought with him, Our Lord's stay in their midst would be recalled, and memories of that stay would cluster round the spot.[239]

After discussing possible routes (as already examined above) he returned to the theme:

With regard to the visit to Glastonbury, the port of export [of Mendip lead], we have the strange hints about a Church built by Our Lord Himself, and the present author ventures to suggest that this refers to a second later visit. Having been taken as a boy by Joseph on this voyage and visited Glastonbury, Our Lord noticed the beauty and quiet of this island. Seeking a quiet retreat in which to spend some years alone before his ministry He returned here as a young man, erected His own small hermitage of mud and wattles, of which houses were erected in the neighbourhood, and then in prayer and meditation prepared for His work and Passion. This house afterwards may have been used by Joseph and his eleven companions as a private chapel.

But can we find any reason other than the mere natural beauty

239 Dobson, April 1936, pp. 20-21; Sept. 1936, p. 20; 1954, p. 23.

of the locality ... to account for the selection of Glastonbury as Our Lord's place of retreat for study and meditation?

The reason may perhaps be found in Druidism, and Glastonbury appears not only to have been itself a centre for this cult, but also within reach of several of its chief centres...[240]

There follows a long discussion, derived largely from Morgan, on Druidism's supposed anticipation of Christianity. Dobson applied his powers of reconstruction to the second visit:

The Home at Glastonbury

We may well visualise the life in that quiet retreat. At the foot of Glastonbury Tor ... is a mystery well of water fed by an invisible spring of great copiousness and of the purest crystal water. Many traditions and legends linger around it. It is known as the Chalice well from a tradition that Joseph dropped the Holy Chalice into it. It was by tradition the spot round which Joseph and his eleven companions erected their houses.

Here, too, we may well think Our Lord erected His humble abode, the well of pure crystal water from which He drank supplied from its invisible source, a symbol of that well of living water which He came to give the world.

We shall not attempt to intrude into the privacy of the life in that quiet abode. As far as we know no one lived near. The mud and wattle village of Godney lay a mile to the North and that of Meare some 2 1/2 miles north-west.[241]

Some ten years later there came a band of refugees, Joseph and his eleven companions, to find a quiet retreat in the place which they knew had already been hallowed by the presence of

---

240 Dobson, April 1936, p. 26.
241 In the 1954 ed., for the last two sentences Dobson substitutes: 'Their [sic] nearest neighbours would be the dwellers in the mud and wattle village of Glastonbury which lay nearby.'

their Master. They erected their own dwellings around the well, as tradition tells us. The small dwelling of Our Lord became their church, in which they met for prayer.

But they came as missionaries, to spread the message of the Saviour Yesu, and proclaim to the Druids the fulfilment of their ancient expectations. This message was welcomed.[242]

Dobson's use of the 'tradition' that Joseph dwelt by the Chalice Well is interesting. It was presumably his own deduction that, if Joseph had dwelt there, then Jesus Himself must previously have done so. The phrase 'an invisible spring of great copiousness and of the purest crystal water' echoes the account of Wright of 1887, who wrote of 'a constant rush of clear, sparkling, wholesome water'.[243] Wright is seemingly the first to record the 'tradition' that the Grail was concealed by Joseph near the Well. He also wrote of 'the disciples, who first landed on the Island, having lived in caves or huts in a very original manner, they really being Anchorites'. This, Wright suggested, was the origin of the name 'The Anchor Inn' by which the Well property had been known, when a public house, at the beginning of the 19th century.[244] It is, perhaps, unlikely that Dobson read Wright's paper himself. The *Proceedings* of the Glastonbury Antiquarian Society in which it appeared ran to only two issues, and, as a publication, was already largely forgotten. It is more likely that he found the idea of early missionaries dwelling around the Well in one of the occasional brochures produced by Alice Buckton in the 1920s to promote her guest house and craft centre. Buckton (1867-1944), who became a friend of Smithett Lewis, ran Chalice Well from 1913 until the end of the 1920s as a centre for the esoterically inclined, staging plays there. Financial difficulties led her to lease the property to the proprietors of what then became Glaston Tor School in 1930, and the death of her long-term companion Annet Schepel in 1931

242 Dobson, April 1936, pp. 29-30; Sept. 1936, 30-31; 1954, pp. 37-38.
243 Wright, 1987, p. 24.
244 Wright, 1887, pp. 34-35.

marked the effective end of the Well as a creative community.[245]

Dobson's booklet attracted correspondence. As he himself recorded in the *CSG* on 12 June 1936: 'The issue of this work has brought further information to hand, and the Editor of this Paper has kindly invited the author to record this in the following brief article.' One of his correspondents had evidently corrected his geography and the 'further information' included the fact that in actuality the river which flows by Glastonbury is the Brue, not the Parrett. It was perhaps the same authority who suggested to him a possible location of 'Paradise' in that very Burnham to which he had, apparently inadvertently, referred as on Joseph's itinerary.

In his newspaper article he enumerated six 'separate and independent traditions'. The fourth was 'That he [Joseph] came with Our Lord in a "ship of Tarshish to the Summerland and sojourned in the place called Paradise."'

Returning to the theme further on he wrote:

'It remains to identify the tradition about "Summerland and the place called Paradise" Adjoining Burnham, and exactly where we should expect to find it, is an area still called Paradise. The Summerland is obviously Somerset.

We are now in a position to reconstruct the story of the visit. … [in Cornwall] They board one of the coastal boats and land at Burnham, where they stay awhile at the village called Paradise. They next make their way in one of the river boats up the Brue to Glastonbury. … From Glastonbury they make their way to the Mendip village of Priddy in the heart of the mining area, and later on returning by the same route to Palestine.

Dobson's newspaper article of 12 June eventually produced a response on the correspondence page of *CSG* on 7 August, 1936. It may stand as typical of the kind of bizarre pseudo-erudition which

---

245 On the life of Alice Buckton, see Benham, 1993, ch. 10 and *passim*.

henceforth was to be the hall-mark of the 'legend', and fill the post-bag of its exponents:

A Glastonbury Tradition

Sir, - One cannot but admire and strongly appreciate the erudition and ability displayed by the Rev. C. C. Dobson in his work "Did our Lord visit Britain?" and the splendid way in which he has collated and presented the evidence obtainable for the Priddy and other traditions. At the same time one must regret certain of his suggestions in his recent article in your Paper. He has by this sadly weakened his case by introducing a modern hamlet and Burnham into his allusions. This hamlet after two thousand years of silting up of its locality by seaborne and river born detritus and blown sand is only at the same level as the part of Glastonbury known by the same name, and which only three hundred and thirty years ago was swamped under twenty or thirty feet of sea water at high tide. The place we now know as Glastonbury was the ancient Celtic Paradise, the Erse Land of the Blessed, long before the Christian Era. It is even said that in ancient India the British Isles were spoken of as "the sacred islands of the West, calling one of them Bretashtan, or the seat and place of religious duty." It was one of the great Druidic Cors or colleges where pupils were sent from abroad for instruction.

Again. Why should metal from the Mendips be sent over the marshes which surrounded the Island to be loaded into boats of the Brue, when the Axe, equally navigable, was only just down over the hill? The trade routes of the Roman period are well known to have been along the Mendips to what is now Uphill, and southward along the ancient British road leading from what we know as Dorchester to Caerleon-upon-Usk, which passed over the Mendips a short distance from Priddy, and about double the distance from the Charterhouse mines. ...

Yours truly, GLASTONIAN.

By September of the same year, in the second edition of his booklet,

Dobson had again refined his account to distinguish 'four separate and entirely independent traditions' concerning the voyage story: the first was that of Cornwall; 'The second is found in Somerset of the coming of Christ and Joseph in a ship of Tarshish, and how they came to the Summer land, and sojourned in a place called Paradise. The third tradition is to be found in the little village of Priddy on top of the Mendip Hills to the effect that Our Lord and Joseph of Arimathea stayed there. Finally, traditions associate Our Lord with Glastonbury. It is to be noted that, while one of these traditions is located in Cornwall, and the other three in Somerset, none is found in Devonshire.'[246]

The edition of September 1936 newly included a map of the journey from St Michael's Mount to Glastonbury,[247] photographs of Chalice Well and Priddy Church, and a photograph of the undistinguished 'Paradise Farm, Burnham, Somerset', beneath a child-like sketch of the 'Jesus Well, near Padstow, Cornwall', another of Dobson's new discoveries, replaced in subsequent editions by a photograph.[248]

By September 1936, the intrepid Dobson had discovered not only the river Brue but, presumably prompted by 'Glastonian', also the River Axe. The passage of April 1936 reconstructing Joseph's route was replaced with a new section headed 'Location of the Traditions'. In this, still echoing Webb, he writes:

(3) In Somerset also is the tradition that they "came in a ship of Tarshish to the Sumerland and sojourned in a place called Paradise". The summerland is clearly Somerset. It was probably known as the land of summer, the land where the summer lingers. Hence Summerset or Somerset.

At the mouth of the Brue river, which runs down from Glastonbury, lies Burnham, and old Ordnance Survey maps give the name of the area round Burnham as "Paradise". It is still

246 Dobson, Sept. 1936, pp. 8-9; 1947, 1954, p. 13.
247 Dobson, Sept. 1936, following title page.
248 Dobson, Sept. 1936, plate preceding p. 7.

known by this name, and there is still a Paradise Farm and a Paradise House. How early the name became attached to this area is not known. A letter in the "Central Somerset Gazette" for 7th August, 1936, and signed "Glastonian", informs us that "Paradise" was also the ancient Celtic Glastonbury. He does not give his authority for the statement.[*][249] About a mile from Glastonbury lies the village of Godney, from which in ancient times river boats went down to Burnham. Godney means God-marsh-island. At Godney a whole village of mud and wattle houses was excavated, and here was found an ancient British river boat intact, which is preserved in the Glastonbury Museum.

The Glastonbury Traditions are mainly concerned with the suggested visit of Our Lord when a man, prior to His Ministry. But, if indeed Glastonbury was the Celtic Paradise then the visit as a boy included this place.

Now lead and copper were mined all around Priddy, and the ore was transported apparently by two main routes. It was taken by the river Axe to what is now Uphill, and thence by coastal ships down to Mount St. Michael or Falmouth to be combined with the export trade of tin.

Another route was by river boat from Godney to Burnham down the Brue and thence by coastal ship.[250]

In the 1954 edition, the name Pilton was substituted for that of Godney in the last sentence quoted above; it seems he must, rather belatedly, have had its 'traditions' brought to his notice.[251] Dobson

249 In the fifth edition of 1947 he added a in footnote: '[*] The name "Paradise" is found attached to several other places. Besides an area in Glastonbury itself, a spot N.E. of the Tor also bears the name, and there is still a "Paradise Lane"'. In the preface to the fifth edition of 1947 he wrote 'As to the Somerset traditions, I learn that the name "Paradise" is found in other places besides Burnham and Glastonbury, and all of these may well have originated in Our Lord's visit.'
250 Dobson, Sept. 1936, pp. 24- 25; corresponding to Dobson, 1954, pp. 31-2; this is inserted into the text found in April 1936 at pp. 24-26.
251 In the preface to his 1947 edition (p. 5) Dobson writes that the 'tradition' is found at Pilton.

(and, for that matter, 'Glastonian') never realised that the Brue's modern outfall to the Severn Sea near Burnham is the result of drainage activities in the later medieval and post-medieval periods. In its original state it meandered around the Glastonbury 'island' on three sides before flowing north through the Bleadney gap to join the Axe on its way to the sea.

Neither was Dobson's engagement with toponymy a happy one; he eventually elaborated his account of the Summerland. For 'the land where the summer lingers. Hence Summerset or Somerset', of September 1936, he substituted, in later editions, 'The terminal "set is the old Celtic word "Saete" or "Setna" meaning place of settlement.' In this he was quite confused. The name 'Somerset' contains no Celtic element and is in reality an Anglo-Saxon folk-name, *Sumorsaete*, literally the 'Summer-settlers'. It relates in an imprecisely understood way to the Anglo-Saxon name of Somerton, the summer-*tun* (enclosure, village, even 'town'), once a royal and administrative centre. Somerset belongs to a series of folk-names which mark a stage of English ethnic interpenetration and expansion in the seventh century, to the west of the older Anglo-Saxon kingdoms, from later Yorkshire to the Channel, including the *Paecsaete*, ('Peak-set'), the *Wrocensaete*, ('Wrekin-set') *etc.*, of which only Dorset now survives on the modern map as its southern neighbour. The water-meadows which surround the boggier parts of the Somerset Levels were, and are, rich summer pasture for cattle, as the world-wide fame of Cheddar cheese confirms, and in earlier days herdsmen would, to some extent, move seasonally with their beasts. The Welsh, looking across the Severn towards its green shores, called Somerset *Aestiva regio* in the Latin of the twelfth century,[252] and in Modern Welsh *Gwlad-yr-Haf*, the Summer Land.

252 Thus in Caradoc of Llancarfan's *Life of Gildas*.

Fig 32. Uphill Parsonage (engr. Rev. William
Barnes, before 1829). Maxwell thought Uphill,
beneath the rocky peninsula of Brean Down, was
an ideal Phoenician harbour. Dobson saw it as a
gateway to Somerset for Joseph and Jesus.

From the thickets of nomenclature, Dobson emerged to reconstruct
the 'first' visit of the Lord. Having become the guardian of Jesus after
the death of Joseph of Nazareth, Joseph of Arimathea brings Him
on a business trip to Mount St Michael. Requiring also to visit the
Mendip mines:

> They take a coastal boat round to the Somerset coast ("a ship
> of Tarshish to the Summerland") and land either at Burnham
> or Uphill. If at Burnham they make their way up by river boat
> to Godney [Pilton, 1954] or Glastonbury and on to Priddy. If at
> Uphill they go up the Axe to Priddy and down to Glastonbury. The
> Paradise at which they sojourn is either Glastonbury or Burnham.
> The return journey would be by the alternative route.[253]

253 Dobson, Sept. 1936, pp. 25-6; 1954, p. 32.

On route they call, perhaps for fresh water, at the oddly named Jesus Well near the mouth of the Camel, which appears in Dobson's work for the first time in September 1936.[254]

As with the other booklets on the subject, Dobson's, as we have seen, attracted correspondence from its public, and mutual admiration among the other champions of the story. In the preface to the third edition of January 1938, Dobson writes:

> With regards to the Cornish tradition ... I was content [in the first two eds.] to quote the bare statement from Baring Gould's "Book of Cornwall"; but Rev. H.A. Lewis, Vicar of Penwerris, Falmouth, writing in the Western Morning News for Nov. 15, 1937, says that the tradition exists at Looe, Portlove, and St Just-in -Roseland, all in the vicinity of Marazion, where the main tradition is found. Another correspondent sends me the charming legend of a hermit named Cledart, who described meeting the Boy Jesus. His cell was at Lammana, where a tiny Priory existed, which belonged to Glastonbury. Space does not permit me to record the story.
>
> As regards the Somerset traditions, I learn that the name "Paradise" is found in other places besides Burnham and Glastonbury, and all of these may well have originated in Our Lord's visit.
>
> I suggested that Our Lord and Joseph landed at Burnham (Paradise), passed up the river Brue to Glastonbury, then on to Priddy, returning by the Axe to Uphill, or vice versa. An anonymous article in the Weston and Somerset Herald for Nov. 13, 1937, makes some interesting suggestions with regard to place names. Between Priddy and Uphill lie the villages of Cross and Christon. Whence their names? ...
>
> A Wells Church dignitary has challenged the antiquity of the Priddy tradition ... But the Vicar of Glastonbury points out ... [etc.]

254 Dobson, Sept. 1936, p. 26.

Fig 33. A Glastonbury Lake-Village-type hut, such
as Dobson thought Jesus had occupied at Chalice
Well, from a painting by V. J. Lee (Dobson,1954).

We should like to have heard more of Cledart as the Hermit of
Lammana. He is presumably to be identified with the saint whose
name is more usually given as St Clether, himself generally identified
also with St Cleer; he is associated with the more northerly Cornish
places which bear those names, and with Brittany. His connection
with Lammana seems to have escaped Hunt, H. A. Lewis, and that
chronicler of the most obscure Cornish saints, Canon Doble. His
experiences there might have provided a better use of space than some
of the speculations for which Dobson did manage to find room.

For his 1954 edition, Dobson selected a picture, a painting by one
V. J. Lee, which has been much reproduced, to illustrate the story of
Jesus' stay at Chalice Well. He explained in an appendix:

Our frontispiece illustration shows a reconstructed mud-and-
wattle hut, as excavated at the Glastonbury Lake Village. ... Our
illustration shows one of the huts, probably somewhat larger than

that constructed and occupied, as we suggest, by Our Lord. ...

The painting shows it as erected near the source of the Chalice Well, which gushes out of the ground at the foot of the Tor Hill.[255]

But he was also mindful of the ancient sanctity claimed for the Old Church on the Abbey site:

The writer has suggested above that the humble wattle home of Our Lord stood by the Chalice Well, and that Joseph and his band erected theirs around it, using it as their own private place of worship.

It may be, however, that this[256] house stood on the site of Joseph's Wattle Church.[257]

Unlike H.A. Lewis, Dobson makes no mention of Bligh Bond and his theories of the circular nature of the oldest church, subsequently enclosed by the rectangular building. Probably, like Smithett Lewis, he was uncomfortable with Bond's spiritualistic methods.

In his 1954 edition, with regard to William Blake's possible knowledge of the tradition, which Miss Hamilton Thompson had questioned, Dobson hazarded the assertion that:

Blake was a common name in Somerset. A Blake family resided in a fine Tudor house in Glastonbury and provided a Mayor in 1762. Another Blake married John Down, owner of Glastonbury Abbey. Whether these were relations of William Blake is not certainly known.[258]

255 Dobson, 1954, p. 48, 'Appendix (8) Glastonbury Lake Village'. Appendices first appear in 1947.
256 Amended to 'His', 1947 ed..
257 *i.e.* the Old Church, Dobson, April 1936, p. 35; 1954, p. 43 adds 'and was a ruin on Joseph's arrival, and that he restored and enlarged it into the wattle church'.
258 Dobson, 1954, p. 47, 'Appendix (4) Note on Blake's "Jerusalem"'

H. A. Lewis anticipated this when in his third edition of 1948 he adds a footnote on Blake and his early drawing of Joseph of Arimathia, and writes 'I am told that one branch of Blake's family lived in or near Glastonbury'.[259]

At Glastonbury, Dobson surmises by the time of his 1947 edition, Jesus 'did not altogether shut Himself up like a hermit, but carried on some quiet work as a teacher'. To the folk of the Lake Villages he would have preached 'the simple principles given later on in Palestine in the Sermon on the Mount. But Glastonbury was a leading Druid centre, and He would meet these Druids, and tell them of the principles of his own Jewish religion.'[260] The two were, of course, in Dobson's view, very much the same.

At some date in the 1940s, Dobson elaborated on his reconstructions in a little-known pamphlet of 31 pages entitled *The Boyhood and Early Manhood of Jesus*. Privately printed, it was available from the author in Hastings or at the 'Gazette' Office in Glastonbury, and saw at least two slightly different impressions. Its cover tells us, ominously, that 'This brief study summarises a larger work now awaiting the Press'. This, thankfully, seems not in fact to have emerged. Dobson tells us that the 'favourable reception and wide circulation' of his previous work 'has led to a further and deeper investigation of the theme, of which this pamphlet is the result'. It added nothing of substance to the 'legend'. Starting from a date of October 6, B.C.4 for the Nativity, it tells how at twelve Jesus went with His parents to visit Jerusalem. On the way 'Mary and Joseph were guests of their uncle Joseph of Arimathea, who had a country house at Arimathea, or Ramah [Ramallah], and a town house at Jerusalem'. Two years later the Arimathean 'asked permission of His parents to take him on one of his journeys to Britain', leaving one less mouth to feed in 'the family's straitened circumstances'. They land in Cornwall and

259 Lewis, H. A., 1948, p. 15.
260 Dobson, 1947, 1954, p. 27; passage not found in 1936 or 1938 eds..

visit the tin mines:

> A well-known tradition quoted by Baring Gould in his "Book of
> the West" is very revealing. He writes:- "Another Cornish story is
> to the effect that Joseph of Arimathea came in a boat to Cornwall,
> and brought the boy Jesus with him, and the latter (Joseph) taught
> Him [*sic*] how to extract tin ...
>
> This ancient tradition reveals a good deal of the boyish
> character of Jesus. It shows Jesus to have been keenly interested
> in all He saw, and anxious to learn all He could. It shows Jesus
> visiting and having intercourse with the miners, and watching the
> processes of their work. It shows Jesus as no idle onlooker, but
> wanting to lend a hand, for he asks to be shown how it is done.
> It implies that those interviews with the miners made so deep
> and lasting an impression and memory, that it has passed into a
> proverb, and has survived even to the present day.[261]

Here Dobson has, of course, and seemingly unconsciously, reversed
the sense of Baring-Gould's story. 'This visit of the boy must have
had one result which vitally influenced His future as will be shown. It
brought Him into His first contact with Druidism. ... He could hardly
not have realised, that Druidism was a preparation for the Salvation
of mankind, which He would accomplish at Jerusalem under the
very name which He bore.' Dobson made much of the resemblance
between the name of Jesus and that of the supposed Celtic divinity
'Hesus'. 'Jesus' first trip to Britain probably occupied the best part
of a year, and at the age of 15 He found Himself back at Nazareth.
The next 4 years, we must assume, were spent at home ... helping
as a Carpenter. ... According to tradition, which we have no reason
to question, Joseph the Carpenter died when Jesus was 19 years of
age, leaving Mary a widow.'

Dobson held the Protestant view of the Holy Family, so Jesus

261 Dobson, n.d., pp. 14-15.

takes the opportunity to 'feel Himself free from home responsibilities' and go off travelling, leaving His mother in the care of His brothers. Dobson's speculations include His going in search of the lost tribes in Armenia, as well as to India, China and Japan. 'Reaching Glastonbury, which had such happy boyhood memories for Him, He settled down, and being a carpenter, was able to erect for Himself a humble dwelling of mud and wattles.' A long discourse on the virtues of druidry follows, ending with the declaration that 'Druidism was Christianity Anticipating Christ. ... We can see Him setting out and tramping the country, and meeting the Druids.' Dobson considers it likely that He even crossed to Ireland to visit the resting place of the Ark at Tara. Throughout, however, 'He never revealed His identity - the expected Saviour of the Druid and equally of the Jew.' In language that seems to hint at anti-Semitism, Dobson writes that before the Passion, 'He pronounced God's coming judgement on the Jew, Palestine and Jerusalem'. Dobson declares that 'Britain was to be Substituted for Palestine to Function in the New Age.'[262]

Dobson's legacy has been kept alive, mainly by those of British Israelite persuasion, and his *Did Our Lord Visit Britain ..?* is still in print. Of a similar character, and also occasionally reprinted, are the pamphlets of Isabel Hill Elder, first written apparently in the 1940s, *Joseph of Arimathea*, *Truth Never Dies*, and *The Story of Glastonbury*. Mrs. Hill Elder presented a framed photograph of the Cup of Nanteos to Glastonbury's Chalice Well in 1963, in the archive of which it is still preserved. In *Truth Never Dies* she writes 'As it is today, so in ages past, the completion of a good education was ever a period of travel. It is not, therefore, surprising that Egypt, India, Tibet and Southern England are mentioned as places to which our Lord travelled.'[263] She goes on to relate that:

The traditional visit or visits of our Lord to these parts have been earnestly recounted for the past 2000 years. In his boyhood with

262 Dobson, n.d., p. 26.
263 Elder, n.d., *Truth Never Dies, p. 31.*

Joseph of Arimathea and in His later years as traversing on foot the hills and swards, is believed and held dear by many Christians, especially in connection with Glastonbury. This tradition is woven into the "warp and woof" of the history of Glastonbury, held sacred by the oldest inhabitants. With them it is not a subject for glib and sceptical discussion, nor for the prying of strangers out of mere curiosity. The lips of the natives are then sealed, but among themselves, in their own homes, they talk about the time in the long ago, when our Lord visited Glastonbury and the surrounding country, and accepted hospitality in their homes. Even to-day there are homes where an extra place is always laid at table in the belief that one day He will return. Does this account for the hallowed atmosphere which seems to pervade Glastonbury and its neighbourhood, recognized even to-day by strangers to the district.[264]

In *The Story of Glastonbury* she writes of Joseph of Arimathea's 'visits to Britain as a metal millionaire', and of the 'strong unvarying tradition that Joseph brought the Boy Jesus with him on some of his visits ... and that part of His school days were spent at the Druidic College at Glastonbury, where, under the Druids, the best education in the world could be obtained. Perhaps with more certainty the belief is held in Glastonbury that our Lord in later years, came there to reside.'[265] With Jesus Christ's school-days at Glastonbury Druidic College we may perhaps safely leave this branch of the 'unvarying tradition'.

Without offering supporting evidence, Smith came to the conclusion that the ultimate source of the voyage story might be found in British Israelite literature of the later nineteenth century. This seems unlikely. Dobson, who seems to have been most influenced by the ideas of British Israel, merely elaborated the story as founded on Jenner, Taylor and Webb; his sources are all identifiable and he had no independent

264 *ibid*. p. 33.
265 Elder, n.d., *The Story of Glastonbury*, p. 7.

knowledge of any 'tradition'. Bennett at Pilton, whose work was unknown to Smith, seems also to have been acquainted with British Israelite ideas, but his role in the development of the 'legend' was peripheral and soon forgotten. More puzzling is Σ, who, as discussed above, *may* be Charles Bennett - or may not. If he is not, then his short query contains no internal evidence to link him with British Israelitism. The adoption of the story by the British Israelites, who took over the publication of Morgan's *St Paul in Britain*, and later of Dobson, seems to be a tertiary development. It has found more recent expression in *Did the Virgin Mary Live and Die in England?* by someone who wrote under the name of Victor Dunstan, and whose publication, by the Megiddo Press Ltd. in 1985, aroused some small notice in the popular press.

14

POST-WAR POSTSCRIPTS

As we have seen, the works of H. A. Lewis and C. C. Dobson spanned the war years of 1939-45 with editions, but even Henry Lewis's Glastonbury supplement of 1946 contained little that was actually new. The same was true of the post-war seventh edition of Smithett Lewis's *Joseph...*, published posthumously in 1955. The British-born Canadian writer George F. Jowett, in *The Drama of the Lost Disciples*, 1961, a highly derivative work published by the British Israelite 'Covenant Books', and re-treading all the now familiar ground, recalled:

> The Rev. Lionel Smithett Lewis, Vicar of Glastonbury, was indefatigable in his research to prove the validity of Jesus and His mother Mary residing in Britain, and painstaking in disclosing the history of Glastonbury from its saintly beginnings at Avalon. In the spring of 1953 he wrote to the writer stating that in the past few years he had recovered much more authoritative information from rare old documents he had discovered concerning Jesus and Mary that would prove revelatory on the subject, his one wish being that he would be privileged to publish this, his last and best work, before he died. He stated, once and for all, that he would prove the validity of the old traditions with incontestable evidence. Unfortunately he died suddenly, a week after writing to the writer, at the age of eighty-six. However, his widow, and co-helper and

Curate, the Rev. Stacey, have carried out his last request.[266]

Lewis died, not inappropriately, on Orangeman's Day, Sunday 12 July, 1953, after a month in hospital at Farnham, where he had settled following his retirement. The funeral at St Thomas-on-the Bourne, Farnham, was conducted 'by his friend and former Assistant Priest, Father Paul Stacey'. The seventh edition of *St Joseph...* carries a brief and non-committal forward by the Rt. Rev. Harold Bradfield, Bishop of Bath and Wells, dated June 11th 1953, but the book did not actually appear until 1955. Lewis's notes were incorporated into appendices which now numbered no less than thirteen. However, there was little which was 'revelatory'.

Somehow or other, Smithett Lewis had made contact with someone whom he thought had provided him with middle-eastern confirmation of the 'tradition'. In a footnote on page 51 he wrote:

Mr. E. V. Duff, Count of the Holy Roman Empire, told the author that in Maronite and Catluei villages in Upper Galilee, there lingers a tradition that as a youth Our Lord came to Britain as a shipwright aboard a trading vessel of Tyre, and that He was storm-bound on the shores of the West of England throughout the winter.[267]

He repeated this story on p.66. On page 54 he wrote a note to his earlier account of Dobson's story of Jesus and Joseph coming 'in a ship of Tarshish to the summer-land, and sojourned in a place called Paradise' - 'Since corroborated to me by Mr. E. V. Duff, who has spent ten years in Palestine and speaks Aramaic, the language which Our Lord spoke.' He mentioned Duff again on page 64, note

266 Jowett, 1961, p. 140. Mention may also be made of Kirsten Parsons' *Reflections on Glastonbury*, also pub. by Covenant in 1965. It retells the story mainly from Dobson, and includes two poems by the author, *The Little Thorntree* and *The Isle of Avalon*, from whom accompanying music was available on cards, as also, apparently, where pots with Holy Thorn leaves set in the glaze.
267 Lewis, 1955, note 5, p. 51-52.

19, observing there that he 'speaks fluently several Eastern languages.' Smith enquired concerning Duff at the library of the School of Oriental and African Studies and elsewhere, and 'tentatively identified "E. V. Duff" as the late Commander Douglas V. Duff, Knight of the Holy Sepulchre', adding that Duff 'was a celebrated raconteur'[268]. Douglas Valder Duff, (born 1901) was a prolific writer, with over ninety titles to his credit, many of them novels, but he also wrote several books in the 1930s about Palestine under the mandate. Duff's story echoes the anecdote of the Rev. Day's told in 1920, (above, p.65) concerning the Patriarch of Damascus, who had evidently read or heard something of Glastonbury lore.

The theme of ships' carpentry recurred in another new report which was included in Lewis's final edition, this time concerning not Joseph of Arimathea but Joseph of Nazareth:

> I have also been informed that at the Ding Dong Mine at Penwith ... the following story is told: that St Joseph, the foster-father of Our Lord, used to come as a ship's carpenter there frequently to get tin, and that on one occasion he brought Our Lord. A former curate at Newlyn, I understand, came across frequent references to the same story when visiting his parishioners, within the last twenty years. This is, of course, a variant of the story of Our Lord coming once with St. Joseph of Arimathea - possibly a confusion very likely to arise in the course of ages.[269]

Lewis returned to the dating of the foundation of Glastonbury, and to the possibility that the Virgin Mary had ended her days there: 'There are two different dates claimed for the founding of Glastonbury Church, A.D.37 and A.D.63. Probably both dates accentuate some special event.' In a footnote he added 'It is quite possible that St. Joseph, familiar with Britain, brought the Blessed Virgin here as her Paranymphos when St. John was at Ephesus, A.D.37, lived with

268 Smith, 1989, p. 75.
269 Lewis 1955 pp. 65- 66.

her here till her *koimesis* [Greek 'falling asleep' = Latin Dormition] fifteen years later, then went to France with St. Philip, was later sent by him to Britain as a missionary in A.D.63.'[270] The ancient belief in the bodily Assumption of the Virgin had only been up-graded to a dogma of the Roman Catholic Church by Pope Pius XII in November 1950. The concept of Joseph of Arimathea as *paranymphos*, Greek 'best man,' to the Virgin may seem a singular one, but is not, in fact, inconsistent with a strand of medieval tradition which saw him as a second Joseph, fulfilling a masculine role at the burial of Christ which echoed that of Joseph of Nazareth at His birth.

Fig 34. Glastonbury Tor, Horace Knowles, detail, (from Chant, 1948). Reproduced in full opp. p1.

270 Lewis 1955 pp. 19- 20.

It is plain that the creative impulse which had driven the development of the 'tradition' had all but run its course, but it had a final surprise to offer. This was *The Legend of Glastonbury* by A. G. (Arthur Guy) Chant, 1948, published by the Epworth Press of 25-35, City Road, London, EC1, decorated and illustrated by Horace J. Knowles. It ran to forty-two pages and was dedicated to William Morton Chant, RAF, and his crew, and retailed for ten shillings and sixpence, all royalties 'being devoted to the Royal Air Force Benevolent Fund'. Written (for the most part) in rhyming couplets, it was designed as a children's book, one of several which Chant wrote. Here the druidical world of the Rev. Morgan and his disciples is confronted by that of Enid Blyton. The result is a kind of *Jesus Goes on Holiday*, in verse more reminiscent of William McGonagall than of William Blake. The most, indeed the only, memorable lines are *The son of God your hill has trod / and its curse is broken.* Cursed it was, for the druids, here no longer primitive Methodists, have reverted to type as presented by the more hard-line Classical authors and as known to archaeology. All is made well, however, when Jesus ascends the Tor to interrupt a human sacrifice on the summit and points out the error of their ways to the astonished druids. His point is underlined when a timely bolt of lightening splits the altar-stone of the cromlech which crowned the summit:

> And Lo! the Tor, that mount of blood and fear,
> Smiles in the morning light, and leaps with joy
> As though the coming of a gentle boy
> Rolls the foul mists away and makes all clear.

The illustrations and decoration, typical of their period, were more competently executed than the text. Horace J. Knowles' career as an illustrator began with Reginald L. Knowles in 1908 with *Legends from Fairy Land*,[271] and he went on to illustrate some ten books,

271 By Holme Lee (pseud. of Miss Harriet Parr), Chatto & Windus, London 1908.

Fig 35. 'And lightnings split the altar stone':
Jesus confounds the Druids on the Tor, H.
Knowles (from Chant, 1948, p. 37).

including his own *Peeps into Fairyland* in 1924.[272] His Glastonbury
connections are first seen when Alice Buckton, in a letter to the
CSG of 27 October 1922, listed a number of people to whom
thanks were due following the completion of her film *Glastonbury
Past and Present*. Included in the list, although with no explanation
of what the thanks were for, was Mr. Horace Knowles of London.
He went on to illustrate the 1931 edition[273] of Alice Buckton's
'Christmas mystery play' *Eager Heart*, originally published in 1904.
Although issued by different publishers, the format, type-face and
paper of this and *The Legend of Glastonbury* are very similar, the
latter volume being clearly modelled on the former. As depicted
by Knowles, Joseph certainly looks the part of the 'enterprising
Semite', if scarcely reassuring as the purveyor of a new faith; one
might, indeed, be wary of purchasing a used donkey from him.
Jesus romps with the shaggy local children as if He has strayed
from the pages of *Peter and Jane*... Even the confrontation on the
Tor is somehow more reminiscent of a *Famous Five* adventure
than of Elijah on Mount Carmel. The whole is, however, quite
charming in its way, and marks the effective end of the creative
development of the 'legend'.

A few Somerset localisations, otherwise unrecorded, are to be
found in the pages of Berta Lawrence's *Somerset Legends* of 1973.[274]
We have already noted her account, apparently from mainly oral
sources, of the legend at Pilton, which reflects the belief of the inter-
war years clearly based on Bennett's play and the depiction of the
story on the church banner. Her remaining material, as at one point
she indicates, is probably of similar age, and she records nothing
which is likely to be independent of the written tradition as already

272 *Peeps into Fairyland*, written & illus. by H.J. Knowles, Thornton Butterworth,
London, 1924.
273 Published by Elkin Mathews & Marrot Ltd., 54, Bloomsbury St. London,
WC1.
274 Berta Lawrence had a considerable acquaintance with traditional rural life
on Sedgemoor, the setting of her 1954 novel *The Bond of Green Withy*, reprinted
by Somerset Press, Tiverton, in 1997.

Fig 36. '"Who'll follow me," He would laugh
and say, "Round Glastonbury My Secret Way?"'
Jesus leads a 'tattered crowd' of village boys and
girls beneath a megalithic Tor. H. Knowles (from
Chant, 1948, pp. 31-33).

examined. She tells how on the night after his arrival at Glastonbury Joseph had a vision in which 'Gabriel commanded him to build a church in honour of the Mother of God. In a second vision Joseph saw Christ himself descend to consecrate the church to the Virgin; this legend, and another, supports the statement that no human hands ever dedicated the *vetusta ecclesia* [the Old Church].'[275] She goes on to tell the Pilton story, and then continues:

> Others think that the boy Jesus made several journeys to Somerset with Joseph and that on two occasions they came, as an old Chapbook relates, to the place now called Burrowbridge.[276] They would have sailed out of Bridgwater Bay into harbour at Combwich ... and then up the soil-brown tidal river Parrett to Burrow bridge, where at that time the tributary river Cary ... flowed into it. ... Joseph and the boy Jesus, following their course up the river Cary, would have landed near the little place now called Beer, a hamlet in the parish of High Ham, on the Bridgwater-Langport road A372. From there they walked to Glastonbury, along a beautiful route that can still be followed.

Ramblers may wish to consult her picturesque description of their route to Turn Hill, High Ham, Pedwell and Ashcott, where it joined the Polden ridgeway, '(A39) and on to Glastonbury'.

> Forty years ago [*i.e.* around the early 1930s] a shepherd in those steep fields on Turn Hill slopes could point out a green path which, he told walkers, was used by Joseph of Arimathea. The place where two of these paths intersected is, according to legend, the site of the present beautiful High Ham church near the village green.

275 Lawrence, 1973, pp. 17-18.
276 The chapbook *The History of that Holy Disciple Joseph of Arimathea*, 1770, p. 7., tells how Joseph 'landed at Barrow-bay [*not* Burrowbridge] in Somersetshire, and then proceeding onwards of his journey eleven miles that day, came to Glastonbury'. This landing post-dates the Crucifixion, and the chapbook makes no mention of Our Lord's visit.

Fig 37. 'They wonder at the leaves, The blossom on the Thorn.' Joseph of Arimathea's miracle, H. Knowles (from Chant, 1948, pp. 43-44).

But the most deeply-rooted of all the legends about journeys of the boy Jesus to Somerset, and one that has passed into the national canon, is his visit to Priddy, that cold, windswept village on the high open top of Mendip that looks to far horizons. ... 'As sure as our Lord came to Priddy' was an expression used in North Somerset until the present century.[277]

Turning to Glastonbury, her material derives from Smithett Lewis and, it would seem, Dobson, although she does not acknowledge the latter in her bibliography. Our Lord's stay there seems to have lengthened:

'A strongly-rooted legend asserts that Jesus spent several of his unchronicled youthful years in Glastonbury, talking with scholars and priests of Druidical faith - a religion of which little is known - who lived in a small community on the Tor. Sometimes he moved among common people like the wild Priddy miners and the Glastonbury fishermen and fowlers. He knew the remarkable, artistically gifted inhabitants of the two Lake Villages ... [who] were to perish about thirty years later. And above all, during this sojourn, Jesus himself built the little church of mud-and-wattle and consecrated it to his Mother.

She concludes her account by quoting from yet another whom the story had stirred to verse. 'The lingering of this story in people's minds is illustrated by several lines from a contemporary verse-drama by Maurice Broadbent ... They took him/ To the Isle of Glass which is their most holy spot/ And there he built a house of boughs/ And twisted wickerwork, and passed his time/ With their young students.'[278] She tells us imaginatively, with a novel chronology, how 'Joseph of Arimathea made other trade-expeditions to Somerset

277 Lawrence, 1973, pp. 20-22.
278 Lawrence, 1973, pp. 22-23, quoting M. Broadbent, 'Apostle unto Britain', *The Cornish Review* (Spring 1969).

after the Romans' arrival in AD 44 for they quickly improved the mining industry on Mendip. He came to the harbour at Uphill, now a suburb of Weston-super-Mare, and was rowed on a small boat up the River Axe.' Joseph 'grew familiar with the new Roman road that replaced the track Jesus had used when he came that way'. Glancing briefly at the well attested sixteenth century tradition of Joseph's burial at Ham Hill, she says 'This legendary site of Joseph's grave seems to link with a little known story that he founded a tiny Christian settlement at Crewkerne and died while visiting it from Glastonbury'.[279] The source of the Crewkerne story is unclear.

In the interest of bibliographical comprehensiveness, reference should also be made to a minor literary curiosity, *Glastonbury: A Legend*, a play published by Lord Brabazon of Tara in 1963. This, as its didactic prologue makes clear, is based on the story as told by L. S. Lewis and Dobson. Dobson's Irish musings seem to have struck his Lordship's imagination for in his play Jesus, who does not appear in person, has acquired an Irish servant called Shaun, a converted robber, while travelling north of 'the great city on the Liffey'. It might be thought a pity that James Joyce omitted to chronicle the doings of the Christ in Dublin.

Equally derivative is the most recent attempt to argue for the credibility of the 'traditions,' the work, to add to confusion, of yet another Lewis. *Did Jesus Come to Britain?* by a professional photographer named Glyn S. Lewis appeared as recently as 2008. This, mistakenly, refers in the captions of two maps to open-cast copper mines at Priddy in addition to lead mines,[280] an idea held

---

279 Lawrence, 1973, pp. 24-26.
280 Lewis, Glyn S., 2008, pp. 56, 60; this author also includes (p.58) 'an old folk song' which says of Joseph 'And he made his way to Priddy/With our dear Lord .. Joseph was a tinner, was he.' This version does not seem to have appeared in print before, but no date or provenance is given, and I have been unable to trace its origin. An equally unprovenanced 'Cornish miners song' (p. 11) sings of three Josephs bringing 'Luck of the Year .. One was a tinner and sailed the sea.' Speculations about St Anthony in Roseland's church (pp.40-50) may be of interest to students of modern Cornish folklore.

earlier by the Rev. Charles Bennett, who derived it from the nearby place-name Green Ore. There are no copper deposits in Somerset, although calamine, the carbonate ore of zinc which was required to add to copper to produce brass, was discovered in the Mendips at Worle, after a nationwide search, in 1566. This led to the growth of a brass industry in the Avon valley using copper ore shipped from Cornwall via the port of Bristol.[281]

Perhaps the most bizarre postscript to the story is found in a pamphlet published by one Norah Cole, *c.* 1975, *The Truth before the World*. From psychic information, Ms Cole tells us (p.2) that

Joseph of Arimathea was the person, naturally, who, being in charge of the Body of Jesus, and knowing the dangers of leaving it where the authorities could have their vengeance on it, took it away in secret, during that first Easter week-end, and so caused the puzzle that has beset the Christian World for nearly 2000 years. He, in all innocence, opened the tomb, left the clothes lying and took the precious body, in his own ship to Britain and Glastonbury.

The resurrection appearances were of a spiritual nature, and the Body, along with that of Mary, still rests at Glastonbury.

A kind of mystic appendix to the 'legend' is to be found in the work of the late Mary Caine, and her artist husband Osmund, in the 1960s and 1970s. Building on the identification of a supposed giant zodiac design in the landscape around Glastonbury by the sculptress Katherine Maltwood in the 1930s, Caine improved upon the original figure of the giant Orion, doubling as Gemini in the Maltwood scheme. Maltwood had a single figure defined by field boundaries and the like, draped over Lollover Hill and neighbouring Dundon Hill, to the south-west of Glastonbury. Caine believed she had identified a second, smaller figure that formed the missing twin

281 See Joan Day, 1973, pp. 15-17.

Fig 38. The face of
Christ, a simulacrum
formed by woods on
Dundon Hill, with Loll-
over Hill forming His
lower body: the Gemini
sign of the Glastonbury
Zodiac (air photo, 1937,
east at top).

Fig 39. Katherine
Maltwood's Orion-
Gemini (1935, left) and
Mary Caine's Christ-
Gemini (1968, right).
Two alternative zodiacal
interpretations.

of Gemini. She also noticed that in an air photograph of Dundon Hill,[282] which forms the head of the original figure, the woods formed a Christ-like face, not unlike that of the Turin Shroud. Whereas Maltwood had perceived only a single arm, raised rather awkwardly over the 'giant's' head, she saw a second arm outlined in the fields, the two wrists bound together. This produced a strikingly moving image which has been called the 'Christ of the Scourging.' Caine quotes Blake, and declares:

> Our Zodiac answers Blake's question with a wonderful affirmative. .. Here is a twin-figure indeed; at once child and man, Bethlehem Babe and suffering Saviour. Katherine Maltwood will I hope forgive this irresistibly beautiful addition to her effigy, which only deepens the meaning of the Zodiac Trinity. She was not one to reject such a cornerstone to her building.
>
> His Messianic aspect mediates between all faiths; for Christlike though he is, he was there long before Christianity.

She relates the tin-trading form of the story, and refers to the Breton legend of St Anne. 'Did He trace the effigies on the old metal-route to the Mendips? They still say "As sure as the Lord was at Priddy" in that little village among prehistoric lead-mines, proudly pointing out the New Inn "where they stayed."[283]

Either she, or Osmund Caine, a painter and stained glass maker, reproduced her interpretation of the figure in a line-drawing in her original publication of 1969, *The Glastonbury Giants*, captioned as her '"Messianic" figure.' Osmund had also painted the image in oils on a large canvas, part of a series illustrating the Caine version of the

282 In *Air Suplement to a Guide to Glastonbury's Temple of the Stars*, K. E. Maltwood, Watkins, London, 1937, Plate V.
283 Caine, Mary, n.d., (1969) vol. 2, From Gemini to Sagittarius, pp 21-23. *The Glastonbury Giants* was originally published as twelve articles in *Prediction* astrological magazine, 1968-9.

Jerusalem

And did those feet in ancient time
Walk upon England's mountains green
And was the Holy Lamb of God
On England's pleasant pastures seen

And did the Countenance Divine
Shine forth upon these clouded hills
And was Jerusalem builded here
Among these dark Satanic mills?

Bring me my bow of burning gold
Bring me my arrows of desire
Bring me my Spear! O clouds unfold!
Bring me my Chariot of Fire!

I will not cease from mental fight
Nor shall my sword sleep in my hand
Till we have built Jerusalem
In England's green and pleasant land

WILLIAM BLAKE

Fig 40. Blake's lyric as illustrated by Mary Caine, c. 1977, with the Dundon 'Christ of the Scourging.'

Glastonbury Zodiac, dated 1964.[284] Their vision of the Zodiac was also recorded in a cine-film, *The Glastobury Zodiac* (56 mins.).[285]

In 1977, in the collaboraive *Glastonbury, Ancient Avalon, New Jerusalem*, edited by Anthony Roberts, she elaborated:

> For lying on or within Mrs. Maltwood's giant babe is a Christ-like figure, his hands bound over his head, his hair and beard uncannily drawn by woods on Dundon Hill's British Camp, his eye its dewpond, his face perfectly profiled by prehistoric fortifications. His head lolls in sleep .. or in death like Christ crucified. .. It satisfactorily accounts for the strange name Lollover Hill on Gemini's lower body.[286]

She avers that 'one imagines' that Blake, whom she believed had once headed the London Order of Druids, knew the images well 'when he wrote, "And did the Countenance Divine shine forth upon these clouded hills?" Blake was well aware of the continuing Glastonbury mystique. ... Blake was conversant from his boyhood with the story of Christ's coming to Britain.'

In her own more ambitious publication, *The Glastonbury Zodiac* of 1978, she adds little, but writes that 'the two arms of the god are bound above his head as if tied to a tree or flagellation-post.' The Zodiac becomes Christ's motive for visiting Britain, perhaps 'urged to it by the astrological Essenes of Qumran, who are thought to have taught his cousin John the Baptist, to study at this famous Druid Open University.' The last page of both this and the previous publication featured a drawing of her own in which she sets out Blake's poem with illuminations of an archer drawing his bow in a chariot as he rides over a dragon, an idealised Jerusalem as a city on a hill, and a

---

284 Oil on canvas, 'Gemini,' 50 x 40 ins., Osmund Caine, 1964 (author's collection).
285 Shown in recent years at Strode Theatre, Street, 20 October, 2006, to accompany a sale of the Zodiac paintings subsequent to Osmund Caine's death.
286 Caine, 1977, p. 41.

Celtic churchyard cross, with the Lamb bearing a cross on its base and the Dundon figure of the 'Christ of the Scourging' in a pictorial panel at the bottom of the shaft.[287]

Having now completed our examination of the printed source-material for the story in the late nineteenth and twentieth centuries, it remains to consider its ultimate origins. Before doing so we should note briefly that only one scholar of any repute since Jenner appears to have taken the story seriously. The American, Valerie M. Lagorio of Iowa, has devoted a number of papers to the subject of Joseph of Arimathea and the Glastonbury versions his legend, scattered throughout various learned journals. Although of very uneven quality, her papers have acquired, in the absence of much competition, a reputation for authority. In *Joseph of Arimathea: The Vita of a Grail Saint*, which appeared in the *Zeitschrift fur Romanische Philologie*, Turbingen, in 1975, and was financed by a research grant from the American Council of Learned Societies, Lagorio gives a credence to the 'legend' which should, by now, occasion the reader some surprise:

> Later legends [than the thirteenth century *L'Estoire del saint Grail*], primarily of Celtic origin, proclaim Joseph of Arimathea as a relative of the Blessed Virgin and hence of Christ. This is a consequence of the prized Welsh tradition, tracing the pedigree of early Welsh rulers back to Anna, a cousin of the virgin Mary.* In one such legend, Joseph of Arimathea is the brother of St. Anne and thus Mary's uncle, who frequently travels to Britain to oversee the family's Mendip tin trade [*sic*].** A variant account tells how Joseph of Arimathea and his nephew Christ came to Britain for a period of years, thereby accounting for the Bible's silence about Jesus from his twelfth to his thirtieth year.*** While such reports must remain in the realm of pious conjecture, Sir Thomas Malory was undoubtedly following this tradition when he amplified his

287 Caine, 1978, pp. 61, 287; 1977, p. 176.

French sources regarding Galahad's family lineage.'[288]

In Malory's *Morte d'Arthur* (*c.* 1470), Lancelot and his Christ-like son Galahad are said to be of the eighth and ninth degree from Christ. Lagorio's motley sources for this remarkable exposition are given as the Rolls Series edition[289] of the *Annales Cambriae* (*), the eccentric *Guardian of the Grail* (**), by John Whitehead,[290] and *King Arthur's Avalon* (***), 1958, by Geoffrey Ashe (see below). Of these, only the first has any independent value, and the Welsh genealogies referred to, mentioned in the introduction to that edition, make no mention of Joseph of Arimathea.[291] With the work of Geoffrey Ashe we move definitively from the shadow of the inter-war years to the modern Glastonbury of the 1960s and their aftermath in which the little former market town has become the world-centre of New Age Spirituality.

288 Lagorio, 1975, p. 67.
289 London, 1860, p.x.
290 London, 1959, p. 49.
291 Welsh pedigrees in Jesus Coll. MS 20, thirteenth century, trace three important dynasties to a hero or demi-god Beli the Great, son of an Anna, described as 'cousin of the Virgin Mary'. G. S. Lewis, 2008 (p.9), attributes the notion that Joseph was the younger brother of Mary's father to the Talmud.

*Fig 41. Dunstan at the feet of Christ, drawn by his own hand.
Note the outline of the Tor between robe and Dunstan's
head. St. Dunstan's 'Classbook'(Bodleian Library, Oxford,
MS.Auct.F.iv.32.fo.1), as redrawn for Marson, 1909.*

15

FORESHADOWINGS

Taking his lead from Geoffrey Ashe, Smith in 1989, in his penultimate section, considered the possibility that 'medieval texts misunderstood' played a role in the evolution of the legend. However, misled by those same eccentric writers of the inter-war years whom we have been examining, his brief account of these texts is both confused and confusing. His failure to engage adequately with them has, therefore, also hampered his assessment of the possible role of William Blake. It is best to begin afresh.

The earliest account of Glastonbury and its legends is to be found in the first *Life* of St Dunstan, *c.* 909-988, Abbot of Glastonbury *c.* 940-957. This was written within a year or two either side of the first millennium, the author identifying himself only by his initial as 'B,' a younger contemporary and acquaintance of Dunstan. As Dunstan was born near and educated at Glastonbury, it is likely that this account echoes the legends as told in Dunstan's boyhood in the earlier tenth century. 'B' records:

> Sharing a boundary [with the place of Dunstan's birth] there was an island, a royal place of former generations, called locally by the ancient name of Glaestonia. It was cut off from other places by broad curving rivers flowing around its spacious and undulating shores, which were slow moving and full of fish. Many poor men tended to use the place, as well as holy men who made up the greatest number, for it was given and dedicated to God. For it was indeed in that very place that the first neophytes of

the Catholic law were directed of old by God to rediscover a church, not built by men's skill, but rather prepared in heaven for the salvation of mankind; afterwards the Maker of the heavens Himself demonstrated by many miraculous deeds and mysteries that this church was consecrated to His Mother [*or, in a second MS,* the Mother of God] Mary. Here also they came to add an oratory built of stone, which at the behest of Christ Himself they dedicated to St Peter the Apostle. Thereafter, a great number of all the faithful round about would gather there, and would humbly frequent the precious place on that island.[292]

The stone church was that traditionally built by Ine, king of Wessex 688-726. The Old Church, called in Latin by 'B' *antiqua ecclesia*, and by William of Malmesbury *vetusta ecclesia*, and *ealde chirche* in Old English, built of wattle and daub, was regarded as in itself a holy relic, anticipating the later cults of Walsingham (of twelfth-century origin) and Loreto (not recorded before the fifteenth century).

Exactly what 'B' wished us to understand by the phrase 'prepared in heaven for the salvation of mankind' is beyond recovery. I have elsewhere drawn attention to the parallel Coptic traditions, of the twelfth century and earlier, of the Burnt Monastery in Middle Egypt.[293] This was regarded as the refuge of the Holy Family in the last phase of their sojourn in Egypt. Following the Ascension and Pentecost, all the Apostles, together with the Virgin Mary, were transported there on the clouds of heaven to be met by Christ, who demonstrated to them the mode of consecration for a church, and celebrated there the first service of holy communion. The building, which is associated with the refuge in the wilderness from the satanic Dragon of the 'woman clothed in the sun,' the cosmic figure of the Virgin in *Revelation* 12, thus becomes the first church in Christendom. I have argued that the account in 'B' is likewise to be understood not as a pseudo-historical account of early missionary activity, but as a supernatural

---

292 The Latin text may be found in Stubbs, 1874, pp. 6-7.
293 Ashdown, 2009.

manifestation of Christ and the Apostles, for it can only be they, in this context, to whom the phrase 'the first neophytes of the Catholic law' can refer. A more familiar apocryphal parallel is the miraculous gathering together of the Apostles from the far ends of the earth to witness the obsequies of the Virgin Mary.

However this may be, it is clear that the focus of the early cult was on the miraculous church building itself, and its special relationship to Christ and His Mother, rather than on those unidentified apostles who discover it. The sober Anglo-Norman historian William of Malmesbury knew the first *Life* of St Dunstan, but clearly found it as problematical as we do. In the *Gesta Regum*, the 'Deeds of the Kings of the English,' of 1140, following the Venerable Bede, he refers to the tradition, found in the *Liber Pontificalis*, the 'Book of the Popes,' of *c*.530, that Pope Eleutherius (*c*.174-89) sent preachers to Britain.[294] 'By these' says William 'was built the ancient church of St Mary of Glastonbury, as faithful tradition has handed down through decaying time.' He continues:

Moreover, there are documents of no small credit, which have been discovered in certain places, to the following effect - 'No other hands than those of the disciples of Christ erected the church of Glastonbury.' Nor is it inconsistent with probability: for if Philip the apostle preached to the Gauls, as Freculphus relates in

294 The often-repeated assertion that this story arose from a confusion with 'Britium' in Mesopotamia rests on nothing more than a speculation of the German scholar Harnack, published in 1904. It was, in fact, probably modelled on a contemporary account of the dispatch of Palladius to the 'Irish believing in Christ' by Pope Leo in 431, to fill a perceived historical gap. See Ashdown, 2004. The Anglo-Saxonist Michael Wood, who recognises the primacy of the Dunstanian account in the development of the Glastobury mythos, writes: 'In the line about "no human skill" we can see the origin of the tale that comes down to Blake's "Jerusalem", the legend that Jesus himself had set foot in Britain.' He interprets B to intend the neophytes to represent the missionaries sent by Pope Eleutherius, mentioned also in the *Anglo-Saxon Chronicle*, finding a church 'consectrated and built "by no human skill". This, of course means by Christ himself. And did those feet ..' (Wood, 1999, p. 57).

the fourth chapter of his second book, it may be believe that he also planted the Word on the hither side of the channel. But that I may not seem to disappoint my reader's expectation by vain imaginations, leaving all doubtful matter, I shall proceed to the relation of substantial truths.[295]

A process of rationalisation has here taken place. No longer of divine origin and merely discovered and repaired by the Apostles, the church is now said to have been actually built by them, or by Eleutherius's second-century missionaries.

This process of rationalisation is taken further in *De antiquitate Glastonie Ecclesie* - 'On the Antiquity of the Church of Glaston', a work originally by William of Malmesbury, written *c.*1129, but surviving only in a version, heavily revised by other hands, of 1247. Here, in chapter one, William's anonymous apostles, sent by St Philip, are said to be twelve in number, adding in a rather non-committal manner: 'Their leader, it is said (*ut ferant*), was Philip's dearest friend, Joseph of Arimathea, who buried the Lord.' This is the first direct reference to Joseph's connection with Glastonbury, although an Old French romance of *c.* 1200, the verse *Joseph d'Arimathie* of Robert de Boron,[296] had already pictured Joseph sending the Grail-company west to the *vaus de Avaron*, the 'vales of Avaron,' generally identified with Glastonbury conceived as Avalon. A later marginal note appended to chapter two of the *De antiquitate* refers to Joseph of Arimathea's role in the various secular Arthurian romances. It was thus in a hesitant and uncertain manner, and for reasons still not well understood, that Joseph's name entered an already well-established body of tradition about Glastonbury.

The main text of the first chapter of *De antiquitate* goes on to relate that the twelve saints 'residing in that desert,' that is in the Somerset levels, build the Old Church as instructed in a vision by the Archangel Gabriel. 'And as it was the first in that region, God's Son

295 Trans. Stephenson, 1854, Llanerch ed., 1989, vol. i, p. 20.
296 Edited by Richard O'Gorman, 1995.

distinguished it with greater dignity by dedicating it in honour of His Mother.' The saints were sustained there 'as the pious believe' by the help and vision (*auxilio ac visione*) of the Virgin herself.

In support of this, reference is made to the 'writings of the elders'. There follows the assertion that 'In the church of St Edmund and also in the church of St Augustine, the apostle of the English, we have seen a work by one of the latter [*i.e.* of the elders], an historian of the Britons, which begins thus: "There is on the western border of Britain a certain royal island…"'. There follows a version of the passage from 'B''s *Life* of Dunstan which we have already quoted, with the emendation that 'It was there that the first English neophytes of the Catholic law, guided by God, repaired an ancient church, not built, they say, by human skill but prepared by God himself for human salvation.' Here it is the first *English* converts, presumably that first generation of West Saxon Christians who occupied Somerset, who find the church, built, we are meant to believe, by the twelve missionaries sent by St Philip, although in contradiction of this, its preparation by God himself still remains embedded in the text. The passage from the Saxon biographer of the tenth-century West Saxon saint has here been wrenched from context and fathered on a 'British' historian, a fact which B's editor Stubbs, writing in 1874 before the intricacies of the 1247 text had been untangled, and therefore regarding the passage as the authentic work of William, thought represented an erroneous expansion of the initial 'B'. There was indeed a copy of the *Life* at St Augustine's Abbey, Canterbury.[297] As already noted, the authentic William of Malmesbury knew the first *Life* of Dunstan, to which he refers in his own biography of the saint, and so his original text of *De antiquitate* may have contained some reference to the passage, but

297 It was a misunderstanding of this reference which led some early seventeenth century antiquaries to believe that the passage was from a letter of St Augustine to the Pope. This was definitively refuted by Stillingfleet in 1685 (pp. 11-12) but the error was never-the-less repeated by Morgan, who was followed by L. S. Lewis and Dobson. It is also to be found in Maxwell, 1927, p. 50.

what form this may have taken is, again, now irrecoverable.

In the *Gesta Regum* (chapter 25), however, William makes a further reference to Christ's special relationship with Glastonbury. St David, towards the end of the sixth century, is said there to have come to Glaston to dedicate the church. 'The antiquity and holiness of the church was established through him by a heavenly vision'. On the night before the proposed ceremony, David had a dream in which the Lord Jesus appeared to him and 'gently asked the reason of his coming.' When David explained:

> the Lord turned him from his purpose, saying that He had long since dedicated the church in honour of His Mother, and it was wrong for such a sacrament to be repeated, and so profaned, by the hand of man. At the same moment, in the dream, the Lord pierced with His finger the palm of his hand, and said: 'Behold a sign that what I have done already must not be repeated. Nevertheless, inasmuch as you were motivated by piety and not presumption, your penalty shall not last long. In the morning, at Mass, when you come to the 'With Him and through Him and in Him,' you shall be fully restored to health and strength.

David awoke to find the wound was real, and 'that his journey might not seem fruitless, he quickly built and dedicated another church'. This story, which was repeated in *De Antiquitate*, was apparently a riposte to the claim made in the first *Life* of St David by Rhygifarch, *c.* 1095, that Glastonbury, along with Bath, was among the churches founded by him.

John of Glastonbury, in his *Chronica* of *c.*1342, has nothing answerable to Pseudo-William's version of the passage from B; but he does refer to Christ's special presence at Glastonbury, the precise meaning of which he leaves unexplained. The introduction, possibly by another hand, headed 'On the antiquity of the Old Church of the Blessed Mary at Glaston ...' states that in the thirty-first year after the Lord's Passion (which, following medieval convention, equates to AD 63) Joseph and eleven companions arrived bringing Christianity to King Arviragus, and here they constructed the first church in 'this kingdom', *i.e.* Britain, making the walls with *virgis torquatis*, 'twisted rods,' that is, of wattle; 'which Christ in honour of his mother and as a burial-place for his servants in his own presence dedicated (*quam Christus in honore sue matris et locum ad sepultam seruorum suorum presencialiter dedicauit*).' It goes on to give the story of St David, concluding 'And though the church, along with the aforesaid addition [by St David], was later often reconstructed and dedicated anew by others, the place always remained consecrated by the most high Lord and by the remains of the saints.'[298] In his first chapter, John says:

No other human hands made the church of Glaston, but Christ's disciples founded and built if by angelic doctrine, an unattractive structure, certainly, but adorned by God with manifold virtue; the High Priest of the heavens himself, the maker and redeemer of humankind, our Lord Jesus Christ, in his true presence dedicated it to himself and his most holy mother .[299]

In his fourteenth chapter, 'On the sanctity of the church of Glaston and its cemetery ..' he says that 'The chief personages of the country would rather await the day of resurrection in the monastery of Glastonbury, in the protection of Mary the ever-virgin Mother of God, than anywhere else'. Later in the same chapter, John gives his reasons why 'that holy earth is so eagerly desired for Christian burial. The first reason is that the Lord dedicated it in his own presence for the burial of his servants.'[300] The story of St David is again repeated in John's thirty-ninth chapter.[301] Finally, John of Glastonbury, writing around 1342, is the first to record Glaston's designation as the

298 Carley, 1985, pp. 2-3.
299 Carley, 1985, pp. 8-9 The Latin of the last clause is *quam ipse summus pontifex celorum fabricator et generis humani redemptor, Dominus noster Ihesus Christus, sibi sueque sanctissime genetrici presencialiter dedicauit.*
300 Carley, 1985, pp. 28-29; 32-33: *Prima causa est quia Dominus eam ad seruorum suorum sepulturam presencialiter dedicauit.*
301 Carley, 1985, p.87.

New Jerusalem. In quoting from the abbey's text of Geoffrey of Monmouth's verse *Life of Merlin* of *c.* 1150, in his second chapter, he gives a version of Geoffrey's description of the Isle of Apples with a significant interpolation:

> *Hec nova Ierusalem fuit, hec fidei quoque lima,*
> *Hec tumulus sanctus, hec scala poli celebratur.*
> *Vix luit inferni penas hic qui tumulatour.*

'This was the new Jerusalem, the faith's refinement, a holy hill, celebrated as the ladder of heaven. He scarcely pays the penalties of hell who lies buried here'.[302] This passage is linked to those previously cited by the *motiv* of the special sanctity of the soil of Glastonbury.

John also included the mysterious Prophecy of Melkin, referred to earlier, in which Joseph of Arimathea lies in a hidden tomb in Avalon with relics of the blood and sweat of the 'prophet' Jesus. When this is found the inhabitants of the island will lack neither water nor 'heavenly dew.'[303]

It is clear that these medieval accounts are relevant to any concept of Christ's presence at Glastonbury in a more special and localised sense than that in which He was considered present among all the faithful through the gift of the Holy Ghost to the Church, and in the sacrament of the Eucharist. Most of them were eventually noted, in one form or another, by Messrs. Lewis, Lewis and Dobson in their attempts to find support for the voyage story. We must recognise, however, that in themselves they give no support to the idea of Jesus coming to Britain in the flesh, either as boy or man, before the commencement of His public ministry in Palestine. They seem to refer rather to some special manifestation of the Risen Christ. One can hardly dissent from Smith's conclusion that 'The story once conceived gave a new meaning, hitherto quite unsuspected, to earlier material

302 Carley, 1985, pp. 12-13.
303 See Ashdown, 2003.

and thus created its own pedigree.'

This does little, however, to help decide the question of when and by whom it was first conceived. As medieval and post-Tridentine Catholic sources seemingly give no hint of the theme of Jesus's voyage with Joseph, the likelihood must be that its background is post-medieval and Protestant. We may even suspect a further process of rationalisation of the medieval texts, anticipating that of Dobson at the very end of the story's twentieth-century evolution. If Jesus built the wooden church at Glastonbury, so the reasoning might have run, then He must have done so during His period as a working carpenter and before the commencement of the public ministry. The medieval stories of the voyages of Joseph, combined with antiquarian speculations, derived from Classical sources, about the Phoenicians and their tin-trading in Cornwall, provided the necessary ways and means to bring Him hither. Were such speculations indeed dependent on the Glastonbury texts, however, or originally wholly independently of them? As Smith points out, the Jesus voyage story is a side shoot or embellishment of the wider Joseph tradition. The relevant question, then, is whether it derived directly from the medieval Grail romances, or from versions, much more accessible in the post-Reformation period, incorporating Glastonbury traditions. It is difficult to believe that it was wholly uninfluenced by these.

Glastonbury's traditions of Joseph of Arimathea took on a new life in the fifteenth century when they were used to bolster the claim of the English Church to an apostolic origin comparable to those maintained (equally spuriously) by the Churches of France, which claimed St Denis as a founder, and Mary Magdalene, Martha and Lazarus for its Mediterranean hinterland, and Spain, which claimed St James the Great at Compostela. The seniority of the national churches within the Conciliar movement, which sought to broaden Church authority by asserting the superiority of a General Council over an array of rival Popes and the then widely discredited institution of the Papacy, was determined by their supposed dates of origin. English delegates, who included Bishops of Bath and Wells and Abbots of Glastonbury, cited Joseph and his mission at the Councils of Pisa

(1409), Constance (1414-18, which coincided with Agincourt), Siena (1424), and Basle (1431-49).[304] The penultimate Abbot, Richard Bere (1494-1525) constructed a crypt dedicated to Joseph beneath the ancient Lady Chapel on the site of the Old Church. A verse *Lyfe of Joseph of Armathia* [sic] was composed at Glastonbury in 1502, and printed by Richard Pynson in 1520.[305] This summarised the literary tradition of Joseph with folkloristic local detail, and related the cures vouchsafed to local petitioners at the newly-established shrine.

The later medieval period saw a renewed attention to genuine ancient history, and the rediscovery of such texts as the lost works of Tacitus, including his account of Britain in the *Agricola*. Britain's legendary history received a check from Renaissance scholarship in the work of Polydore Vergil, an Italian who came to England in 1502 and was asked by Henry VII to write a history of England. Ironically, given that the monarch had come to the throne as *map darogan*, 'son of prophecy,' fulfilling the ancient Welsh expectation of an Arthurian restoration, Vergil became convinced that the works of Geoffrey of Monmouth, in which the legendary history was enshrined, were but fables. His *Anglica Historia* was finally published abroad in 1534, long after Henry VIII had succeeded his father. It aroused a storm of controversy, and John Leland, the King's librarian and antiquary, set out to vindicate the traditional account, undertaking several journeys visiting historic sites and the soon-to-be-destroyed monastic libraries, including that of Glastonbury, recording invaluable information.

Leland died insane in 1552. The work of preserving precious manuscripts was to be continued by Matthew Parker (1504-1575), from 1559 Elizabeth I's Archbishop of Canterbury, the father of Anglo-Saxon studies, and in this he was assisted by Elizabeth's great minister William Cecil, Lord Burghley. Parker believed he could find in the pre-Conquest English Church traces of a true Christianity destroyed by the (Papally sanctioned) Norman invasion and subsequent growth

304 On the use of the Joseph legend at the Councils, see Lagorio, 1971, pp. 220-224.
305 Ed. Skeat, 1871, 1996.

of Papal authority, and only restored by the Protestantism of his own time. Many of his manuscripts found a permanent home in the library of his old college, Corpus Christi, Cambridge. Such careful scholarship was not enough, however. After Henry VIII's break with Rome, it was felt desirable by Protestant historians and polemicists to establish a case for an origin for the newly independent Church of England which did not derive from Papal authority. Late Antique speculations about British Christian origins were sought out in the asides of the Church Fathers and in obscure Byzantine church histories and lists of saints. Such efforts were summed up in those enduringly popular works, Foxe's *Acts and Monuments*.., commonly known as *Foxe's Book of Martyrs*, and John Camden's *Britannia*, first published in 1586 and subsequently much enlarged.

Camden (1551-1623) cites the opinions of the scurrilous Protestant writer John Bale (1495-1563), a Suffolk man sometime Bishop of Ossary, and Matthew Parker, that Claudia Rufina, 'a British dame passing well learned,' whom the Roman poet Martial commemorates, was 'the very same woman of whom St Paul maketh mention in his latter Epistle to Timothy ... howsoever others be of a contrary opinion.' He defends the possible authenticity of the story of King Lucius, citing Tertullian's statement that parts of Britain inaccessible to the Romans had been won for Christ. He goes on, however, to note the alternative, apostolic, antiquarian model for the arrival of Christianity in Britain, writing:

> But our Ecclesiastical writers who have employed both time and diligence in the consideration of this point endevor and labour to prove, and that out of ancient authors of credit, that this before this time, in the very dawning and infancies of the Church, Britanny [*i.e.* Britain] had received the Christian religion: and namely that Joseph of Arimathea a noble Senator, sailed out of Gaule into Britanny, and that Claudia Rufina the wife of Aulus Pudens, which woman, as is credibly thought, S. Paul nameth in his later epistle to Timothy, and whom the Poet Martiall so highly commendeth, was a Britan borne. They cite also the testimony of Dorotheus, who

commonly goeth under the name of the Bishop of Tyre, who in his *Synopsis* hath recorded, that Simon Zelotes, after he had travelled through Mauritania, was at last slaine and buried in Britanny [Britain]: as also that Aristobulus, whom S. Paul mentioneth in his Epistle to the Romanes, was made Bishop of Britanny [Britain] (whereto Nicephorus inclineth), notwithstanding he speaketh of Britania and not Britannia. They report likewise upon the authority of Simeon that great Metaphrast, and of the Greeks *Menology* that S. Peter came hither and spred abroad the light of Gods word: out of Sophronius also and Theodoret, that S. Paul after his second imprisonment in Rome, visited this our country. Whereupon Venantius Fortunatus, if he may be beleeved as a Poet, writeth thus of him, unlesse he speaketh of his doctrine:

> *Pass'd over Seas, where any Ile makes either port or bay,*
> *And lands, so far as Britans coast or cape of Thule lay.*

But to this purpose maketh especially that which erewhile I alleged out of Tertullian, as also that which Origen recordeth how the Britans with one consent embraced the Faith, and made way themselves unto God by meanes of the Druidae, who alwaies did beat upon this article of beleefe, that there was but one God. And verily of great moment and importance is that with me, that Gildas, after he had mentioned the rebellion of Boodicia and treated of the revenge thereof, *Meane while* quoth he, *Christ that true Sun, shining with his most glittering brightnesse upon the universall world, not from the temporall skie and firmament, but even from the highest cope of heaven, exceeding all times, vouchsaved first His beames, that is to say His precepts, and doctrine in the time, as we know, of Tiberius Caesar, unto this frozen I[s]land full of Ice, and lying out as it were in a long tract of earth remote from the visible sunne.*[306]

The poet and hymn-writer Venantius Fortunatus (*c.*530-*c.*603),

306 Camden, *Britannia* (1610), Romans in Britaine, 65.

however, an Italian resident in Gaul and familiar with Armorica and its islands who had become Bishop of Poitiers, as Camden's caveat suggests, had merely stated that the *writings* of St Paul had crossed the Ocean to Britain and *ultima Thule*, the furthest north-western extremities of the then-known world.

Camden's work in this regard was continued by his friend James Ussher (or Usher) (1581-1656). Of aristocratic ancestry, Ussher was born and educated in Dublin, where in 1607 he became Professor of Divinity and Chancellor of St Patrick's Cathedral. A frequent visitor to England, James VI & I made him Bishop of Meath in 1621. In 1622 he published his *Discourse of the Religion anciently Professed by the Irish and British*, in which he first established the myth of what eventually came to be known as the 'Celtic Church.' This had, naturally, been in agreement with the contemporary Church of England and hostile to that of Rome. The following year King James recalled him to England the better to carry out his politically useful researches into the history of the ancient British churches, and in 1625 he was nominated to the ancient Irish primatial see of Armagh, returning to Ireland to take up his charge in 1626. In 1639 he published in Dublin his influential *Britanicarum Ecclesiarum Antiquitates* (Antiquities of the British Churches) in which the Glastonbury traditions were fully expounded, including valuable sixteenth-century material derived from the last generation to know the Abbey as a living institution.

Ussher was not just a scholar, but an active pastor and administrator. He was again in England, however, when the Irish rebellion of 1641 broke out, and he never saw his native country again. It was a measure of the respect in which he was held that, despite his episcopal orders and identification with the Royalist cause, on his death in 1656, Cromwell as Lord Protector sanctioned his burial in Westminster Abbey. It is sad and ironical that he is now remembered mainly with derision for his *Annales Veteris et Novi Testamenti* (Annals of the Old and New Testaments, 1650-54). In this he sought to use historical method, and ancient sources independent of the Bible, to produce an accurate Biblical chronology, in the course of which he suggested a date for the creation of the world in 4004 BC. Given the

data with which he had to work, and contemporary lack of scientific
knowledge to the contrary, there was nothing very unreasonable in this
conjecture. It was not Ussher's fault that his dates were subsequently
inserted by some unknown authority into the margins of reference
editions of the Authorised Version, giving them for the uncritical a
spurious appearance of Divine sanction.

The Glastonbury traditions figured influentially in the seventeenth
century not only in the work of Ussher but in that Sir Henry Spelman.
Spelman (*c*.1564-1641), of Norfolk gentry stock, was another friend
and contemporary of Camden, and of Sir Robert Cotton, a collector
whose manuscripts eventually formed the nucleus of the British
Museum's library, in the Society of Antiquaries. His most important
work, *Console, decreta, leges, constitutiones in re ecclesiorum orbis
britannici* 'is an attempt to place English church history on a basis
of genuine documents.' The first volume (1636), which occupied him
for seven years, came down to 1066. A second volume was edited
by Dugdale in 1664.[307] Spelman gave some prominence to the Greek
text of Metaphrastes which connected St Peter with Britain, and to
Glastonbury's traditions of Joseph of Arimathea, which he attributed
to William of Malmesbury. He published a valuable illustration of
a metal plate, now lost, salvaged from a pillar in the Abbey, which
bore a written version of the Joseph legend, and also an imaginative
reconstruction of the 'pyramids,' inscribed and figured cross-shafts,
which Malmesbury had recorded in the ancient cemetery. Spelman's
most influential legacy, however, was another 'conjectural' restoration,
that of the Old Church itself, identified as the oldest church in the
whole world (*totius orbis*). This was shown as a structure of woven
wattles, without daub, with a thatched roof of shaggy reeds, its overall

307 The antiquary Sir William Dugdale (1605-1686) published his national
survey from monastic records, *Monasticon Anglicanum*, in Latin, successively in
single volumes in 1655, 1664 and 1673. An abridged English edition appeared
in 1693 as *Monasticon Anglicanum, or The History Of the Ancient Abbies, and
other Monasteries, Hospitals, Cathedral and Collegiate Churches, in England and
Wales. With Divers French, Irish, and Scotch Monasteries Formerly relating to
England (Translated from the Latin)*, London (available online).

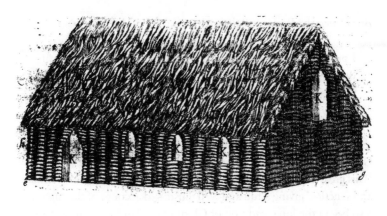

Fig 42. *Sir Henry Spelman's much-imitated 'conjectural' restoration of the Old Church, Concilia, 1636, p. 11.*

Milton, careful Classical scholar as he was, was sceptical about the Glastonbury traditions. Stillingfleet, as we have seen, argued that St Paul (and not Joseph of Arimathea) had brought the gospel to Britain. In *Origines Britannicae, or the Antiquities of the British Churches*, 1685, he discussed those medieval texts which maintained the Old Church at Glastonbury was consecrated by Christ Himself. Noting that the Roman Catholics Alford and Cressy 'are much displeased with Sir H. Spelman for calling it into question' he concluded sceptically that any who believe it 'are past all confutation by reason, having their minds naturally framed to believe legends.'[308]

'B"s *Life* of Dunstan, with the oldest account of the Glastonbury legends, was also printed for the first time in 1685, albeit on the Continent by those industrious Roman Catholic scholars, the Bollandists.

John Aubrey (1626-1697), pioneer of something approaching field archaeology, born near Malmesbury, Wiltshire, and with family in Somerset, knew Glastonbury, noting in particular in his *Monumenta*

308 Stillingfleet, 1685, p. 11.

Britannica the Ponter's Ball earthwork:

> I presume that this work was raised by the Britons to fortify
> themselves within this neck of land. Perhaps it [Avalon] might
> take its denomination from this vallum, rather than from aval (an
> apple). Before the Romans settled here, here were only crabs.[309]

The renowned antiquary William Stukeley (1687-1765) also visited
Glastonbury and in his *Itinerarium Curiosum* of 1724 observed that
'This great monastery in superstitious times held the first place for fame
and sanctity,' giving a full and well illustrated account of the ruins. He
also began the long tradition of Glastonbury landscape mysteries:

> In this county of Somerstshire are three remarkable hills, that make
> an exact triangle twelve miles each side, much talked of by the
> country people; Camalet castle, Glassenbury torr, and Montacute.
> They have a notion that king Arthur obtained from some saint,
> that no serpent or venomous creature should ever be found in this
> compass, though frequent all around it.[310]

An edition of John of Glastonbury's fourteenth-century *Chronica*
by the antiquary Thomas Hearne (satirised as Wurmius - 'To
future ages may thy dulness last / As thou preserv'st the dulness
of the past!' in Pope's *Dunciad*, 1728) was printed in 1726. This
was followed by his edition of Adam of Domerham's older, late-
thirteenth-century, Chronicle, including with it the *De antiquitate*
of William of Malmesbury, in 1727. All the major primary sources
for the Glastonbury *mythos*, therefore, were readily available to
antiquaries and others from the third decade of the eighteenth century.
The oddities contained in John of Glastonbury's pages, asserting

309 Fowles 1880, p. 894.
310 *Itinerarium Curiosum*, rep. 1969 by Gregg International Publishers, Farn-
borough, Hants., p. 150. On Stukeley's role in the popularisation of the Druids,
see conveniently Piggott, 1968.

Christ's consecration of the Old Church and its churchyard 'in his own true presence,' did not escape notice.

From 1772 to 1787 there appeared the six volumes of *The Antiquities of England and Wales* by Francis Grose. In volume five he writes of the Old Church being constructed of wattles by Joseph of Arimathea and his eleven companions. He adds that 'The legend says it was consecrated by Christ in person, and by him dedicated to the honour of his mother,' going on to relate the story of St David. This is a reasonable paraphrase of John of Glastonbury, but one perhaps liable to misinterpretation, especially in view of the lack of context and attribution.[311]

Grose (*c*.1730-1791), the son of a Swiss jeweller settled at Richmond, became a soldier in his teens, and from 1755-1763 was Richmond Herald. Returning to the military, he rose to Captain in the Surrey militia. He began sketching medieval buildings as early as 1749, sought to become a professional illustrator, and was elected to the Society of Antiquaries in 1757. His *Antiquities of England and Wales*, combining engravings with text, brought him both income and fame. On an antiquarian tour of Scotland in 1789 he became friendly with Robert Burns, who honoured him in two poems, and he is credited with inspiring Burns to write *Tam O' Shanter* to accompany his sketch of Alloway kirk. He also wrote important works on dialect and the vulgar speech of the day.

The splendidly-named but anonymous *Britannica curiosa: or a description of the most remarkable curiosities, natural and artificial, of the island of Great Britain, in the several counties, cities, towns, villages, &c...*, of 1775, tells us of Glastonbury, with an element of hyperbole, that 'This town, for antiquity, claims pre-eminence over every other in the country. Here being an abbey, formerly the richest and most magnificent in the world .. The foundation of this abbey is by some carried back as far as the time of our Saviour, and said to be consecrated by him in person, and by him dedicated to his mother.' He

311 *Op. cit.*, vol. 5, 'Somersetshire,' pp. 28-9.

went on to record that 'Joseph of Arimathea, St. Patrick, and St. David are said by some to have resided here; which has been controverted by others, though it strongly appears, that it was the popular opinion of its being the burial place of Joseph of Arimathea.[312] This too, of course, is merely a somewhat prosaic rendering of the substance of John of Glastonbury, but the matter-of-factness of its reference to Christ, more marked even than in Grose's version, must have puzzled some readers unfamiliar with the medieval Latin original.

Most commentators, however, continued to dwell on the more familiar story of Arimathean Joseph. Virtually alone of the saints in England, Joseph of Arimathea retained a following of a sort in the aftermath of the Reformation, becoming almost, in a paradoxical way, the Patron Saint of English Protestantism. The traditions concerning him continued to grow. The medieval versions of his legend were elaborated in the tradition of the Holy Thorn. By 1677,[313] if not before, the winter-flowering thorn, first mentioned in the Glastonbury verse *Lyfe* of Joseph in 1502, but not there explicitly connected with him, was regarded as having sprouted from his staff or, in some versions, from a slip of the Crown of Thorns, planted by him. The trees, both at Glastonbury and elsewhere throughout England, received much attention following the reform of the calendar in 1752, when many watched them to see whether they would blossom on Christmas Day New Style, or, as proved to be the case, would continue to observe the old date.

The eighteenth-century chapbook *The Holy Disciple, or, The History of Joseph of Arimathea, containing a true account of his birth and parentage; his country education, piety; his begging of Pontius*

---

312 *Op. cit.* vol. 3 (of 6), pp. 261-2. Of onomastic interest is the statement concerning Glastonbury that 'its present name is derived from *Glaustrum*, i.e. Dyers Woad, which abounds in these parts.' I am grateful to Dr Adam Stout for this and the previous reference.

313 See Dr. Robert Plot, 1677, pp. 156-7. Stout, 2007, p. 5, notes the entertainment organised by James Montague, Bishop of Bath and Wells 1608-16, in which the character of Joseph presented James I's queen, Anne of Denmark, with two boughs from the Thorn, citing Richard Broughton, *The Ecclesiastical History of Great Britaine*, Douai, 1633, pp. 110-111.

*Pilate the body of our blessed Saviour, and burying in a sepulchre of
his own. Also, how he came to England and first preach'd the gospel at
Glastenbury [sic] in Somerset-shire, in memory of which, there is still
growing the noted white thorn, that buds every Christmas-day in the
morning, blossoms at noon, and fades at night, where he first pitch'd
his staff in the ground. With his life, death and burial* is now a rare
item. Only around twenty copies survive, with slight variations of title,
but it seems to have been popular and widely distributed in its day.
Its exact date and textual history are uncertain. The British Library
catalogue lists the earliest example as printed by Samuel Farley at
Bath and Bristol in 1719.[314] Another copy may have been printed in
Newcastle around 1740. Seemingly for the first time, it has Joseph
landing at Barrow bay and, after planting his staff at Glastonbury,
going on to conduct mass baptisms in the future episcopal city of
Wells. A version entitled *The History of that Holy Disciple Joseph of
Arimathea* (tentatively dated to 1770) tell us:

> Besides [his work at Glastonbury], as Eusebius, Sozomenes, and
> Ruffinus, three most faithful ecclesiastical writers relate, he baptized
> at the city of Wells, which is within four miles of Glastonbury,
> eighteen thousand persons one day;[315]

Joseph's name was also linked with the mid-eighteenth-century
attempt to establish Glastonbury as a spa following the miraculous
cure claimed by one Matthew Chancellor in May 1751. Chancellor
had been directed by an angel in a dream to drink the water from
a conduit near the Chaingate on Magdalene Street for the relief of
his asthma. The potency of the waters at the Chaingate, to the west

314 Shelfmark RB.23.a.3217.
315 Op. cit. p. 7, Glastonbury Abbey Archive GLSGA: 1988/1436 A23. I am
grateful to Dr. Ball for providing me with a photocopy. Needless to say, the ancient
authors cited make no reference to Joseph or his work at Wells. On the history of
this chapbook, and its relationship to another, *The Wonderful Works of God..,*
concerned with the calendar dispute of 1753, see Stout, 2007, pp. 38-41; (notes)
59-60.

Fig 43. St. Joseph of Arimathea leaning on his staff, and
the Holy Thorn, from the chapbook The History of that
Holy Disciple.., ?1719 (various editions).

of the Abbey, was jocularly associated with the healing influence of
the dust of Joseph and his fellow saints lying in the Abbey grounds,
through which the waters filtered. The water was bottled, and sold
at apothecaries in the Strand in London, an enterprise with which
Henry Fielding, the Glastonbury-born author of Tom Jones, was
associated. The poet-laureate Robert Southey (1774-1843), himself
of a Somerset family, recorded the curious case of a young man who
took fright at the ghost in a performance of Hamlet at Drury Lane.
His humour turned to the king's evil; all other medicines having
failed, he eventually tried Glastonbury waters, and 'Faith healed the
ailment which fear had produced'.[316]

A curious Protestant, and perhaps specifically Quaker, variant of
the medieval versions of the dedication of the Old Church by Christ

316 Gray, 1943, pp. 56-7.

Himself was included by John Clark in the 9th edition, of 1848, of his *Avalonian Guide to the Town of Glastonbury and its Environs*, originally published in 1810. Clark tells us that it is recorded that 'St Joseph and his companions occasionally passed over the water [from Avalon], to *the Place of the great Wells*, afterwards called by the Romans, THEO-DORO-DONUM, or, "The Gift of God," - and where many of the Britons, from the hills of *Mune-depe*, were converted to the Christian faith.' The picture of Joseph evangelising at Wells derives from the mid-eighteenth-century chapbook noted above. The name *Theodorodunum* comes from Camden, who took it from Leland ('but whence he had it I wot not').[317]

Opposite a plate showing a reconstruction of the ancient wooden church, 'The Original Chapel of St. Joseph of Arimathea,' Clark further tells us that:

> It is also recorded by several ancient historians, that after the erection of the Chapel, by Joseph of Arimathea, he was about to *consecrate* the structure to the memory of Mary, the Mother of Christ: but that he was prevented from so doing by Jesus, the Christ, *in propria persona*, informing him that he himself had already consecrated it to the glory and honour of GOD, he alone being worthy of adoration, from everlasting to everlasting.[318]

This attributes to Joseph an experience similar to that vouchsafed to St David in earlier versions, although without the *stigmata*, but completely reverses the sense of these sources, in which it is Christ

---

317 Camden, Somersetshire, 19: 'Southward, not farre from the foresaid [Wookey] hole, where Mendip slopeth downe with a stonie descent, a little citie with an Episcopall Sea is situat beneath at the hill foot, sometime called (as saith Leland), but whence he had it I wot not, *Thodorodunum*, now Welles, so named of the Springs or Wels which boile and walme [well] up here, like as Susa in Persia, Croia in Dalamatia, and Pagase in Macedonia were named of the like fountaines in their countrey speech, whereupon this also in Latine, is called *Fontanensis ecclesia*, as one would say, Fountain-Church.

318 Clark, 1848, p. 5.

Himself who dedicates the church to His mother.

John Clark was born at Greinton in 1785, the son of Thomas Clark, a minister of the Society of Friends, who died at the age of 91 in 1850. Himself an active Quaker, John Clark was also something of an inventor, who projected an electric telegraph, took out a patent for the construction of india rubber air beds and cushions, and, also in 1848, published a 'description of a machine for composing hexameter Latin verses.' The expansion of his section on Joseph of Arimathea in the 9th edition of the *Avalonian Guide* seems to have been stimulated by the appearance of the Rev. W. Phelps' *History and Antiquities of Somersetshire* in 1836, to which work he refers in his introduction. Although he makes no mention of Joseph following the tin-trader's routes, as suggested by Phelps, he did record that the spot where Joseph's Holy Thorn was thought to have grown 'is

Fig 44. Memorial stone on Glastonbury's Wirrall (Wearyall) Hill, marking the supposed site of the Holy Thorn (19th century). The present small specimen tree beside it was planted in 1951 to mark the Festival of Britain. The original Thorn was actually further south-west, beside modern Roman Way.

*Fig 45. The Old Church as reconstructed in
Clark, Avalonian Guide, 1848, p. 4. Here,
appropriate wattle panels have been inserted
between the massive oak trunks as imagined in
Phelps, 1836 (see above p. 24).*

now [1848] marked by a Monumental Stone, laid on the ground,
and bearing the inscription, I.A. A.D. XXXI.' The stone still exists,
although the inscription may now hardly be discerned. The date of
AD 31, so much earlier than that of AD 63 claimed by the medieval
abbey, reflects Phelps' reference to Spelman's (erroneous) attribution
to Gildas of the statement that Joseph brought the Gospel to Britain
in AD 33.[319] Clark followed Phelps in including in his 9th edition
a woodcut of the 'Old Church', derived from that of Spelman but
more 'authentic' in that it showed panels of wicker-work between
wooden uprights.

The appearance of Christ at Glastonbury in his own 'very
person', and referring to His own past actions there, is suggestive.
The Glastonbury *mythos* was beginning a renewed local evolution
in unexpected directions. The *Avalonian Guide* was widely used by
visitors to the town, and after John Clark's death at Bridgwater in

319 Phelps, 1836, vol. 1, p. 42.

1853, two further editions, in 1855 and 1857, were revised by his son Thomas.

Alfred, Lord Tennyson in 1869 published *The Holy Grail and Other Poems*. *The Holy Grail* formed part of his Arthurian cycle, *The Idylls of the King*. In this he remedied the omission of the Holy Grail from Glastonbury's own medieval legendary accounts of itself, and, perhaps for the first time, had Joseph bring the Cup - 'the phantom of a cup that comes and goes' - itself thither. Having taken the cowl in a monastery 'far away from Camelot,' Sir Percivale tells a fellow-monk of:

> 'The cup, the cup itself, from which our Lord
> Drank at the last sad supper with his own,
> This, from the blessed land of Aromat -
> After the day of darkness, when the dead
> Went wandering o'er Moriah[320] - the good saint
> Arimathean Joseph, journeying brought
> To Glastonbury, where the winter thorn
> Blossoms at Christmas, mindful of our Lord.
> And ther awhile it bode; and if a man
> Could touch or see it, he was heal'd at once,
> By faith, of all his ills. But then the times
> Grew to such evil that the holy cup
> Was caught away to Heaven, and disappear'd.'

Tennyson's wife, Emily, *née* Sellwood, believed herself to be 'of the same name and race' as the fifteenth-century Abbot of Glastonbury, John Selwood, and Tennyson had visited Glastonbury with her in 1850 in the course of a honeymoon tour. Tennyson was briefly there again in 1854.[321]

---

320 Moriah is a biblical name applied to Jerusalem, especially to the Temple Mount. The reference is to the breaking open of tombs in an earthquake which accompanied Christ's death on the Cross, and the dead rising and going 'into the holy city,' as told in *Matthew* 27:52-3.
321 Tennyson, Hallam, 1906, pp. 278-79; 316-17.

Emily had encouraged her husband to overcome his reluctance to write the poem, and its Avalonian elements may have been a tribute to her.

Tennyson's poetic cycle had great influence on the Victorian revival of interest in things Arthurian. His poems were a source of inspiration to the artists of the Pre-Raphaelite Brotherhood, whose interpretations were formative to the Victorian visual imagination, and embraced both the biblical and the romantically historical. In 1850, John Everett Millais' painting, now in the Tate, of *Christ in the House of His Parents* had shocked contemporaries with its vivid departure from the conventions of religious art. The Christ-child - 'a hideous .. red-haired boy in a night-gown,' according to Charles Dickens - has injured the palm of his hand in Joseph the Carpenter's workshop, the blood dripping onto his foot, foreshadowing the nail-wounds of the Crucifixion. As His parents comfort Him, His cousin John the Baptist fetches a bowl of water, seemingly to cleanse the wound, while through the doorway we see sheep penned in a pastoral landscape. The workaday realism of the scene anticipates the blend of the mystical and the prosaic which we find in the voyage-story, and despite an attempt at Middle-Eastern authenticity in the inclusion of a *shaduf* or water-raising device in the background, it has a very English feel.

Of closely allied sensibility is Holman Hunt's *A Converted British Family Sheltering a Christian Priest from the Persecution of the Druids*, now in the Ashmolean Museum, Oxford, which hung beside his friend Millais' work in that same Royal Academy exhibition of 1850. In a shelter of boughs, with eucharistic corn-stalks and grapevines woven into its thatch, beside reedy water, which may well be intended to reflect marshy Glastonbury and the 'church of boughs,' slumps an exhausted Roman figure in alb and mantle, tended by a group of agitated and shaggy Britons. His Christ-like character is emphasised by a wound on his brow, which a young, red-haired, well-dressed, girl is about to bathe with a bowl of water, while (presumably) her sister, bare-foot and naked to the waist, her long hair flowing, stoops to remove a bramble which has snagged in his alb by his sandled feet.

Fig 46. Christ in the House of His Parents, 1849, John Everett Millais (1829-1896), Tate Britain, London.

Fig 47. A Converted British Family Sheltering a Christian Priest from the Persecution of the Druids, 1850, William Holman Hunt (1827-1910), Ashmolean Museum, Oxford. The renowned Lizzie Siddal modelled the two 'sisters.'

We are seemingly intended to see in these two a reminder of practical Martha of Bethany, and of her sister Mary in the persona of the Magdalene, the sinner who bathed Christ's feet with her hair. In the background we see a second missionary-priest being apprehended by a hostile crowd urged on by a druid, who stands within a stone circle. This setting places the notional date at some point prior to Roman military occupation. Here we have biblical imagery set quite consciously in the south of Britain in the context of the apostolic era. The voyage-story might almost represent a blending of these two well-known and linked Victorian paintings.

Probably as a reflection of Tennyson's *The Holy Grail*, there arose at Glastonbury a local belief that Joseph had hidden the Grail at Glastonbury's Chalice Well or on nearby Chalice Hill. Although the suggestive names are apparently as old as the eighteenth century, they seem to be a corruption of the older *Chilkwell*, signifying a mineral spring, preserved in Chilkwell Street. As we have noted, the association with the Grail was first recorded in 1886 in a talk by G. W. Wright to the Glastonbury Antiquarian Society.[322] In the previous year, the property containing the Well had been acquired by a French Roman Catholic order as a seminary. Its chapel served local Roman Catholics as a place of worship, they having no parish church at this date, and the seminarians actively promoted the idea of the Well and its waters as not merely therapeutic, but holy.

This last development brings us to the period immediately before the appearance in print of the Jesus-voyage 'tradition' in 1895. The broad period between the appearance of Heane's edition of John of Glastonbury in 1728, and *c.*1890, then, is probably the one in which we should seek the emergence of the story. Central to this period was the life of William Blake (1757-1827), to whose possible place in its development we should now turn.

---

322 Printed in their *Proceedings* in the following year, Wright 1887. See also Ashdown, 2005.

Fig 48. *Joseph of Arimathea Among the Rocks of Albion*, an engraving by William Blake (1757-1827) in its second state of c. 1800-1810, British Library.

16

AND DID THOSE FEET IN ANCIENT TIME ...?

It was the often perceptive writings of Geoffrey Ashe and fashionable developments in 'Arthurian' archaeology which were largely responsible for a revival of enthusiasm for Glastonbury in the 1960s. For the first time since the 'Avalonian' high tide of the early 1920s, Glastonbury came to be seen as a focus for a sense of national identity which ran deeper than the surface-currents of football and royal matrimony. *King Arthur's Avalon, the Story of Glastonbury*, appeared in 1957. Writing from a Roman Catholic background and with an awareness of the historical importance there of the cult of the Virgin Mary, in the dedication of the first edition Geoffrey expressed the hope that England might again 'become conscious of Glastonbury'. He can hardly have foreseen the scale of his success. Of the voyage story he wrote:

> Blake's poem *And did those feet in ancient time* (a true alternative National Anthem) is doubtless the finest piece of writing which Glastonbury has so far inspired. Characteristically, Blake uses one of the strangest fancies of all. No medieval Benedictine would have dared affirm such a thing: it was left to the Age of Reason to devise it. This fancy, of course, is the supposition that Christ himself came to Glastonbury as a youth with Joseph of Arimathea. It is presumably based on two passages in the early historians - the reference in the *Life of Dunstan* to a church "not built by art of man, but prepared by God himself," and the vision of St. David in William of Malmesbury ... From these texts taken together it is

possible to extract the notion that the Incarnate God visited Britain and built the church, before beginning his public ministry.

Where did this fable come from? I do not know. There are said to be some wild scraps of Cornish and Mendip folk-lore with a bearing on it, and there is certainly a connection with eighteenth-century academic extravaganzas about the druids. By embedding it in his verse, Blake ensures that he would be misunderstood; most people who read or sing his lines take them in a not very lucid metaphorical sense, because the literal sense is too far-fetched to occur to them. Yet Blake's instinct was sound. Glastonbury is England's only real national shrine, and a Glastonbury legend, however unlikely, is one of the few adequate themes for a national hymn.[323]

His assurance that Blake's 'lyric' was indeed based on Glastonbury legend was endorsed by no less a literary luminary than Robert Graves, who felt that a few references in *The White Goddess*, 1948, had made him an expert on Glastonbury tradition. In a sneering review in *Time and Tide* he wrote 'Mr. Ashe ... likes to believe that the Joseph of Arimathea legend is not necessarily a lie. Here he is, of course, in good company. William Blake liked to believe in the legend that the child Jesus himself visited Glastonbury in Joseph of Arimathea's company: *And did those feet in ancient times ...*'[324] A quarter of a century later, Geoffrey Ashe himself was less certain, both of medieval hints and of Blake's cognisance. In *Avalonian Quest*, 1982, he wrote:

One further belief is famous, beloved, and impossible to trace to its source. ... Part of the belief is that 'Christ walked in Priddy',[325] a village on the Mendips. Sceptics maintain that the whole notion began with a children's play, written in Victorian days by the village

323 Ashe, 1957, pp. 350-351.
324 Graves, R., 1958, p. 46.
325 This seems to offer yet another variant on the Mendip 'saying'.

schoolmistress: an innocent piece of fantasy which, like other pieces of fantasy, became an ancient Somerset legend. However, William Blake's lines ... might be held to imply a previous version. No one knows. What is morally certain is that if the belief had existed in the Middle Ages, as an authentic local folk-tale, Glastonbury's monks would have exploited such a stupendous distinction. They never even hint at it.[326]

In between these two accounts, he had written *Camelot and the Vision of Albion*, 1971, for which he had made a more detailed study of the relevant writings of Blake, doubtless discovering the scantiness of the evidence for Blake's knowledge of the 'legend.' Here he wrote:

Blake may be referring to one of the odder offshoots of the Arthur-Grail imbroglio, the belief that Jesus visited Britain as a boy, lived at Priddy in the Mendips, and built the first wattle cabin at Glastonbury. This tale seems to have arisen quite recently - perhaps, indeed, too recently for Blake to have heard it - from a misunderstanding of one of the legends about the Old Church.[327]

Edith Ditmas, in her workmanlike *Traditions and Legends of Glastonbury*, 1979, was perhaps influenced by this assessment when she wrote: 'The visit of Christ as a boy to Britain, some say to Cornwall, others to Somerset, is an attractive proposition but it probably stems from romantic speculations of the Victorian era'.[328] In truth, and sadly for supporters of the antiquity of the voyage-story, Blake paid but scant attention to Somerset in his writings. 'And the Forty Counties of England are thus divided in the Gates [of Jerusalem]: ... Judah: Somerset, Gloster, Wiltshire' [*Jerusalem*

326 Ashe, 1982, pp.96-97.
327 Ashe, 1971 [p. 180 pbk ed.]
328 Ditmas, 1979, p. 14.

K637];[329] Judah is, indeed, the tribe of Christ. The Severn, 'Sabrina beautiful', is counted among the 'lovely Daughters of Albion' [*Jerusalem* K624]; Kwantok is numbered among 'the terrible sons ... of Albion' [*Jerusalem* K623 etc.] but although his name echoes that of the Quantock Hills, he represents John Guantock, M.P., a judge at Blake's trial for sedition in 1804. Bath is, perhaps predictably, the 'healing City ... mild Physician of Eternity, mysterious power Whose springs are unsearchable & knowledge infinite' [*Jerusalem* K675-6]. Blake included him, in preference to his episcopal twin, Wells, among the Cathedral Cities. He is identified as 'Legions' (*recte* Caerleon) in *Jerusalem* [K668], although in *Milton* [K531] he ranks 'London & Bath & Legions & Edinburgh' as Albion's 'rocks .. the four pillars of his Throne.' In *Jerusalem*, in a darker aspect:

> And Rahab, Babylon the Great, hath destroyed Jerusalem.
> Bath stood upon the Severn with Merlin & Bladud & Arthur,
> The Cup of Rahab in his hand, her Poisons Twenty-seven-fold.
>
> [K715]

Bladud is the legendary pre-Roman British king who supposedly founded Bath, and Rahab the Jericho working-girl from the *Book of Joshua* who stands in for the Whore of Babylon in the writings of Blake, who gives her a complex mythology of her own. This is a meagre harvest for those who would see in Somerset's Mendip Hills those 'England's mountains green' of Blake's most famous lines, rendering superfluous Dobson's unsupported speculations about distant connections with Somerset families of Blakes. He showed no interest in Glastonbury itself. Neither under that name, nor as Avalon, does it figure in his list of the Cathedral Cities of Britain, nor among the many names of British places which he interwove

---

329 References to Blake's writings are by page to the edition of Geoffrey Keynes [K..], Oxford Standard Authors, 1966 *et seq.* (see p.53, note 69 above).

with Biblical ones throughout his poetry.[330] This in itself is rather odd, as the two figures most closely associated with Glastonbury in tradition, Joseph of Arimathea and Arthur, figure as major presences in the works of Blake.

As an apprentice of sixteen, Blake engraved the figure of a man taken from a centurion in Michaelangelo's 'Crucifixion of St Peter' in the Pauline Chapel in Rome. It is his earliest surviving original engraving. On the unique impression of the first state he wrote 'Engraved when I was a beginner at Basire's, from a drawing of Salviati[331] after Michael Angelo'. Blake was apprenticed to James Basire, of Great Queen Street, to learn the 'Art and Mystery' of engraving in 1772. Basire sent him out to make drawings of the tombs in Westminster Abbey, where he learned a love of the English Gothic, and, as he said, experienced 'his 'earliest and most sacred recollections'.[332] He was present at the opening of the tomb of Edward I in 1774. 'Probably after 1800'[333] he almost completely re-worked the plate of his engraving with the inscription:

'Joseph of Arimathea among The Rocks of Albion. This is One of the Gothic Artists who Built the Cathedrals in what we call the Dark Ages, Wandering about in sheep skins & goat skins, of whom the World was not worthy; such were the Christians in all Ages. Michael Angelo Pinxit. Engraved by W. Blake 1773 from an old Italian Drawing.' [K604][334]

The description of the early Christians is adapted from *Hebrews* 11:37-38, on the prophets. The reference to Joseph as a builder, with its Masonic ring, might be a reference to his building of Glastonbury's

---

330 Eg. 'Jehovah stood among the Druids in the Valley of Annandale', *Jerusalem*, K696.

331 The engraving was in fact by Beatrizet. Bindman, 1977, plate 1.

332 Ackroyd, 1995, p. 44.

333 Wilson, 1927/1971, p. 6, footnote.

334 Line engraving, 22.8 x 12 cm., British Library; Raine, 1970, illus. 3, p.10 (b&w).

Fig 49. Blake's engraving of Joseph of Arimathea, approx.
23 x 12 cm.' first state, 1773 (left, in private hands) and
second state, c.1800-10 (right, British Library), compared.

first church and is so taken by Damon;[335] but Joseph was also linked
to London, having supposedly carved a crucifix, the 'Rood at the
North Door,' which found a home over the north door of Old St Paul's
and became a focus of pilgrimage. According to the chronicler John
Hardynge (before 1457) it was cast into the sea near Caerleon and
was eventually washed up in the Thames at London in the time of

335 Damon, 1965, 1979, pp. 224-5.

King Lucius. This crucifix was also mentioned in Glastonbury's verse *Lyfe of Joseph of Armathea* [sic] of 1502, and in William Dugdale's *History of St Paul's Cathedral* of 1658, from whence the tradition might have found its way to Blake.[336]

Some have thought Blake's title an after-thought, but Ackroyd writes: 'He was, for Blake the first Gothic architect and the direct progenitor of Westminster Abbey, which was soon to encompass and engross him.' He notes Joseph's role in Protestant iconography, and his inclusion by John Foxe in his 'Book of Martyrs.' Blake, indeed, may have been following Foxe in dissociating Joseph from Glastonbury, for in his pages, although the tradition of Joseph's coming is approved of, Glastonbury is not mentioned in connection with him. Foxe followed those sources which regarded Glastonbury as a foundation of the Saxon king Ine (688-728), and Dunstan, Glastonbury's greatest abbot, is not portrayed sympathetically in his history.

Ackroyd suggests that Joseph could be seen as an English prophet and that Blake, also, could be set in the tradition of London's Dissenting prophets of the sixteenth and seventeenth centuries. He remarks that 'an entire culture of urban dissent and religious radicalism may be momentarily glimpsed in Blake's work of this kind. There was once an oral tradition, conveying beliefs and attitudes from generation to generation of Londoners, which is now quite lost - in the poems and images of Blake, however, we seem partially able to recall it before it slips once more into darkness.'[337] He further notes that in a poem written while Blake was still an apprentice is the line 'Liberty shall stand upon the cliffs of Albion', virtually duplicating the 'Rocks of Albion.' He thinks one source for the Joseph figure is an image of a druid in William Stukeley's *Stonehenge: A Temple Restored to the British Druids* (1740), and takes this to indicate that, even when young, 'his interest in British

---

336 Riddy, 1991, pp. 325-6; Dugdale, *op. cit.*, 1658, p. 20; Skeat, 1871/1996, pp. xlvii, 44, lines 217-24. See also D. Keene et. al, eds. St Paul's, the Cathedral Church of London, Yale, 2004, p. 40.
337 Ackroyd, 1995, pp. 40-41.

antiquity and in ancient religion was not confined to his engraving work for Basire.' Ackroyd states that 'there may also be a more homely connection' in that the sister of Henry Pars, proprieter of the drawing school in the Strand which Blake attended from from 1767 to 1772, and who taught there, 'had just been depicting Joseph of Arimathea on some Wedgwood crockery for the Empress of Russia.'[338] This is the so-called 'Green Frog Service,' called 'perhaps the most famous dinner service in Europe,' now in the Hermitage Museum, St Petersburg. The little creature appears on many items as a crest, the original Finnish name for the location of the palace for which it was intended translating as 'frog marsh.' It is a splendid creamware dinner and dessert service of 944 pieces, depicting picturesque British scenes for the Anglophile Catherine II. Ordered in 1773, it was exhibited in Wedgwood's London showrooms at Portland House, Greek Street, Soho, before despatch in 1774. However, although it includes views (among many other places) of Glastonbury and its ruins from contemporary drawings, including three by Francis Grose (see below), it does not show Joseph of Arimathea. Anne Pars, a ceramic painter and sister to the artists Henry and William Pars, did indeed work on the service at Chelsea in June 1774, but only on the twig baskets, which have no views.[339]

Blake himself clearly valued his image, keeping the plate for the rest of his life, re-engraving it a quarter of a century later, and making proofs as late as 1825. In *The Four Zoas* (1795-1804) Joseph is equated with Los, Blake's Hephaistos-like figure, who represents creative imagination and artistic labour:

> Los took the Body from the Cross, Jerusalem weeping over;
> They bore it to the Sepulchre which Los had hewn in the rock
> Of Eternity for himself: he hew'd it despairing of Life Eternal.
>
> [K349 see also 356]

338 Ackroyd, 1995, p. 42.
339 Raeburn *etc.*, 1995, pp. 16; 27; 40; 72; 77; 331-2; 416-7.

Joseph also figures in what Damon calls an 'enigmatic trifle' in a MS notebook of 1808-11:

> I will tell you what Joseph of Arimathea
> Said to my Fairy - was not it very queer?
> Pliny and Trajan! What are you here?
> Come listen to Joseph of Arimathea:
> Listen patient, & when Joseph has done
> 'Twill make a fool laugh & a Fairy Fun.
>
> [K552]

Trajan and Pliny the Younger had corresponded about the suppression of Christians in Asia Minor, where Pliny was a governor, in AD 112. Blake may be thinking of the folk-belief that the coming of Christianity had frightened the fairies away, and implying that his - and Joseph's - brand held no threat for them.

There also exists a coloured relief-etching of 1794 by Blake, featuring a patriarchal figure in white holding a staff, sometimes called *Joseph of Arimathea Preaching to the Inhabitants of Britain*.[340] Similarly depicted, in white with a staff, but here also holding an urn of spices, Joseph is the dominant figure in *The Procession from Calvary* or *The Body of Christ Borne to the Tomb*, *c.* 1799-1800.[341] Joseph also appears, with Nicodemus, in the pen and watercolour work *The Entombment* or *Joseph Burying Jesus*, of c. *1805*, with the three Marys (here, Mary the Virgin, Mary Magdalene and Mary, wife of Cleophas) standing in the doorway of the tomb.[342] Joseph, then, was a figure of personal significance to Blake during most of

340 7.7 x 10.7 cm, British Library; Raine, 1970, illus. 70, p.92 (colour). Damon, 1965, p. 225, however, questions the validity of this title on subjective grounds.
341 Tempura on canvas, 26.6 x 37.7 cm., Tate Gallery; Raine, 1970, illus. 78, p.103 (b&w); Ackroyd, 1997, colour plate, un-numbered.
342 Pen and watercolour, 417x310 cm., Tate Gallery, Butlin, 1990, p. 130 & plate 48. A small tempera painting of 1799-1800, also called *The Entombmet*, features either Joseph or Nicodemus (*ibid.*).

his creative life.

The figure of Arthur loomed even larger. From May to September 1809 Blake staged an exhibition at his brother's shop in Broad Street, Soho. One painting was of *The Bard, from Gray*. This, however, was not the major work. 'Dominating the exhibition was a painting, since lost, which he considered his most important work and was unlike anything else he ever did'.[343] Entitled *The Ancient Britons*, it was at fourteen feet by ten his largest work, far larger, in fact, than most of his pictures. The poet Southey thought it 'one of his worst pictures - which is saying much', although one of Swinburne's informants was more favourably impressed. It depicts the aftermath of Arthur's last battle. In his *Descriptive Catalogue* for the exhibition, Blake gave a long descriptive explanation of the painting :

NUMBER V
The Ancient Britons

In the last Battle of King Arthur, only Three Britons escaped; these were the Strongest Man, the Beautifullest Man, and the Ugliest Man; these three marched through the field unsubdued, as Gods, and the Sun of Britain set, but shall arise again with tenfold splendour when Arthur shall awake from sleep, and resume his dominion over earth and ocean.

... The British Antiquities are now in the Artist's hands; all his visionary contemplations, relating to his own country and its ancient glory, when it was, as it again shall be, the source of learning and inspiration. Arthur was a name for the constellation Arcturus, or Bootes, the keeper of the North Pole. And all the fables of Arthur and his round table; of the war-like naked Britons; of Merlin; of Arthur's conquest of the whole world; of his death, or sleep, and promise to return again; of the Druid monuments or temples; ... of the elemental beings called by us by the general

343 Williams, Gwyn A. 1994, p.187.

name of fairies; and of these three who escaped, namely Beauty, Strength, and Ugliness. Mr. B. [Blake] has in his hands poems of the highest antiquity. Adam was a Druid, and Noah; also Abraham was called to succeed the Druidical age, which began to turn allegoric and mental signification into corporeal command, whereby human sacrifice would have depopulated the earth. All these things are written in Eden. The artist is an inhabitant of that happy country; and if every thing goes on as it has begun, the world of vegetation and generation may expect to be opened again to Heaven, through Eden, as it was in the beginning.

The Strong Man represents the human sublime. The Beautiful Man represents the human pathetic, which was in the wars of Eden divided into male and female. The Ugly Man represents the human reason. They were originally one man, who was fourfold; he was selfdivided, and his real humanity slain on the stems of generation, and the form of the fourth was like the Son of God. How he became divided is a subject of great sublimity and pathos. The Artist [Blake] has written it under inspiration, and will, if God please, publish it; it is voluminous, and contains the ancient history of Britain, and the world of Satan and Adam.

In the mean time he has painted this Picture, which supposes that in the reign of that British Prince, who lived in the fifth century, there were remains of those naked Heroes in the Welch Mountains; they are there now, Gray saw them in the person of his bard on Snowdon; there they dwell in naked simplicity; happy is he who can see and converse with them above the shadows of generation and death. The giant Albion, was Patriarch of the Atlantic; he is the Atlas of the Greeks, one of those the Greeks called Titans. The stories of Arthur are the acts of Albion, applied to a Prince of the fifth century, who conquered Europe, and held the Empire of the world in the dark age, which the Romans never again recovered. In this Picture, believing with Milton the ancient British History, Mr. B. has done as the ancients did … and not in the dull way that some Historians pretend, who, being weakly organised themselves, cannot see either miracle or prodigy; all is to them a dull round of probabilities and possibilities; but the history of all times and places is nothing else but improbabilities and impossibilities; what we should say was impossible if we did not see it always before our eyes.

> The antiquities of every Nation under Heaven, is no less sacred than that of the Jews. ... All had originally one language, and one religion: this was the religion of Jesus, the everlasting Gospel. Antiquity preaches the Gospel of Jesus. [Kqw577-579]

Here, in his own words, Blake explains his use of history, both legendary and Biblical. His interest is in the mythic, the cosmic, significance, not in the letter. Even within the old 'British History' of Geoffrey of Monmouth, which conventional historians no longer believed, and of Malory, Arthur's last battle of Camlan was fought against the British rebels of his wicked nephew-son Mordred, as Blake would well have know, but for the purposes of his picture, Blake imagines his antagonists to have been the Romans. It is, on one level, an aspect of the struggle between Classicism and the Gothic for Britain's artistic soul, one of his favourite themes and the context of his famous 'lyric' (see below).

Blake's acquaintance with antiquarian lore is, none the less, not to be underestimated. In the advertisement for the exhibition, Blake's painting is further described:

THE ANCIENT BRITONS - Three Ancient Britons overthrowing the Army of armed Romans; the Figures full as large as Life -

From the Welch Triades.
In the last Battle that Arthur fought,
the most Beautiful was one
That return'd, and the most Strong another:
with them also return'd
The most Ugly, and no other beside
return'd from the bloody Field.
The most Beautiful, the Roman Warriors

> trembled before and worshipped;
> The most Strong, they melted before him
> and dissolved in his presence:
> The most Ugly they fled with outcries
> and contortion of their Limbs.

[K560]

Of these six lines of verse, the Welsh historian Gwyn Williams writes: 'This seems to be the first English translation of an authentic Welsh triad of the Middle Ages', although it is, in fact, of the nature of a paraphrase.[344] Its actual source was no. 85 of the 'Welch Triades' in the *Myvyrian Archaiology* (1st series, ii, London 1801-7). Blake's source was William Owen (1759-1835), born in Merioneth, who came to London in 1776. Owen, who later changed his name to Owen Pughe, did much of the work on the *Archaiology*. It was he who apparently commissioned, and subsequently bought, *The Ancient Britons*, or a copy of it. Owen probably became acquainted with Blake through the engraver William Sharp, himself a devotee of Richard Brothers and Joanna Southcott. 'Pughe was one of Joanna Southcott's "Elders" and was open to all forms of millenarian belief; he had once been a political radical, during the revolutionary years of the previous century, but now espoused a complicated mixture of Druidic allegory, Arthurian lore and comparative mythology that made so powerful an appeal to Blake himself.'[345]

Robert Southey, who had been interested by Blake's Exhibition, went to see Blake in 1811. As his friend Crabb Robinson recorded in his diary:

Late to C. Lamb's. Found a very large party there. Southey had been with Blake & admired both his designs & his poetic talents

---

344 Williams, 1994, p.188. Damon, 1965, p. 443, pleasingly and economically describes the Triads as 'a mnemonic and aphoristic form, peculiar to the Welsh bards, in which characters or statements were arranged in groups of three'.
345 Ackroyd, 1995, p. 305, with refs.

at the same time that he held him for a decided madman. Blake, he says, spoke of his visions with the diffidence that is usual with such people & did not seem to expect that he shd. be believed. He showed S[outhey] a perfectly mad poem called *Jerusalem*. Oxford Street is in Jerusalem.[346]

Nearly twenty years later Southey described the visit with hindsight:

Much as he is to be admired, he was at the time so evidently insane, that the predominant feeling in conversing with him, or even looking at him, could only be sorrow and compassion. His wife partook of his insanity in the same way (but more happily) as Taylor the pagan's wife caught her husband's paganism. And there are always crazy people enough in the world to feed and foster such craziness as his. My old acquaintance William Owen, now Owen Pugh, who, for love of his native tongue, composed a most laborious Welsh Dictionary, without the slightest remuneration for his labour, when he was in straitened circumstances, and has, since he became rich, translated *Paradise Lost* into Welsh verse, found our Blake after the death of Joanna Southcote, one of whose four-and-twenty elders he was. Poor Owen found everything which he wished to find in the Bardic system, and there he found Blake's notions, and thus Blake and his wife were persuaded that his dreams were old patriarchal truths, long forgotten, and now re-revealed. They told me this, and I, who well knew the muddy nature of Owen's head, knew what his opinion upon such a subject was worth. I came away from the visit with so sad a feeling that I never repeated it. ... You could not have delighted in him [Blake] - his madness was too evident, too fearful. It gave his eyes an expression such as you would expect to see in one who was possessed.[347]

346 24 July, 1811. Quoted by Wilson, M., 1948/1971, p. 268.
347 *Correspondence*, Dublin, 1881, p.194, quoted by Wilson, M., 1948/1971 p.269.

A less patronising view of Owen may be found in Gwyn Williams'
Madoc, 1979, and the supposed adventures of the medieval Welsh
Prince Madoc in the Americas furnished Southey himself with a poetic
theme. Owen edited the medieval *Llywarch Hen* poems in 1792,
and his Welsh dictionary was produced between 1793 and 1803.[348]
Southey was mistaken in believing Blake's acquaintance with Owen
to date only from Joanna Southcotte's death in 1814. Owen was a
member of a group of nationalistically minded London Welshmen led
by another friend of Southey's, Edward Williams (1747-1826), better
remembered by his bardic name of Iolo Morganwg. Williams was a
druidic enthusiast, who founded the *Gorsedd* of the Order of Bards,
the origin of the Welsh National Eisteddford. The first gathering
was held on Primrose Hill in London in 1792, a site which has held
significance for neo-druids ever since. Williams and Owen, with one
Owen Jones, who financed it, were the joint editors of the *Myvyrian
Archaiology of Wales*, whose title refers to Jones's nickname of *Myfyr*
(Scholar). This group was active, and sometimes creative, in the study
of Welsh antiquities. Williams has acquired a reputation similar to
that of the Scot Macpherson, who 'faked' the Ossian cycle of poetry
from ancient Gaelic fragments and from his own imagination.

If Blake was not interested in Glastonbury, Williams, who spent
a year in Somerset in 1785, may have been. In the 'Third Series of
Triads' in the *Myvyrian Archaiology*, 1801, compiled by Williams
from unknown sources, is the first record of a triad (no. 84) which
names Glastonbury among the 'Three chief perpetual choirs of the
Island of Britain'.[349] In *Y Greal* 7, in 1807, an edition of the longer,
B, text of the Welsh *Buchedd Collen*, (*Life of St Collen*), part of
which is set in Glastonbury, was published from 'a book loaned from
Llanvynydd to Iolo Morganwg ... February, 1800'.

Merlin and Gwinivera (as well as Boadicea and Brittannia, figures
not found in the 'British History') also have a minor role in the
mythology which Blake spun for Britain. Gwyn Williams suggests that

348 Williams, 1979, pp. 108-9.
349 Trans. *c.* 1823 by W. Probert; ed. Malcolm Smith, 1977, p. 57.

Blake's depiction of Milton in his poem of that name, the location of
And did those feet ..?, is influenced by the figure of the Welsh mystic
bard Taliesin as well as that of Virgil. In assessing Blake's contribution
to Arthurian art and literature he writes 'This breathtaking perception
of Arthur as a symbol of humanity, shot through with a mystic vision
of aboriginal human unity centred on Albion - Britain - was the most
unexpected and rapid reincarnation the Hero of the Britons ever
experienced.'[350] This view of Arthur is instructive. William Owen, in
his *Cambrian History*, 1803,[351] identified Arthur with the constellation
of the Great Bear and suggested that the circumpolar constellations
were the origin of the Round Table. Blake likewise makes Arthur
the keeper of the Pole. However, Arthur's association with war, and
the courtly love of Arthurian romance, and Arthur's own cuckoldry,
productive, according to Blake, of an unhealthy and unbalanced
female dominance, were uncongenial to him. It is Arthur as a symbol,
not as an historical or even legendary figure, who interests Blake.

In the same decade in which Blake penned *And did those feet ..?*
then, he was deep in Arthurian study under the influence of the London
Welsh antiquaries, whose interests also touched the Glastonbury
legends as seen from a Welsh perspective. Glastonbury's own supposed
connection with druidry and ancient British paganism became a *topos*
with the appearance of Warner's *An History of the Abbey of Glaston;
and of the Town of Glastonbury* in 1826,[352] and it may not have been
new speculation even then. Blake had much to say about the Druids,
deriving his ideas from Milton and from Stukeley and the antiquaries
and mythologisers who followed him. But unlike Williams and Owen,
his attitude to them was at best ambiguous. He accepted them as
demonstrative of Britain's place as the ancient seat of the religion of
the patriarchs, but he also felt that they had degenerated to a cult of
false moral codes, guilt and blood-sacrifice. 'Hence the Infernal Veil
grows in the disobedient Female, Which Jesus rends & the whole

350 Williams, Gwyn A. 1994, p.187-9.
351 p. 15.
352 Warner, 1826, p. xxiii.

Druid Law removes away From the Inner Sanctuary …' [*Jerusalem* K708], the reference being to the Veil of the Temple, rent from top to bottom at the Crucifixion.[353] Unlike Stukeley, the Welsh mystics, and their successors from Morgan to Bligh Bond and Dobson, Blake did not identify druidry with the 'Everlasting Gospel' of Jesus.[354] His vision of them was more akin to that of A. G. Chant.

Blake's Albion, a personification taken from Holinshed and Spencer, is 'patriarch of the Atlantic Continent, whose History Preceded that of the Hebrews & in whose Sleep, or Chaos, Creation began'.[355] For Blake (anticipating modern plate tectonics), the Atlantic continent embraced America and the British Isles, before the Flood submerged much of it and sundered the two. This antediluvian epoch, rather than the first century of our era, is, in all probability, the 'ancient time' of *And did those feet ..?* Atlantis is the site of Eden, as in later pseudo-histories of the nineteenth century, and in particular the use of that myth by Helena Blavatsky, founder of the Theosophical Society; in a manner, also, anticipating the Mormons, for whom, far from being 'unvisited, unblessed,' the Americas had had their own revelation.

It is quite likely, too, that Blake would have read the popularising topography of the anonymous *Britannica curiosa* of 1775, which appeared when he was engaged in antiquarian study while apprenticed at Basire's and seemingly already drawn to the figure of Joseph of Arimathea, which recorded of Glastonbury that 'The foundation of this abbey is by some carried back as far as the time of our Saviour, and said to be consecrated by him in person, and by him dedicated to his mother,' and *The Antiquities of England and Wales* of Francis Grose, completed by 1787, who wrote of the wattle church constructed by Joseph that 'The legend says it was consecrated by Christ in person, and by him dedicated to the honour of his mother.'

---

353 And perhaps, in Blake's strange personal 'tantra,' to the biological maidenhead. See his illustration to *Vala or The Four Zoas*, reproduced in Schuchard, p. 42.
354 On Blake and the Druids see Fisher, 1959; Damon, 1965, 1979, pp. 108-110.
355 *A Vision of the Last Judgement*, K609.

Some might consider these references alone, divorced as they are from their true historical context, sufficient stimulus to Blake's brooding and mystical imagination, reinforced as this constantly was by the *milieu* in which he moved.

Blake's links with the world of the esoteric and the occult were considerable and of long standing. His mother is now known to have worshipped, before her marriage to Blake's father, at the Moravian Chapel in Fetter Lane which also played host to Emanuel Swedenborg. Besides Swedenborg, Blake himself was also influenced by the older alchemical writings of Paracelsus, and of Jocob Boehme (whom he knew as Behmen), and he was close to personalities in the first nineteenth-century revival of ceremonial magic.[356] Although Blake himself does not seem to have been a Freemason, the Freemason's Hall and Tavern stood opposite Basire's in Great Queen Street where he was seven years an apprentice. His father is recorded as having been a Mason between 1757 and 1761.[357] Many of his friends were Masons and Masonic imagery occurs in his work, most familiarly in *The Ancient of Days*, 1794, in which the God of the Old Testament (albeit illustrating *Proverbs* 8:27 - 'he set a compass upon the face of the depth') holds the compasses of the Masonic 'Great Architect of the Universe.'

In a little-known watercolour of the boy Jesus, set in a wooden-framed building representing the workshop at Nazareth and entitled *The Humility of the Saviour*, or *Christ in the Carpenter's Shop c. 1803*,[358] a naked Christ-child amazes his parents by inscribing a design on the floor, in the manner of medieval cathedral architects, with a large pair of compasses held in his right hand while in his left

356 On Blake and the occult, see Ackroyd, *passim*, and especially pp. 218-20, and, with some caution, Schuchard, 2006, who also documents the Moravian links of Blake's mother.

357 Schuchard, 2006, p. 144 & n. 7, p. 370.

358 Walsall New Gallery, 1973.004.GR, watercolour and ink on paper, 13½. x 12 ins. (34.5 x 31.5 cm). This is one of a series of Bible illustrations commissioned by Blake's friend and patron Thomas Butts. Eight others are in London's Tate Gallery.

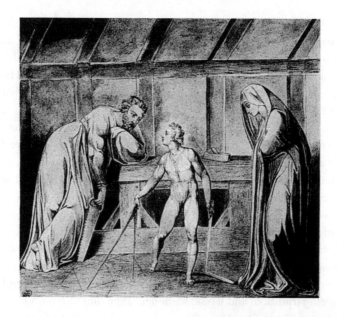

Fig 50. The Humility of the Saviour, William
Blake, c. 1803-05. Lower caption: 'And he
went down with them, and came to Nazareth,
and was subject unto them.' Garman Ryan
Collection, The New Art Gallery, Walsall,
with kind assistance and permission.

he supports a set-square. He is looking at Joseph, who is leaning on a
work-bench and holding a saw, at His rear right, while Mary stands
to His left, the design at her feet. Jesus appears to have the facial
features of Blake himself. He seems to be demonstrating to Joseph
the geometrical exercise of 'doubling the square', a fundamental of
medieval Gothic design, regarded as a mason's secret.

In some respects Blake's composition anticipates Millais, whose
Christ in the House of His Parents may have been inspired by it, but
the scene is intended to illustrate Luke 2:51, 'And He went down
with them, and came to Nazareth, and was subject unto them: but
His mother kept all these sayings in her heart.' This text comes at
the end of the story which tells how when Jesus was twelve years

old, His parents took him to Jerusalem for the Passover, as was their custom. In the homeward caravan, they discover He is missing, and return to look for Him. They find Him in the Temple, astonishing the doctors of the law with His precocity. When Mary chides Him, He replies tartly 'How is it that you sought me? Wist ye not that I must be about my Father's business?' In the picture, He still does not look particularly humble, and is, in fact, clearly demonstrating to Joseph the carpenter and builder how to design a building properly, just as He had set to rights the doctors of the law in the Temple. The Temple connection is subtly emphasised by the compasses and set-square, which are the primary Masonic symbols.

This picture is intriguing in view of the ancient tradition of Christ consecrating the wooden-framed, wattle and daub church at Glastonbury to His mother, which Blake could have known through Grose and the *Britannica curiosa*, and perhaps Spelman's 'conjectural' picture. It places a youthful Christ firmly within the Masonic temple-building tradition, and would seemingly align him also with Joseph of Arimathea as 'One of the Gothic Artists who Built the Cathedrals in what we call the Dark Ages' of the *c.* 1800 re-engraving of Blake's oldest picture, and dates from the same period or slightly later, contemporary with *And did those feet ...?*

Contemporary antiquarian speculations about Cornish tin being transported in Hiram's ships for the building of the Temple in Jerusalem, too, might have had a special appeal to Freemasons.

Blake's world, then, intersected with numerous circles in which he *might* have come across the Jesus voyage story, seemingly offering support to Jenner's inference when he wrote, in 1934, that 'William Blake ... seems to have known some form of it.' Is this a correct inference however? Blake's most memorable lines occur in a rather unexpected context, at the end of a short prose passage which forms the preface to *Milton, a Poem in 2 Books.*[359] Blake is attacking the influence of Classicism on poets, sculptors, painters and architects,

359 Mary Lynn Johnson writes that 'the prose half of the Preface harks back to Milton's polemical pamphlets,' Johnson, 2003, p. 237.

which he felt had tainted both Shakespeare and Milton:

> Rouze up, O Young Men of the New Age! ... We do not want either Greek or Roman Models if we are but just & true to our own Imaginations, those Worlds of Eternity in which we shall live for ever in Jesus our Lord.

And did those feet in ancient time
Walk upon England's mountains green?
And was the holy Lamb of God
On England's pleasant pastures seen?

And did the Countenance Divine
Shine forth upon our clouded hills?
And was Jerusalem builded here
Among these dark Satanic Mills?

Bring me my Bow of burning gold:
Bring me my Arrows of desire:
Bring me my Spear:O clouds unfold!
Bring me my Chariot of fire.

I will not cease from Mental Fight,
Nor shall my Sword sleep in my hand
Till we have built Jerusalem
In England's green & pleasant Land.

"Would to God that all the Lord's people were Prophets."
Numbers, xi. ch., 29 v. [K480-1]

'The concluding motto, also paraphrased by Milton in *Areopagitica*, reaffirms Moses' rebuke of Joshua's complaint about

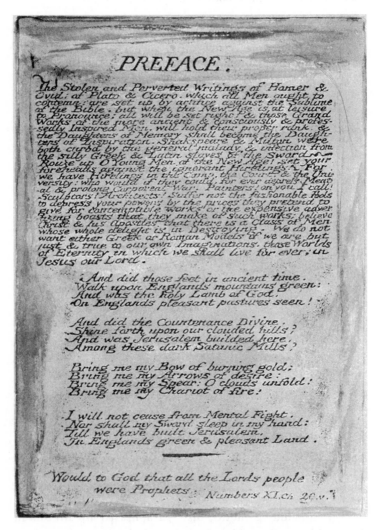

PREFACE.

the Stolen and Perverted Writings of Homer & Ovid; of Plato & Cicero. which all Men ought to contemn; are set up by artifice against the Sublime of the Bible; but when the New Age is at leisure to Pronounce; all will be set right & those Grand Works of the more ancient & consciously & professedly Inspired Men, will hold their proper rank, & the Daughters of Memory shall become the Daughters of Inspiration. Shakspeare & Milton were both curbd by the general malady & infection from the silly Greek & Latin slaves of the Sword. Rouze up O Young Men of the New Age! set your foreheads against the ignorant Hirelings. For we have Hirelings in the Camp, the Court & the University: who would if they could, for ever depress Mental & prolong Corporeal War. Painters! on you I call! Sculptors! Architects! Suffer not the fashionable Fools to depress your powers by the prices they pretend to give for contemptible works or the expensive advertizing boasts that they make of such works; believe Christ & his Apostles that there is a Class of Men whose whole delight is in Destroying. We do not want either Greek or Roman Models if we are but just & true to our own Imaginations. those Worlds of Eternity in which we shall live for ever; in Jesus our Lord.

And did those feet in ancient time.
Walk upon Englands mountains green:
And was the holy Lamb of God,
On Englands pleasant pastures seen!

And did the Countenance Divine,
Shine forth upon our clouded hills?
And was Jerusalem builded here,
Among these dark Satanic Mills?

Bring me my Bow of burning gold;
Bring me my Arrows of desire:
Bring me my Spear: O clouds unfold!
Bring me my Chariot of fire!

I will not cease from Mental Fight,
Nor shall my Sword sleep in my hand:
Till we have built Jerusalem,
In Englands green & pleasant Land.

Would to God that all the Lords people
were Prophets   Numbers XI.ch 29.v.

Fig 51. And did those feet... in its original context as plate 2 of Blake's engraved book Milton, copy c. 1808-9.

upstart prophets.'[360] The poet-prophet looks back to a Golden Age of unfettered inspiration and proclaims a 'New Age' in which it may return; the poem proper opens with an appeal to the 'Muses who inspire the Poet's Song', in echo of Milton's own invocation of the 'Heav'nly Muse' which opens *Paradise Lost*. In those first years of the nineteenth century, Blake steeped himself in the works, and the image, of Milton. It is far from obvious, however, why Blake felt these verse stanzas particularly appropriate here. Their closest parallels in language and imagery are, in fact, to be found in another poem on which he was working contemporaneously, entitled *Jerusalem*. The title pages of both are dated 1804, presumably when the plates were etched, but this is not the date of either works' completion. They were both etched over a considerable period, 1804-1808 for *Milton* and 1804-1820 for *Jerusalem*, of which Southey saw but a draft. It is likely, in fact, that *Milton* was begun between 1800 and 1803, while the Blake's rented a cottage at Felpham, Sussex. Ackroyd quotes from verse in a letter which Blake wrote at this time, 'With the bows of my Mind & the Arrows of Thought ... My arrows glow in their golden sheaves'. Wilson writes 'The greater part of the symbolic book *Milton* was also probably drafted at Felpham'.[361] It was at Felpham that Blake's world intersected with yet another circle in which he might have come across the voyage-story, or at least had his awareness of those Glastonbury traditions which lay behind it reinforced. This was the one period in which, singular personality as he was, Blake can be shown to have been directly influenced in significant ways by another individual, the poet, aesthete, and biographer of Milton and Cowper, William Hayley (1745-1820).

Ackroyd speculates that their paths may first have crossed thirty years earlier, when Blake was apprenticed at Basire's, and Hayley lived with his mother at 5 Great Queen Street, just yards away. In 1784 the sculptor John Flaxman sent Hayley a copy of Blake's *Poetical Sketches*. Although disregarded now, Hayley was a popular poet in

360 Johnson, 2003, p. 237.
361 Wilson, 1927/1971, p. 190.

his day, and even declined the Laureateship. Thomas Hayley (1780-1800), William Hayley's illegitimate and crippled son, a precocious sculptor, sought Blake's acquaintance as early as 1796 when he was living in London, and the Blake's resided at Lambeth.[362] Three years later, when Tom was dying, his father sought an engraver to make plates of two of his son's drawings and undertake a portrait of the youth for a memorial volume. Flaxman recommended Blake. The commission was still unfinished when Tom died on 2 May 1800, and Blake first visited Felpham in July. The decision was then made that Blake would rent a nearby cottage and work under Hayley's patronage. The Blakes moved in early September. It was at Felpham that Blake first saw the sea, and walking along its shore he fancied he saw the spirits of ancient poets and prophets as 'majestic shadows.'[363] At first, too, the Blakes found their country cottage enchanting, and Blake witnessed a fairy funeral in the garden.[364] Later, they were both to suffer from the damp.

Hayley himself had only moved to his 'marine hermitage' at Felpham from his old family home at Eartham earlier in 1800. He added a turret to the property to accommodate his study and voluminous library, in what was subsequently known as Turret House. One of Blake's first tasks for Hayley was to make painted medallions of the busts of Hayley's literary heroes in tempura to decorate its walls. Hayley liked to think of Blake as his secretary and Blake became his daily companion, with regular access to this library. Hayley liked to act as mentor for marginalised literary figures, including that other 'mad poet,' William Cowper, who had died but two weeks before his son Tom. Blake worked on illustrations for Hayley's *Life of Cowper* (published in 1803). He was well aware that, like Cowper, the world viewed him as mad. In a marginal note in a book on insanity, he later wrote 'Cowper came to me and said ..".. Can you not make me truly insane? .. You retain

362 Ackroyd, 1995, pp.2521-3.
363 Ackroyd, 1995, p.239.
364 Wilson, 1927/1971, p. 181.

health and yet are as mad as any of us all - over us all - mad as a refuge from unbelief - from Bacon, Newton and Locke."'[365]

In the Turret library, Hayley taught Blake Latin and Greek, and, discovering in middle life an aptitude for languages, Blake went on to study Hebrew, French and Italian. Hayley had been the first to translate Dante into English. It seem that the increasing prominence of Milton in Blake's thought at this time was also, in part, due to Hayley's influence.[366] He also believed himself Blake's teacher in the art of miniature painting, and Blake acknowledged the value of Hayley's example in the practicalities of publishing. Hayley liked to excerpt a controlling influence over his friends and *protégés*, and Blake seems to have filled Cowper's place for him for a time, and perhaps Tom's too, until he at length rebelled against Hayley's patronising and busy philanthropy. Although there was no dramatic quarrel, Blake and his wife returned to London, partly for reasons of her poor health, in the autumn of 1803. The influence of William Hayley upon Blake, and his own possible role in the voyage story, however, are matters to which we shall have occasion to return.

Both at Felpham and elsewhere Blake was recorded as 'composing or improvising' tunes for his lyrics, and singing them for the entertainment of his guests. One recalled him singing a 'devotional air'. Ackroyd writes 'It is interesting to consider Blake singing, then, in the study of Hayley's home in Felpham, And did those feet ... It is not necessarily a fanciful notion, either ... So the famous lyric now known as 'Jerusalem' might have been written at a little cottage by the Sussex shore.'[367]

What tune might Blake have employed for his lyric, if not some composition of his own? Some folk-air or a tune from the metrical Psalter so beloved of Nonconformists would be most likely. Given that Blake wrote it at the height of his Miltonic phase, it is worthy of remark that the words fit rather well to the tune *Old Hundredth*, supposedly

365 Wilson, 1927/1971, p. 156.
366 Ackroyd, 1995, pp.248-9.
367 Ackroyd, 1995, pp.235-8.

Is it again to plunge into deeper affliction? behold me Ready to obey, but pity thou my Shadow of Delight Enter my Cottage, comfort her, for she is sick with fatigue

Blakes Cottage at Felpham

Fig 52. *Blake's depiction of himself walking in his Felpham cottage garden and beholding Ololon, the 'Virgin of Providence.' Milton, copy c. 1808-9, plate 36.*

the battle-hymn of Cromwell's New Model Army. This certainly gives them a rather more martial tone than does Parry's familiar music, one not inappropriate to their setting in the Preface to *Milton*.

Blake scholars, unfamiliar, perhaps, with the true complexity of the Glastonbury *mythos*, have been rather more sympathetic to the view that Blake was influenced by some form of the voyage story than have the more sober historians of Glastonbury itself, despite the strictures of Beatrice Hamilton Thompson. Kathleen Raine, in her volume *William Blake*, 1970, in the accessible and influential Thames and Hudson *World of Art Library* series, wrote: 'Blake's interest in English history extended into legendary prehistory. Joseph of Arimathea is said to have brought Christianity to England, accompanied, some say, by Jesus himself. This legend could give credibility to the lines: "And did those feet in ancient time/Walk upon England's mountains green?"'³⁶⁸ Mona Wilson, in 1927, connected those same lines, from the 'beautiful quatrains' which 'have been set to music, and are sung at religious and social assemblies' with the 'the idea common among Celtic revivalists of his day that England was the birthplace of the "patriarchal religion" from which all later forms of religion were derived', which Blake 'appears to have adopted', implying an intended historicity.³⁶⁹ Others have seen the nexus more metaphysically. Blake's Introduction to *Songs of Experience* (1789-1794) begins:

> Hear the voice of the Bard!
> Who Present, Past, & Future sees;
> Whose ears have heard
> The Holy Word
> That walk'd among the ancient trees,
>
> [K210]

The American Northrop Frye wrote in 1957: 'England, along with America, is also the historic form of what in the imagination is the kingdom of Atlantis, which included both, but now lies under the "Sea of Time and Space" flooding the fallen mind. We begin at this point to see the connection between our present poem and the famous lyric ... As all imaginative places are the same place, Atlantis, Eden, and the Promised Land are the same place; hence when Christ walked in the Garden of Eden in the cool of the day he was also walking on the spiritual form of England's mountains green, among the "Druid" oaks.'³⁷⁰ Is the question of Blake's connection with the Jesus-voyage tradition, therefore, to be answered in simplistic terms of yes or no?

The defining characteristic of the Universal Church, and of its major surviving fragments, has been historicity. In its presentation of

---

368 Raine, 1970, p. 92, caption to colour plate 70, *Joseph of Arimathea preaching to the Inhabitants of Britain*.
369 Wilson, M., 1927/1971, p. 190.
370 Frye, 1957, pp. 26-27. In the conventions of Christian art, God. walking in the Garden of Eden as in *Genesis*, is usually depicted in the form of Christ.

itself, it was founded by God, incarnate as Jesus, and born of Mary on a specific, if imprecisely known, date, Who did or experienced certain things at certain times. Blake rejected the Roman and Anglican churches and the mainstream Nonconformist sects. His Christianity, or at any rate his mythology, is, by contrast, of a Gnostic character, and, like that Gnostic penumbra of the Church as it seeped into the pagan world in its first centuries, it deals with a dimension beyond space and time. Yeshu the Nazarine, who wrote in the dust of Palestine, felt the blows of the Roman *flagrum*, and, as the creeds remind us, 'was crucified under Pontius Pilate,' bears the same relation, we feel, to the Jesus of Blake's poetry (as opposed to some of his visual art) as does Arthur the Soldier of the *British History* to Albion, Universal Father and Patriarch of the Altlantic. It is not the Jesus of history of whom Blake writes.

Now there was at Glastonbury an 'esoteric tradition' which we sense, rather than see, which, like some water creature, just breaks the surface from time to time, but is never wholly visible, and is never explained.[371] We glimpse it mostly in the earlier texts. Although I do not suggest that Blake read him directly, 'B''s statement in the *Life* of Dunstan that the church of Glaston was built by no hand of man, but made in heaven for the salvation of mankind, is of a kind which comes very close to Blake's vision when he asked *and did those feet …?* Blake's second question, which has been little noticed in discussion, *and was Jerusalem builded here …?* resonates with the lines quoted by John of Glastonbury in 1342, *this was the New Jerusalem*. It is, at least, curious that Blake's rhetorical question *And did those feet …?* is answerable in terms of the tradition in John of Glastonbury of its consecration by Him 'in His own presence'. This might, perhaps, be nothing more than coincidence; but his second question, *and was Jerusalem builded here ..?* invokes in response a second Glastonbury *motiv*, that of the immanence of the New Jerusalem in *England's green and pleasant land*. To find not one, but two, Glastonbury themes

371 See Carley, 1981, who first uses the phrase.

within the eight short lines of the first two stanzas should give us pause. The whole 'lyric' might be read as a particularly thoughtful meditation upon the various lines of John of Glastonbury.

Blake did not wholly share the anti-monastic prejudices of most of his Protestant contemporaries. In the poem which begins 'I saw a monk of Charlemaine ..' (in the original draft, 'a monk of Constantine') at the end of his address 'To the Deists' [*Jerusalem* K683], Blake defends the Grey Monk from his Enlightenment critics, Gibbon and Voltaire. Hayley had visited Glastonbury in 1773,[372] and it might be pleasant to imagine Blake picking his way through the Latin of John of Glastonbury's opening chapters in Hearne's edition in the library-tower of Hayley beside the sea, but neither of Hearne's Glastonbury volumes appears in the extensive catalogue of the sale of Hayley's library following his death.[373] Even if Blake had come across them elsewhere, however, or had them expounded to him by Owen or some other antiquarian or druidic friend, it must be recognised that he does not himself take the argument any further than did John of Glastonbury. The crucial element of the sea-voyage is missing. It is not Jesus the Galileen child or working man, at home in the carpenter's shop or the fishing-boats of Gallilee, Whom we see in Blake's prophetic books. St Dunstan in his *Classbook*, in his famous drawing of himself at the feet of Jesus (*see illustration* p. 214), seems to picture the Christ of Judgement over Glastonbury Tor. Likewise at the climax of *Milton*, Blake writes that 'Jesus wept & walked forth From Felpham's Vale clothed in Clouds of blood' at the commencement of the general Resurrection and the Judgement. Blake takes up the themes, and the phrases, of his famous 'lyric' again and again in *Jerusalem*, where it is the cosmic Christ (the *Pantocrator* of Eastern Christianity, a term with which Blake was familiar), transcending space and time, whom we see specially linked

372 Bishop, 1951, p. 47.
373 Munby, 1971, vol. II, pp. 83-173.

to England, and to Albion, through Jerusalem as His spouse:

> ...Then Albion stood before Jesus in the Clouds
> Of Heaven, Fourfold among the Visions of God in Eternity.
> "Awake, Awake, Jerusalem! O lovely Emanation[374] of Albion,
> "Awake and overspred all Nations as in Ancient Time;
> "For lo! the Night of Death is past and the Eternal Day
> "Appears upon our Hills. Awake, Jerusalem, and come away!"
>
> So spake the Vision of Albion,
> & in him so spake in my hearing The Universal Father.
> Then Albion streach'd his hand into Infinitude
> And took his Bow. Fourfold the Vision;
> for bright beaming Urizen
> Lay'd his hand on the South
> & took a breathing Bow of carved Gold ...
>
> > [*Jerusalem* K744]

His four manifestations united as one, Albion, mankind's 'Universal Father', annihilates with his fourfold bow, and fiery arrows, the 'Druid Spectre' and 'Eternity is achieved in the mystical union of all things'[375]

Earlier in *Jerusalem*, Blake ends his address 'To the Christians' with the verses:

> England! awake! awake! awake!
> Jerusalem thy Sister calls!
> Why wilt thou sleep the sleep of death
> And close her from thy ancient walls? ...

---

374 An Emanation, for Blake, is the feminine portion of an individual or nation, separated off, sometimes problematically, in lower levels of existence, but re-united in Eternity (see Damon, 1965, pp. 120-2). The idea corresponds to the male-female, *shiva-shakti*, compassion-wisdom pairings of Indian and Tibetan tantric art, of which Blake was dimly aware.

375 Damon, 1965, p. 13.

> And now the time returns again:
> Our souls exult, & London's towers
> Receive the Lamb of God to dwell
> In England's green & pleasant bowers.
> [*Jerusalem* K718]

In 'To the Jews' Blake puts his vision most explicitly:

Jerusalem the Emanation of the Giant Albion! Can it be? Is it a Truth that the Learned have explored? Was Britain the Primitive Seat of the Patriarchal Religion? If it is true, my title-page is also True, that Jerusalem was and is the Emanation of the Giant Albion. It is True and cannot be controverted. Ye are united, O ye Inhabitants of Earth, in One Religion, the Religion of Jesus, the most Ancient, the Eternal & Everlasting Gospel. The Wicked will turn it to Wickedness, the Righteous to Righteousness. Amen! Huzza! Selah! "All things Begin & End in Albion's Ancient Druid Rocky Shore."

Your Ancestors derived their origin from Abraham, Heber, Shem and Noah, who were Druids, as the Druid Temples (which are the Patriarchal Pillars & Oak Groves) over the whole Earth witness to this day.

You have a tradition, that Man anciently contain'd in his mighty limbs all things in Heaven & Earth: this you received from the Druids.

"But now the Starry Heavens are fled from the mighty limbs of Albion."

Albion was the Parent of the Druids, & in his Chaotic State of Sleep, Satan & Adam & the whole World was Created by the Elohim.

> The fields from Islington to Marybone,
> To Primrose Hill and Saint John's Wood,
> Were builded over with pillars of gold,
> And there Jerusalem's pillars stood.

Her Little-ones ran on the fields,
The Lamb of God among them seen,
And fair Jerusalem his Bride,
Among the little meadows green. ...

She walks upon our meadows green,
The Lamb of God walks by her side,
And every English Child is seen
Children of Jesus and his Bride.
[*Jerusalem* K649-50]

What we do not find is any explicit reference to the Jesus voyage tradition. Although for many, including the present writer, Blake is a supreme Christian artist, his Christianity was of a highly unorthodox, not to say heretical, stamp. For instance, he did not credit the Virgin Birth, but regarded Joseph of Nazareth's acceptance of the pregnant Mary, in St Matthew's Gospel, as a supreme example of the forgiveness of sins. The image of Jesus as a ship-wright or miner, or as a weary, travel-stained, companion to the Arimathean, might well, we may think, have been especially congenial to him, and we might perhaps have expected him to have used it more explicitly in his art or the less 'prophetic' poetry had he himself known or credited it; but, as Peter Fisher noted in 1959, Blake 'made use of the materials of Celtic myth to communicate his own vision'.[376] The paths of his imagination seldom followed an expected or consistent course. Blake was a creative genius standing at the cross-roads where romantic antiquarianism, nascent Welsh nationalism, and social and political radicalism met with Nonconformity in its most gnostic aspects, Freemasonry, alchemy and the occult. This is precisely the kind of background from which we might envisage the Jesus voyage-tradition as emerging. We might also remember Peter Ackroyd's perceptive words concerning Blake and Joseph of Arimathea, quoted above,

376 Fisher, 1959, p. 162.

'that an entire culture of urban dissent and religious radicalism may be momentarily glimpsed in Blake's work,' and his invocation of the oral traditions of generations of Londoners which are now wholly lost to us.

On the present evidence it is not possible, therefore, to say with any assurance that Blake did *not* hear the 'tradition' in some form from the London Welsh, or from esoteric Freemasons, or from the sectarian artisans with whom he was in daily contact, and use it imaginatively, if subtly and partially, in his poetry. Alternatively, and this possibility does not seem to have been given much consideration, Blake's own poetic statements concerning the appearance of the Lamb of God in England may have been taken literally in just such circles, and in particular by some or other of his artisan associates. It should not be forgotten that as an engraver, his actual trade, Blake himself was a worker in metal, and a regular purchaser of metal sheets, his copper plates sometimes of 'the thickness of a half crown'. He wrote in 1809 that in forty years he had 'never suspended his Labours on Copper for a single Day.'[377] This is not very far removed from the world of the makers of tin organ-pipes in the north of London. Blake's poetic imaginings, blending with the Glastonbury *mythos* as known, at whatever remove, from the antiquaries and from popularisers like Grose and the *Britannica curiosa* (and familiar, in a general way, to Blake himself), and speculations rooted in the Old Testament concerning a Tyrian metal trade with Cornwall, might have developed an independent life of their own. The resulting 'craft tradition' could have survived among London metal-workers to be picked up by Jenner's friend's friend, James Baillie Hamilton, the inventor of the vocalion, less than seventy years after Blake's death. This may, perhaps, offer the best solution to the problem.

But could such an essentially London-based 'tradition' have filtered back to the West Country, to influence the lore of the miners of Priddy or Cornwall, which we seem to hear faintly echoed in Σ's

377 Ackroyd, 1995, p.34.

query in *SDNQ* in 1895 and in the memories of the Rev. Henry Lewis's elderly Cornish parishioners? Possibly. The idea that ordinary country people never went more than a few miles from the village of their birth before the dawn of the railway age is a fallacy. The exigencies of humdrum domestic service took many a village lad and lass between town and country in the perambulations of their betters. The fluctuations of their industry took the skills of the West-Country miners, which included ordinary tunnelling of all kinds, far and wide. Romany tinkers and horse-dealers were as at home on the fringes of the Metropolis as on the High Mendip or beside the Atlantic breakers.

Itinerant Nonconformist preachers too, and perhaps more especially those of the less conventional groups, may have played a larger role in our story than surviving records reveal, and it may be their voices we hear echoed in John Clark's *Avalonian Guide* of 1857. The Moravians, or United Brethren, that enigmatic, originally German, sect to whom, according to Marsha Schuchard's researches, Blake's mother had belonged, maintained their chapel in Fetter Lane until it was destroyed by a German bomb in 1941. They were by no means exclusive to London, however. In 1851 a low-church farmer named John Whitehead, from the village of Baltonsborough, near Glastonbury, came upon them while visiting Bath for his health, and was impressed. Already disgruntled with the Anglo-Catholic leanings of the local squire-vicar, he and some like-minded neighbours built a chapel on land opposite the 'Cob Cottage' that marked the traditional birthplace of St Dunstan, to whom the parish church is dedicated. Among the subscribers were the Austin family, one of whom went on to become the last private owner of Glastonbury Abbey. The Moravians were invited to provide a minister, and they maintained a congregation in Baltonsborough from 1852 until 1956, when the last service was held.[378] It may be supposed that by the 1850s the Brethren had abandoned the psycho-sexual practices documented of the 1740s by Schuchard, when the Swedish mystic Emanuel Swedenborg studied their techniques. A sect of not dissimilar leanings, however, established its *Agapamone* or 'Abode of Love' at Spaxton, near Bridgwater, in 1846. The New Church, founded by Swedenborg himself, had congregations in Bath and Taunton in 1851, when the Mormons were also represented in Bridgwater, Chard, Wincanton and Bath.[379]

The railways came to both Glastonbury and Wells in the 1850s, as England found itself a rather smaller place. There were various channels, then, by which ordinary folk could have come to hear of metropolitan 'traditions.' If any new information on the story is to emerge, indeed, it is just as likely to be by chance from the letters and diaries of the unlearned as from the leather-bound volumes of forgotten antiquaries. A hitherto little-regarded piece of the jigsaw-puzzle, however, did in fact come to light, within some manuscript pages written in a Georgian mad-house and preserved among just such dusty tomes in a Suffolk country-gentleman's library, as recently as 1938.

378 Clapp, 2000, pp. 80-86. As we have seen, from 1906-1916 the village also harboured an early congregation of Anglican nuns, their priest residing in 'The Beehive,' or 'Cob Cottage,' opposite the Moravian Chapel. The community was overseen by Dom Aelred Carlyle.
379 Dunning, 1975, pp. 86-89.

*Fig 53. Christopher Smart (1722-71) at Pembroke College,
Cambridge, c.1745, showing a letter from Alexander Pope.*

17

THE MADNESS OF KIT SMART

If Blake's actual referencing of the Glastonbury legends is open to question, the same is not true of a composition by a poet of the previous generation who was also considered quite mad by his contemporaries, but whose work has remained little known outside of literary circles. Christopher Smart (1722-71), in the remarkable manuscript entitled *Jubilate Agno*, 'Rejoice in the Lamb,' written between 1758 and 1763, makes the explicit statement that 'The Lord was at Glastonbury in the body and blessed the thorn,' adding for good measure that 'The Lord was at Bristol and blessed the waters there,' referring to the then-fashionable spa at the Hotwells. Here, then, would appear to be an obvious source for William Blake - were it not for the fact that the work was unpublished in Smart's own lifetime, the manuscript was lost, and it did not appear in print, in fact, until as late as 1939. As with Blake, also, it is far from certain whether it is an early - indeed the earliest - attestation of the voyage story, or an independent personal extension of well-known Glastonbury material by a poet of very special sensibility.

Smart was born, apparently premature and of a delicate constitution, at Shipbourne, Kent, on 11 April 1722. He had two older sisters. His father, Peter Smart, was himself of gentry background, and had moved to Kent from Durham to take over the stewardship of Fairlawn, an estate belonging to the aristocratic Vane family, whose principal seat was Raby Castle in County Durham. Earlier forebears included another Peter Smart, a prominent Puritan divine, prebendary of Durham Cathedral in the reign of Charles I and headmaster of Durham School, who was jailed for ten years for publishing 'a fierce

antiprelatical sermon' in 1628. 'Another ancestor through his father
was the sixteenth-century preacher Bernard Gilpin, the "Apostle of the
North," renowned on the opposite side for his steadfast adherence to
Catholic principles.' Peter Smart had himself originally been intended
for holy orders, and had a taste for literature, and possible esoteric
interests. 'If, as seems likely, this Peter Smart was the same one whose
signature appears on the translation of an important Rosicrucian
document dated 1714, Christopher Smart's interest in the supernatural
and occult may have begun early.'[380] He was to write in *Jubilate Agno*
(B2) 'For I am the Lord's builder and free and accepted MASON in
CHRIST JESUS.'

Christopher's mother was Winifred, *née* Griffiths, of a Radnorshire
family. He was proud of her Welsh blood, proclaiming in *Jubilate
Agno* 'For I am of the seed of the WELCH WOMAN and speak the
truth from my heart.' Peter Smart prospered sufficiently to purchase
a substantial property of his own, a mansion with farmland, called
Hall-Place in East Barming. Christopher remembered the Kentish
countryside of his earliest childhood with fondness in his later
poetry.

The young Christopher was evidently precocious in both literature
and love. At the age of four he wrote a short poem in which he
challenged a rival to the affections of a girl of twelve. He began his
education at Maidstone Grammar School. His father died in 1733
when he was eleven, and his mother, having sold of much of their
property to pay off debt, moved to live near relatives at Durham,
where he finished his schooling. He spent the holidays at Raby Castle,
where he formed a romantic attachment with Anne, the daughter of
Henry Vane, Earl of Darlington.

According to a story related by Smart's daughter, Elizabeth Le
Noir, in a letter to E. H. Barker (circa 1825), and corroborated by

---

380 Christopher Smart (1722 - 1771), internet essay on The Poetry Foundation
website, www.poetryfoundation.org/archive/poet/html?id=6348, by Karina Williamson, of St. Hilda's College, Oxford, and University of Edinburgh.

allusions in *Jubilate Agno*, he had a youthful love affair with the daughter of Lord Barnard, Anne Vane; she is said to have been the subject of an amorous poem that Smart claimed to have written at the age of thirteen: "To Ethelinda, on her doing my verses the honour of wearing them in her bosom"[381] Le Noir relates that "this very spirited ode had taken such effect that these young lovers had actually set off on a runaway match together; they were however timely prevented and saved." Whatever the truth of this colourful story, Smart never forgot Anne Vane, who is recalled by name or other reference with loving frequency in *Jubilate Agno*.[382]

It was her uncle and aunt, the Duke and Duchess of Cleveland, who sponsored his entry, aged seventeen, into Pembroke College, Cambridge, in 1739. He became a fellow in 1745.

He wrote both Latin and English verse, but also took to drinking and living the high life, and he was arrested for debt for the first time in 1747. In the same year he produced and acted in a farce of his own composition, *The Grateful Fair; or, A Trip to Cambridge*. The poet Thomas Gray, future author of *Elegy Written in a Country Churchyard* (1751) and poems on Norse and Celtic subjects, including *The Bard* (1759), then an undergraduate at Peterhouse, wrote an entertaining account of this production in a letter of March 1747 to William Mason, foretelling with impressively druidic accuracy that Smart's drunkenness, extravagance, and wild behaviour would inevitably lead him to jail or to Bedlam. While at Cambridge Smart embarked on his second love affair, an 'unsuccessful passion" for Harriote Pratt, the sister of a fellow student and daughter of a Norfolk landowner. He addressed several poems to her and remembered her with fondness in *Jubilate Agno*.

In 1749 he was granted a 'leave of absence' from college and moved to London, beginning a career as a professional writer, editing and supplying copy for literary magazines, including the *Student* (1750-

381 First published in *Poems on Several Occasions*, 1752.
382 Williamson, Karina, 2..., *op.cit.*.

1751), the *Midwife* (1750-1753), and other titles of the publisher John Newberry, who lived at Canonbury House, Islington. There Smart was 'a constant visitor,' and became acquainted with Newberry's step-daughter Anne Maria Carnan, 'Nancy,' who, like her mother, was a Roman Catholic. A romance developed and, apparently at St. Bride's Church, Fleet Street, in 1752, they entered into a 'clandestine marriage' without Newberry's consent. The marriage obliged Smart to give up his Pembroke fellowship. Newberry apparently soon forgave the couple, and Smart moved into Canonbury House. The marriage seems to have been happy at first, and a daughter, Marianne, was born in 1753, followed by a second, Elizabeth, in 1754.

In 1750 Smart had competed for the newly inaugurated 'Seatonian Prize,' offered annually for the best volume of poems by a Cambridge Master of Arts on 'one or other of the perfections or attributes of the Supreme Being.' He won with *On the Eternity of the Supreme Being*, and continued to win with succeeding annual volumes, *On the Immensity..*, *the Omniscience..*, *the Power..*, and *the Goodness..*

Fig 54. Sharpham Manor, near Glaston-bury, the birthplace in 1707 of Henry Fielding. Carved fragments from the Abbey are set over the door. A. E. Webb, 1929, p. 99.

of that exalted personage. He translated Horace into prose for the benefit of students in 1756.

Not all his work was so high-minded, however. He wrote songs and sketches for theatres and pleasure gardens; including 'a series of popular entertainments' called *Mrs. Midnight's Oratory*, sponsored by Newberry. These 'entertainments' were 'something between a music-hall show and a circus, with songs, recitations, dances, performing animals, and other acts. Smart himself is said to have taken the part of "Mrs. Midnight" on some occasions.' Mrs Mary Midnight was the transvestite comic character of an old woman, whose outspoken commentaries on the social scene would seem to have had something in common with those of that present-day creation of Mr Barry Humphries, Dame Edna Everidge. Some of Smart's lighter 'fables' were compared by contemporaries for their social observation to the work of John Gay (1685-1732), still famous for *The Beggar's Opera* (1728). Smart branched into satire with *The Hilliad* (1753) in which he attacked a literary enemy of himself and of Henry Fielding, with whom he had become acquainted.

Henry Fielding (1707-1754), writer and London magistrate, co-founder, with his half-brother, of the Bow Street Runners, had been born at Sharpham Manor near Glastonbury, scene of the arrest of the last abbot of Glastonbury, the Blessed Richard Whiting, by the agents of Thomas Cromwell in September 1539.[383]

Reminiscences of his childhood there underlie certain rural descriptions in his most famous novel, *Tom Jones* (1749), whose hero is adopted as a foundling by Squire Allworthy of 'Paradise Farm,' reflecting Glastonbury's 'Paradise' place-names as noted above. Fielding had been active in promoting the sale of Glastonbury Water in London during its brief vogue as a panacea in 1751. In the humorous

---

383 Fielding was born in the so-called 'Harlequin's Chamber,' a small room over the chapel, on St George's Day, 23 April, 1707. The old manor house, largely rebuilt in the 19th and 20th centuries as Sharpham Park Farm, was also the birthplace of the Elizabethan courtier and poet Sir Edward Dyer (1543-1607), a friend of Sir Philip Sidney. Dyer's most famous line, *My mind to me a kingdom is..*, might well apply to Smart.

The Midwife or The Old Woman's Magazine, however, edited by
Smart as Mary Midnight, appeared an item satirising the Glastonbury
claims and the type of testimonies produced in their support:

Some Account of a new Mill to Grind old People Young.
  It is strange that we are ever ready to believe all that is
incredible, and to doubt of everything that is demonstrable ...
In order therefore to satisfy the credulous I have inserted an
Account of some Miracles affected by a new Mill lately built
near Glastenbury [*sic*].
  The case of Mrs. Martha Sprigings. Whereas I (MS), was
violently afflicted with that inevitable Disease old age, I do declare
that I am perfectly cured by being ground in Mr. Whacum's Mill
near Glastenbury, and when a Year ago I was upwards of Ninety
Nine, I am at this present writing, not quite Eighteen Years Old.

Mrs Richard Fumble, '70 years and upwards,' testified that 'by
being ground in the Glastenbury Mill, I am perfectly recovered and
restored to Youth, insomuch that I am as much a Child as ever I was.'
Mrs William Capari, 'lately aged Eighty-three,' wrote that:

I am no more than twenty-five, being ground so down to that Age
precisely, in the Glastenbury Mill, which I sincerely recommend
to the old Women of all faculties.
  N.B. The Mill is adapted for Females only, so no Gentleman
who does not make it appear that he has been an old Woman,
can possibly be ground.[384]

The concluding caveat might be supposed to have left Smart, who
did on occasion make it appear that he was an old woman, still eligible
for the rejuvenating mill. He was soon, however, to find a different
path to re-birth. In 1756 Smart published his *Hymn to the Supreme*

384 *The Midwife*, London, 1751-3, published in book form (2: 172-4); see Reid,
2000, p. 5.

Being on Recovery from a Dangerous Fit of Illness. The illness seems to have been partly physical, a type of fever, but was accompanied by a classic conversion experience, and so was linked to the form taken by Smart's subsequent mental disorder. He wrote that Christ 'pitying did a second birth bestow.' Henceforward the poet vowed to consecrate all his acts and abilities to the glorification of God. Though linked thematically to the Seatonian poems, the *Hymn* abandons Miltonic blank verse for stanzas of regular metrical pattern and rhyme. 'The abandonment of blank verse also signalled a more radical shift from Miltonic to Hebraic conceptions of poetry.'[385]

Smart's recovery of health was short-lived, and in less than a year he plunged into apparent insanity. He was forcibly confined in St. Luke's Hospital for Lunatics on Windmill Hill in London, and, from 1759-63, in a private home for the insane in Bethnal Green. His illness manifested itself in a compulsion to engage in public prayer. Dr. Samuel Johnson wrote 'My poor friend Smart shewed the disturbance of his mind, by falling upon his knees, and saying his prayers in the street, or in any other unusual place. .. I did not think he ought to be shut up. His infirmities were not noxious to society. He insisted on people praying with him' and concluded with the quip 'and I'd as lief pray with Kit Smart as anyone else.' Smart himself wrote in *Jubilate Agno*: 'For I blessed God in St James's Park till I routed all the company. For the officers of the peace are at variance with me, and the watchman smites me with his staff.' His condition has been considered to be of a manic-depressive, or, as it would now be termed, a bi-polar, nature

Mad or not, his apparently attractive personality had won and retained him the friendship not only of Johnson, but of actor-manager David Garrick, who in 1759 gave a benefit performance of Voltaire's *Mérope* on his behalf, playwright Oliver Goldsmith, the musicologist Charles Burney, and eventually his daughter Fanny Burney (born 1752), the future pioneering female novelist. During

385 Williamson, Karina, 2..., .

his incarceration he was able to keep a cat, 'surpassing in beauty,' of which he was very fond, and to work in the garden. But his confinement coincided with a permanent estrangement from his wife, who moved with her two daughters to Dublin, where she opened a shop. She subsequently sent the daughters to a convent in France for a while. She returned after two years and settled in Reading, where she edited a newspaper, the *Reading Mercury*, for her stepfather, but seemingly made no attempt to visit her husband throughout the last ten years of his life. Religious differences may have come to the fore, for he makes slighting allusions to her Catholicism in *Jubilate Agno*. He also seems to have believed, apparently groundlessly, that she had cuckolded him. Fanny Burney, in her journal for 1769, quoted him as saying that 'he knew not if the horrid *old Cat* - as he once politely called his wife, be dead yet or not,' adding 'she had really used him uncommonly ill, even cruelly.'

His seven years of captivity, as he saw it, can, however, be seen in retrospect as his most brilliant and original literary period. He wrote *A Song to David*, in which he identified himself with the poet as prophet, and most, if not all of *A Translation of the Psalms of David* and *Hymns and Spiritual Songs for the Fasts and Festivals of the Church of England* (published together in 1765). He was released, apparently cured, in 1763, in which year *A Song to David*, his best-known poem before the twentieth century re-discovery of *Jubilate Agno*, was published, although his friend and fellow-poet William Mason, on reading it, concluded he was 'as mad as ever.' Others have found a 'sensuous brilliance' in it, and, although it accords little with modern taste, it was much admired by Browning and by Dante Gabriel Rossetti, who in an undated letter to T. Hall Caine, called it 'the only accomplished poem of the last century.' It was also during his confinement that he produced the lengthy manuscript of *Jubilate Agno*, whose surviving fragments, of more than seventeen hundred verses, represent only about a third of what he actually wrote. His release was followed with more poems and hymns. He wrote the libretto for an oratorio, *Hannah* (1764), with a score by John Worgan; a second oratorio, *Abimelech* (1768), was performed only once in his lifetime.

Sadness continued to dog his life, however, and he again fell into poverty and debt, for which he was again confined, in April 1770, this time in the Kings Bench prison. Once more, his imprisonment was not wholly onerous. He was allowed the freedom of St. George's Fields, an area around the prison with shops, public houses, and open ground for walking. His friend Charles Burney organised a small fund for him, from which he in turn would assist needy fellow prisoners, among whom he was popular. Fanny Burney wrote, in her *Memoirs of Dr. Burney* (1832), that he alternated between 'partial aberration of intellect, and bacchanalian forgetfulness of misfortune.' Here he wrote his final work, *Hymns for the Amusement of Children*, which has been compared to Blake's *Songs of Innocence* (1789); and here he died, after a short illness of the liver, on 20 May, 1771.

Smart's reputation with his contemporaries did not long outlast his death. Thomas Percy (1729-1811), whose landmark compilation *Reliques of Ancient English Poetry* had appeared in 1765, described him in a letter to Edmond Malone of 17 October 1786 as 'poor Smart the mad poet.' He fell into general neglect until the twentieth century, when still, as the *Cambridge Guide to English Literature* (1983) remarked, he 'remains, on the whole, a scholar's poet; in spite of his obvious gifts, his chosen subject keeps him at a distance from most general readers.'[386]

It is the sixteen surviving loose sheets, written on both sides, of his free-verse manuscript the *Jubilate Agno*, 'Rejoice in the Lamb,' unpublished in his lifetime, which now constitute his greatest claim to literary fame. Parts of it were set to music in Benjamin Britten's festival cantata, *Rejoice in the Lamb* (1943), and, among contemporary poets, it is said to have been admired by Allen Ginsberg and others. It has been described as 'Smart's "prophetic, book": a doxology, evangelical and philosophical manifesto, personal diary, and commonplace book all in one, as

386 Michael Stapleton, 1983, p. 816.

Fig 55. Smart caricatured by a contemporary as a Mad Poet, addicted to gambling: 'Nor Worth nor Honours this great Child regards, But whimpers still for horses, cocks and cards.' From Tommy Tagg's book, pub. by John Newbery.

Fig 56. A manuscript page from the Jubilate Agno, as discovered in 1938.

well as a remarkable experiment in poetic form.' It consists of two sets of pages. With but three exceptions, every line on one set begins with the word 'Let' and every line on the other set begins with the word 'For,' in a rough pattern of vesicle and response. The whole would seem to be inspired by the Matins canticles *Benedicte, omnia opera*, 'All ye Works of the Lord, bless ye the Lord,' and Psalm 100, *Jubilate Deo*, 'O Be joyful in the Lord ..,' and the Evensong canticle Psalm 98, *Cantate Domino*, 'O Sing unto the Lord..,' as found in the Anglican Book of Common Prayer. Smart himself referred to it as 'my Magnificat,' with reference to the Virgin Mary's song, also included as a part of Evensong in the Book of Common Prayer. It also accords with the principles of ancient Hebrew poetry as expounded in the ground-breaking work of Robert Lowth, *De Sacra Poesi Hebraeorum* (1753), a work with which Smart was familiar.

Jubilate Agno would seem to be an intensely personal celebration of the Creation, with a most extraordinary array of animal, vegetable, biblical and scientific references. Its existence only became generally known in 1938, when W. Force Stead published an article, 'A Christopher Smart Manuscript: Anticipations of "A Song to David," in *The Times Literary Supplement*, announcing that he was preparing it for publication. His edition appeared in 1939 under the title *Rejoice in the Lamb: A Song from Bedlam*, and many, indeed, would still consider it to be quite mad. Its perhaps most famous section begins 'For I will consider my cat Jeoffrey, For he is the servant of the Living God duly and daily serving him,' and continues for 70 lines.[387] This has been separately anthologised and is, as the *Wikipedia* article on Smart observes, 'popular among cat-lovers.' The madness of *Jubilate Agno*, however, as Stead himself recognised, is often merely superficial. Smart combines here the playfulness of an Edward Lear or a Lewis Carroll with occasional flashes of the mystic grandeur of a Blake. Stead wrote that he 'broke through the literary conventions which

387 In fragment B4.

had dwarfed him .. There are no rhymes and no iambic blank verse; yet the arrangement of the lines and their rhythm show that the composition is not intended as prose, and one should therefore take it as an eighteenth-century excursion in free verse.'[388]

The importance of *Jubilate Agno* for us lies in a section in Fragment B2 which has as an intermittent theme the evangelisation of Britain:

225 Let Apollos rejoice with Astacus, but St Paul is the Agent for England.
…[5 intervening stanzas]
231 Let Gaius rejoice with the Water-Tortoise - Paul & Tychicus were in England with Agricola my father.
232 Let Aristarchus rejoice with Cynoglossus - The Lord was at Glastonbury in the body and blessed the thorn.
233 Let Alexander rejoice with the Sea-Urchin - The Lord was at Bristol and blessed the waters there.
234 Let Sopater rejoice with Elacate - The waters of Bath were blessed by St Matthias.

Unfamiliar with the intricacies of Glastonbury legend, Smart's editors have experienced some puzzlement at these references. W. H. Bond, in his 1954 edition of the text, wrote in a footnote: 'St. Paul as the *Agent for England* remains unexplained; possibly Smart is thinking of St. Paul's Cathedral.'[389] Readers of these pages, however, will by now be familiar with Camden's reference, and with Stillingfleet's influential opinion of 1685, which is duly noted by Karina Williamson in her definitive edition of the *Jubilate Agno*.[390]

Apollos, an Alexandrian Jew, was a disciple of John the Baptist, whose teaching he was spreading in Asia Minor until he was converted to full-blown Christian belief at Ephesus by Aquilla and his wife

388 Stead, 1938.
389 Bond, W. H., 1954, p. 78, n. 1.
390 Williamson, 1980, p. 50, n. 225.

Priscilla, associates of St Paul (*Acts* 18:24-28). Leaving Ephesus, where Paul, arriving soon after, had to complete the imperfect Johanine teachings he had left there (*Acts* 19:1-7), he went on to preach at Corinth, where some, indeed wished to set him up as a rival to Paul (*I Cor.* 1:12, 3:4 *etc.*), although Paul retained confidence in him (*I Cor.* 16:12; *Titus* 3:13).

The Astacus, with whom Apollos is paired, is the Roman natural historian Pliny's name for a crayfish or crab.[391]

Gaius is the name of four minor characters in the New Testament, three of them linked to St Paul. The most significant is a Macedonian who, with fellow-Macedonian Aristarchus of Smart's next verse, was dragged into the amphitheatre at Ephesus by a hostile crowd during civil disturbances there occasioned by Paul's preaching (*Acts* 19:29). Aristarchus does not seem to have been too badly hurt, because after the riot he accompanied Paul into Macedonia and Asia Minor (*Acts* 20:1-4). He was subsequently a fellow-voyager of Paul's to Rome (*Acts* 29:2) and, as Paul himself records, his fellow-prisoner there (*Col.* 4:10). Paul calls him his fellow-labourer in his *Epistle to Philemon* (verse 24), also written from prison. As Paul's apocryphal mission to Spain and Britain was supposed to have occurred after his first Roman imprisonment, Aristarchus is a logical choice as a fellow-evangelist.[392] The Cynoglossus, with which Aristarchus was to rejoice, is glossed by Stead as '(literally dog-tongued) a plant, hound's tongue, in Pliny, a fish in Artedi, and Willughby [*sic*], *Hist. Pisc.*, p. 101 (where it = citharus, [of Smart's] line 8 above).' The Elecate of line 234 is likewise a fish, being used by Pliny of the tunny or tuna.[393]

Tychicus was another co-worker of St Paul, accompanying him into Macedonia along with Gaius, Aristarchus, and Sopater of Smart's line 234 (*Acts* 20:4). He was charged by Paul with carrying the apostle's *Epistle to the Ephesians* (6:21), and *Epistle to the*

---

391 Stead, 1939, p. 222.
392 This point is also made with regard to Tychicus by Williamson, 1980, p. 51.
393 Stead, 1939, p. 222.

Colossians (4:7), where he is called beloved brother, faithful minister and fellowservant in the Lord. Paul considered sending him as a messenger to Titus in Crete (*Titus* 3:12) and afterwards sent him back to Ephesus (*II Tim.* 6:12).

Alexander is not the Macedonian warrior-king but one of the four New Testament characters of that name, probably either the man present with Gaius and Aristarchus in the amphitheatre during the Ephesus disturbances (*Acts* 19:33), or the son of that Simon of Cyrene who had carried Christ's cross (*Mark* 15:21), if, indeed, for Smart they were not identical, for elsewhere in *Jubilate Agno* he identifies himself with Simon: 'Let CHRISTOPHER, who is Simon of Cyrene, rejoice with the Rough [*i.e.* the Ruff, a wadding bird]' (B2).

It is notable that Smart singles out in this section those of Paul's associates who were linked with the disturbances at Ephesus. There, on his third missionary journey, Paul taught for over two years in the city of the temple of the goddess Artemis (Roman Diana) which was accounted one of the Seven Wonders of the ancient world. Finding his living endangered by Paul's preaching, one Demetrius, a silversmith who made 'shrines for the goddess' as souvenirs for pilgrims, stirred up a riot to the chant of 'Great is Diana of the Ephesians,' in which the mob took over the city's amphitheatre. Paul wanted to go into the arena to address the crowd, but was prevented from doing so by well-wishers. After two hours, the rioters were eventually persuaded to disperse by the town clerk (*Acts* 19:24-41). It might seem here that Smart is not only identifying himself with Paul, who famously underwent a conversion experience and was beaten and imprisoned for preaching the gospel, but equating the Ephesian riot with the disturbance in St James's Park when he 'routed all the company,' the officers of the peace were at variance with him over his exhortations to prayer, and the watchman beat him with his staff.

Of Smart's assertion that 'Paul & Tychicus were in England with Agricola my father,' Stead comments: 'Smart had a variety of fathers, on a previous page (VIII) he claimed to be a 'son of Abraham' and on the same page referred to 'Thomas Becket my father.'[394] Karina Williamson adds that their journey 'could also have coincided with Agricola's first visit to England [*sic*] as a military tribune in AD 61.' Gnaeus Julius Agricola (AD 40-93) was father-in-law to the Roman historian Tacitus (who thus becomes a putative brother-in-law to Smart) who wrote a famous biography of him. He served as a military tribune on the staff of Suetonius Paulinus, governor of Britain AD 59-61, at the time of the revolt of Boudica during which he acquired invaluable military experience. After various postings on the continent, he sided with Vespasian in the Roman civil war, and was returned to Britain to command the Twentieth Legion, AD 70-73. With consular rank, he returned to Britain once more as her most celebrated Roman governor (AD 78-84). St Paul was traditionally supposed to have been martyred at Rome during the persecution of Nero which followed the Great Fire of Rome of AD 64, and, as noted by Camden, the British historian Gildas apparently synchronises the arrival of Christianity in Britain with the Boudican rising.

Thus far, therefore, we see nothing but, for contemporaries, reasonable conjecture based on the New Testament, Camden and Stillingfleet. With Smart's assertion that the waters of Bath were blessed by St Matthias, however, we seemingly enter the world of his own imagination. St Matthias's visit to Bath, Williamson writes, 'is Smart's invention, presumably based on the tradition that some of the apostles preached the gospel in England.'[395]

Smart certainly valued that 'tradition.' In his *Hymns and Spiritual Songs for the Feasts and Fasts of the Church of England*, 1765, in Hymn XXVII for St Simon and St Jude (28 October) he writes:

394 Stead, 1939, p. 222.
395 Williamson, 1980, p. 51, n. 224. She cites Robert Nelson, A Companion for the Festivals and Fasts of the Church of England, [1704, 16th ed., 1736] p. 137 [*recte* 96-7].

'Simon well may claim a place
In our book of Common Pray'r;
Here he likewise planted grace
By his apostolic care.

He his pilgrimage perform'd
Far as the Britannic coast,
And the ready converts swarm'd
To recieve the Holy Ghost.[396]

This is the Byzantine Greek ecclesiastical speculation that St Simon Zelotes had been crucified and buried in Britain, popularised in England from the sixteenth century in Foxe's 'Book of Martyrs'[397] as well as by Camden, Ussher, and other antiquaries. As Walsh and Williamson note, Samuel Johnson used it in his *Upon the Feast of St Simon and St Jude*, 1726. But while the legend of Simon the Zealot is attested and general, Smart's reference to Matthias is both specific and apparently unique.

The Greek form *Matthias* tends to be retained in English usage to distinguish the lesser-known figure who (in *Acts* 1:23-26) is chosen by lot after Pentecost to fill the vacant place of Judas among the Twelve Apostles from his namesake (in Greek) St Matthew the Evangelist (also called Levi), the former tax-collector, who had been called by Jesus Himself. The two were anciently sometimes confused. St Matthias is commemorated in the *Book of Common Prayer* on 24 February. Early writers have him preach in Ethiopia (as, likewise, Matthew the Evangelist), and a belief exited that the Empress Helena had brought his relics to Trier, but no other tradition connects him with western Europe.

An apocryphal *Acts of Andrew and Matthias*, of Egyptian origin, existed in Greek, Syriac and, according to M. R. James, 'in part in Latin,' and was rendered into Anglo-Saxon alliterative poetry as

396 Ll. 9-16, Walsh & Williamson, 1983, pp. 81-2; 418-19 (notes).
397 John Foxe, Acts and Monuments, 1570 ed. p. 66. The assertion is found in pseudo-Dorotheus, Nicephorus and the Greek Menologies for 10 May. Walsh & Williamson quote Nelson's version.

Andreas, preserved in the Vercelli Book (in which, however, *Matthias* is mistakenly identified with the Evangelist). Here the apostles divide the countries of the world between them, casting lots, and it falls to poor Matthias to evangelise in the land of the *anthropophagi*, the cannibals, in the city of Mermidona, where they eat no bread and drink no wine, but feed on the flesh of men, first drugging them to rob them of their wits and putting out their eyes. Matthias is blinded and put in prison, but the poisonous draft has no effect on him, and he continues to pray. A light appears, with a voice which announces the restoration of his sight, and promises that Andrew will rescue him. Three days before Matthias is due to be killed, the Lord tells Andrew to go to his aid. Andrew asks how he can get there in time, and is told to go to the shore next day where he will find a ship. He does so and finds a little boat with three men. The pilot is Jesus, and the other two are angels, all in disguise, and they convey Andrew and his followers to the shore of the cannibal's land. They fall asleep and are taken the rest of the way by the angels. On awakening, Andrew effects the rescue of Matthias and his fellow prisoners, dispatching them on a cloud with his disciples to 'the mount where Peter was teaching, and there they remained.'[398]

It is unclear where Smart might have found this story, which was not well known in the West, being omitted, for example, from the *Golden Legend*, and the Vercelli Book was not discovered until 1822. Had he done so, however, he might have identified with Matthias in his confinement, perhaps in the administration of unwanted medication, and in the restoration of spiritual blindness. A satirical turn of mind might have equated fashionable Bath with the city of the cannibals. Although Bath has no ancient church dedicated to either Matthias or Matthew, the cathedral of its episcopal twin, Wells (joint seat of the Bishops of Bath and Wells), is dedicated to St Andrew, as is the adjacent ancient spring, the 'wells' from which the town is named, rising in a pool in the Bishop's garden, whose

398 James, 1924, pp. 453-8.

waters then flow in a channel beside the High Street. The (implicit) twinning of the names Andrew and Matthias, and the two healing pools of Wells and Bath, would be consistent with the character of the *Jubilate Agno* and the watery themes of this section, and this may, in fact, be the simplest solution.

Smart refers to 'Christ the seaman' in his *Ode to Admiral Sir George Pocock*, and to Christ as helmsman in his Hymn XXVI on the Accession of King George III in *Hymns and Spiritual Songs*.[399] Tantalising as the image of Jesus as sailor is, however, Smart's knowledge of the legend remains pure speculation.

Old traditions did link St Matthew the Evangelist with Brittany. At the foot of the lighthouse at Pointe de St-Mathieu, in Finistère, one of the candidates for Brittany's Land's End, are the remains of a great abbey which stood until the Revolution. Supposedly founded in the sixth century, it claimed St Matthew's skull, which local sailors had journeyed all the way to Ethiopia to collect, until this was translated to Salerno in the tenth century. Godfrey of Viterbo in the twelfth century told a story, from a *History of Enoch and Elias* he claimed to have found at St Matthew's monastery, of a party of Galilean monks, disciples of St Matthew, who having converted Brittany and Spain, sailed west and encountered Enoch and Elijah on an island, returning to find three centuries had passed. 'We seem to have here,' wrote David Dumville, 'a Latin version of a local ecclesiastical legend which was itself an adaptation of an apocryphon to the story-types of Celtic literature.'[400] The Bretton tradition of St Matthew might perhaps have influenced Smart's thinking about Matthias, although his hymn for St Matthias' Day in *Hymns and Spiritual Songs* contains nothing of note.

Having examined the surrounding references, we may now turn to the central matter of Smart's statement of the Glastonbury tradition - 'The Lord was at Glastonbury in the body and blessed the thorn,' and his seemingly unique assertion that 'The Lord was

399 Walsh & Williamson, 1983, pp. 80; 418 (note).
400 Dumville, 1973, pp. 309-11.

at Bristol and blessed the waters there.' W. H. Bond, in 1954, was as puzzled by this as by the reference to St Paul: 'The *Glastonbury Thorn* was said to have been planted by Joseph of Arimathea. The references to Christ and Matthias in England .. remain unexplained.'[401] Karina Williamson, in 1980, managed rather better. 'The root of Smart's idea that Christ visited the west of England must be the legend recorded by William of Malmesbury that the church at Glastonbury was dedicated by Christ in person. Though discredited by Stillingfteet (*Origines Britannicae*, 1685), the story was still being quoted in Rapin's *History of England* (1725-31) which Smart read at Cambridge. *The thorn*: the Glastonbury thorn is supposed to bud on Christmas-day; cf. Hymn 32. 31—2.' It was the mission of Joseph which Stillingfteet 'discredited,' preferring the rival suggestion of St Paul, rather than mystic ideas of Christ at Glastonbury, and Rapin's history, translated from the French, hardly touches the matter. Although she does not allude to it, Williamson's comments seems influenced by recollections of the later voyage tradition.

The Thorn, which does indeed bud, and flower, at Christmas-tide, was referred to again by Smart in his description of mid-winter in *A Song to David* (1763), verse LXIII:

> The cheerful holly, pensive yew,
> And holy thorn, their trim renew;
> The squirrel hoards his nuts;
> All creatures batten o'er their stores,
> And careful nature all her doors
> For ADORATION shuts.

In Hymn XXXII for the Nativity in his *Hymns and Spiritual Songs for the Feasts and Fasts of the Church of England*, London,

401 Bond, W. H., 1954, p. 78, n. 5.

1765, he writes:

> Spinks and ouzles sing sublimely.
> 'We too have a Saviour born;'
> Whiter blossoms burst untimely
> On the blest Mosaic thorn.

Walsh and Williamson cite suggestions that 'the word "Mosaic" connects this image with another blossoming staff, the rod of Aaron, which burst into bloom in the tabernacle as a sign of the selection of the Levites to be priests (Numbers xvii),' and that Smart implies here that the English have become the chosen priesthood.[402] The link is explicit in the chapbook *The History of the Holy Disciple Joseph of Arimathea*, which includes a wood-cut of Joseph leaning on a staff beside a flowering tree, and tells that on arriving at Glastonbury and 'fixing his pilgrim's staff in the ground, it was no sooner set in the earth, but just like Aarons rod .. it was presently turned into a blossoming thorn.'[403] Smart may well have been inspired by this very pamphlet. In the context of the Nativity, we may perhaps think also of Joseph of Nazareth's staff, which flowered overnight in the Temple to announce his selection by God as a husband for the Virgin Mary in a formerly well-known apocryphal story. Smart's use of the Glastonbury traditions would seem, then, not to have been casual but rather deliberate and, for him, deeply symbolic.

Williamson makes no specific comments on Smart's reference to Christ at Bristol, the most surprising element among his assertions. Bristol's Hot Well discharges below the level of the River Avon, except at low tide for one and a half hours each day. The water emerges hot, at 76° F (25° C), effervescent, and 170 times more radio-active than ordinary tap-water.

---

402 Walsh & Williamson, 1983, pp. 88-89; 426-7 (note).
403 *Op. cit.* p. 7. Although the tree in the woodcut has both thorns and flowers, the leaves are not lobed like those of a hawthorn, but rather resemble apple leaves. See illustration p.234.

The known history of the spring goes back to the fifteenth century, and in the 1630s a John Bruckshaw obtained a licence from the Crown to 'take in' the Hot Well water, making baths for visitors. A glass-making industry developed in the city in part to facilitate the export of bottled Hot Well water. The Mayor of Clifton and the Society of Merchant Venturers bought the spring, and in 1677 the water was patronised by Queen Catherine of Braganza. In 1680 a diabetic Bristol baker named Gagg dreamed that he must drink Hot Well water, and was supposedly cured within days. This became widely known, and the episode may well have provided the model for the similar dream of Matthew Chancelor and the subsequent exploitation of the Chalice Well water at Glastonbury seventy years later. At Bristol the facilities continued to expand and an Assembly Rooms was opened in 1723. Rival springs were developed at Jacob's Wells and the New Hot Well, later known as St Vincent's Spring,

Fig 57. The Bristol Hotwells complex from the south bank of the Avon, as painted by Nicholas Pocock, 1791.

further up the Avon Gorge, which was patronised by John Wesley in 1754, although as a resort this did nor outlast the eighteenth century. The Hot Well spa would be used by Smart's young friend Fanny Burney as the setting for part of her first novel *Evelina, or The History of a Young Lady's Entrance into the World*, published in 1778, a social comedy which provided an inspiration for Jane Austen. The spa saw intermittent attempts at revival into the first decades of the twentieth century.[404]

While other sections feature birds and land animals, the entire 'B2' section of Smart's poem has an aquatic flavour, linking the praise of a whole array of biblical figures with those of various sea-creatures and fresh-water fishes. We read: 'Let Joseph of Arimathea rejoice with the Barbel - a good coffin and a tomb-stone without grudging!' The watery imagery is perhaps also particularly appropriate for those other transmarine apostolic missionaries, St Paul, who had famously survived shipwreck, and his companions. It continues with the focus on the eighteenth century's three most prominent therapeutic spas in the West of England, Bath, Bristol, and Glastonbury, for although the Glastonbury Waters are not mentioned explicitly by Smart, they may be assumed. As we have seen, Smart's friend Fielding had been marketing them in London, and the 'discovery' of their healing powers by Matthew Chancellor in 1751 had occasioned national celebrity, and a satirical response in Smart's *The Midwife*. Indeed, the 'Mosaic thorn' of *Hymns and Spiritual Songs* may also reference the rod with which Moses struck the rock to release a spring of water in the Sinai desert for the thirsty Israelites (*Ex* 17:1-7). The underlying theme is of 'living water,' with its millenarian echoes of the *Book of Revelation* (and, whether or not Smart read him, of 'Melkin's Prophecy' in the pages of John of Glastonbury). As Smart himself put it in fragment 'B2,' 'For the FOUNTAINS and SPRINGS are the life of the waters

404 Watson, 1991, pp. 60-77.

working up to God.'

The theme of Britain's blessing through water runs on into the staunchly patriotic and imperial strain in Smart's work, which echoes that of the famous lyric *Rule, Britannia!* from *Alfred, a Masque* (1740), co-written by James Thomson and David Mallet and set to music by Smart's London contemporary, Thomas Arne (1710-1778). This was first performed at Cliveden, country home of Frederick, Prince of Wales, on 1 August 1740, to commemorate the accession of George II and the birthday of Princess Augusta:

> When Britain first, at Heaven's command
> Arose from out the azure main;
> This was the charter of the land,
> And guardian angels sang this strain:
>
> 'Rule, Britannia! rule the waves:
> 'Britons never will be slaves.' *etc.*

This became well-known as an independent lyric from 1745, and in 1755 Mallet included a version, known as *Married To A Mermaid*, in his masque *Britannia* which he produced at Drury Lane Theatre, and which also became extremely popular.

In comparison it is worth quoting the whole of Smart's Hymn XXVI, from *Hymns and Spiritual Songs*, 1765, for the anniversary of the Accession of King George III (who came to the throne, at the age of 22, in 1760, the first Hanoverian monarch to rejoice in his Englishness):

> BY me, says Wisdom, monarchs reign,
> And princes right decree;
> The conduct of the land and main
> Is minister'd by me.

Where neither Philip's son[405] was sped,
  Nor Roman eagles flew,
The English standard rears its head,
  To storm and to subdue.

Our gallant fleets have won success,
  Christ Jesus at the helm,
And let us therefore kneel and bless
  The sovereign of the realm.

This day the youth began his race,
  With angels for allies,
And God shall give him strength and grace
  To claim the naval prize.

His righteous spirit he fatigu'd
  To speak the nation's peace;
Yet more and more the Papists leagu'd
  To mar the world's increase.

The Lord accept his good intent,
  And be his great defence,
And may his enemies repent
  At no prescrib'd expence.

As yet this isle the proof has stood,
  Which God from all disjoins;
O make him singularly good,
  And bless with fruit his loins.

His eastern, western bounds enlarge,
  Which swarms in vain contest,

405 Alexander the Great, son of Philip of Macedon.

> And keep the people of his charge
> In wealth and godly rest.

This remarkable lyric, whose entreaties look forward to *Land of Hope and Glory*, is to be understood in the light of the now largely forgotten Anglican millenarian expectations which accompanied Britain's emergence as a world power in the later seventeenth and early eighteenth centuries.[406] The radical millenarians of the Civil War and Commonwealth, Levellers, Fifth-Monarchy Men and others, had rejected the established episcopal church. Something of their sensibility, however, seems to have been taken up by the 'latitude-men' or latitudinarians within the Restoration church, influenced by the Cambridge Platonists Moore and Cudworth, who included the scientists Boyle and Newton, and Bishop Edward Stillingfleet (he who believed St Paul had brought the gospel to Britain). They advocated a moderate English Protestantism, such as might hope to embrace the maximum number of Dissenters, in which belief was underpinned by reason and natural science as they understood it. They differed from their Enlightenment successors in believing themselves to be uncovering the mechanisms by which God ordered the world and its affairs, in which the British were a new chosen people. 'History would end at the second coming, and the saints led by the English church would reign triumphantly in the millennial paradise.'[407]

The Glorious Revolution of 1688-9 presented a difficulty for Anglicans who had endorsed the divine right of kings and the duty of loyalty to the sovereign. These uncertainties were resolved by the belief that the Revolution, too, had been a step in God's plan for a Protestant victory in Europe, as witnessed, for instance, by the 'Protestant Wind' which landed the Prince of Orange at Brixham harbour, Devon, so appropriately on the fifth of November, 1688. In

---

406 This Anglican millenarianism is discussed by Jacob, 1976, especially in her chapter 3, pp. 100-142.
407 Jacob, 1976, p. 58.

1692 John Tillotson, William III's personal appointee as Archbishop of Canterbury, who had been a Presbyterian before the Restoration and had married a niece of Cromwell, could write of William and Mary in his private common-place book: 'I look at the King and Queen as two angels in human shape sent down to pluck a whole nation out of Sodom that we may not be destroyed.'[408] During the War of the Spanish Succession (1701-14), Protestant writers equated the French king, Louis XIV, with the Beast of *Revelation*. In 1704 the Bishop of Gloucester, Edward Fowler, celebrated Marlborough's great victory over the French forces at Blenheim as a prefiguration of the Second Coming. In the same year, William Lloyd, Bishop of Worcester, an advisor to Queen Anne, who had earlier discussed his expectations with Queen Mary II, predicted that the world would end in 1736. 'At which time Rome shall be burnt, the papacy destroyed, and Jerusalem rebuilt.'[409] This would be preceded by Britain's humiliation of that instrument of Catholic tyranny, the French Empire. These views were shared by that strange being, the mathematician, historian, and theologian William Whiston (1667-1752), like Tillotson sometime a scholar of Clare College, Cambridge, and Newton's successor as Lucasian Professor of Mathematics in that University. Ordained by Lloyd in 1693, he elevated the continental struggle 'to the status of a holy war.'[410] The work of Newton and Halley had led to an awareness (rather similar to that of today) of the possibility of collision with comets as a mechanism of global catastrophe. Whiston's *A New Theory of the Earth from its Original to the Consummation of All Things* (1696) suggested Noah's Flood had been caused by a comet. Whiston subsequently developed anti-trinitarian views which made him *persona non grata* in Cambridge. He lectured on his theology instead in the coffee-houses of London, Tunbridge Wells, and Bath, and eventually became a Baptist. His translation of the works of the ancient Jewish historian Josephus (1736), with copious scholarly

408 Jacob, 1976, p. 124.
409 Jacob, 1976, pp. 128; 255.
410 Jacob, 1976, p. 131.

notes, remained the standard edition until quite recently, being frequently reprinted. As we have seen, Josephus in his *Jewish Wars* (II, 8:11) wrote of the Essenes in connection with the Western Islands of the Blessed.

Smart's mature works were written against the background of the (also, now, rather forgotten) Seven Years' War (1756-63), in which Britain, allied with Protestant Prussia under Frederick the Great, again confronted the Catholic power, France, this time allied to Austria, Russia and, eventually, Spain, in a world-conflict which established a British naval supremacy which was to endure until the twentieth century. Clive's victory over the French at Plassy (1757) opened the door to Britain's eventual subjugation of the entire Indian sub-continent; in Canada, a British expedition took Quebec with great heroism and the death of the British commander, General Wolfe (13 September. 1759). Nearer home, in that same *annus mirabilis* of 1759, Anglo-Hanoverian troops crushed the French at Minden (1 August). The French had devised a fantastical plan to invade Britain which involved the union of their Mediterranean and Atlantic fleets off Brittany to conduct troops first to the west of Scotland as a distraction and then, sailing round the north of Britain, pick up their main forces from the Low Countries to invade the south-east of England. This cunning plan was shattered when the Toulon fleet was dispersed by Admiral Boscawen off the Portuguese coast in the Battle of Lagos (19 August, 1759). Then followed the decisive defeat by Admiral Hawke of the French Atlantic fleet in Quiberon Bay, Brittany (20-21 November, 1759). Great Britain was subsequently able to dictate peace-terms to the French in the Treaty of Paris, 1763, which confirmed her domination of North America and India.

It was not, therefore, his own mental disorder but an infectious wave of popular enthusiasm which prompted Smart, in *Jubilate Agno* (B382), to write in January 1760, the New Year following the *annus mirabilis*, that 'this is the twelfth day of the MILLENNIUM of the MILLENNIUM foretold by the prophets - give glory to God ONE THOUSAND SEVEN HUNDRED AND SIXTY.'

Christopher Reid quotes from the sermon of one Richard Price, delivered on the day of official thanksgiving for Quiberon Bay and the other victories (29 November 1759), that the 'season fixed by prophecy for the destruction of the man of sin [the Antichrist, generally identified with the Pope] cannot be far distant, and the glorious light of the latter days seems now to be dawning upon mankind from this happy Island,' and that the British are the Lord's 'peculiar and favourite people.'[411] For Smart, too, Britain is 'The land of God's selected sheep' (Hymn V for 30 January) and in *Jubilate Agno* (B2) he writes 'I am descended from the steward of the island - blessed be the name of the Lord Jesus king of England.' He declares 'For I bless God that the CHURCH of ENGLAND is one of the SEVEN[412] ev'n the candlestick of the Lord,' and prophesies 'For the ENGLISH TONGUE shall be the language of the WEST.' One of the more surprising discoveries of this study has been the way in which popular attitudes and myth-making during the Seven Years' War anticipate those which we have already examined surrounding the closing phases of the later World War of 1914-1918.

Smart maintained allegiance in the *Jubilate Agno* to the Old Style Julian calendar, which, according to Reid, was 'associated in Smart's work with a view of the origins of the English Church and with its appointed role as an instrument of the millennium.' It was also inseparably associated in the mid-eighteenth century with Glastonbury and its legends. The Julian calendar had been replaced in Britain, by act of Parliament of 1751, with its newer Gregorian rival, associated in the popular mind with Roman Catholicism.[413] September 1752 was declared to be a month of only nineteen days, the 2nd being followed directly by the 14th. This aroused widespread resentment at the government's 'theft' of eleven days, a disquiet which peaked in Christmas-tide 1752/3, the first major festival to follow the

411 Reid, 2000.
412 The reference is to 'the seven churches that are in Asia' to which *Revelation* is addressed.
413 The Gregorian calendar, instituted by Pope Gregory XIII in October 1582, with the loss of 10 days to rectify the gradual drift of Julian reckoning from the solar year, had been adopted by most of continental Europe.

reform. The Glastonbury Thorn, of which many cuttings had been planted up and down the country as a whimsical curiosity before the destruction of the original specimen by an iconoclast shortly before 1649, was regarded by the discontented as a natural (or divine) arbiter of calendrical correctness. In several parts of the country newspapers reported the vigil of large gatherings of people around Glastonbury Thorns to observe their behaviour at midnight on Christmas Eves Old and New Style, including at Glastonbury itself. The trees displayed a preference for the old reckoning, as they continue to do.[414]

Reid drew attention to the little-known 'Pilgrimage of John Jackson,' of Wakefield, Yorkshire, a stonecutter and clock-repairer who, although aged 71, set off on foot in November 1755 to observe the flowering of the Thorn at Glastonbury for himself, and recorded his travels in a journal.[415] His journey has been placed firmly in its Glastonbury context by Adam Stout in his brilliant and ground-breaking study, *The Thorn and the Waters: Miraculous Glastonbury in the Eighteenth Century* (2007), and Stout himself retraced Jackson's route on foot in the last weeks of 2008. Jackson represents and articulates a popular and rural resentment of the belittling of time-honoured social and calendrical custom by an urban intellectual elite, and he fully shares Smart's mystic nationalism. Smart's views seem to have evolved following his conversion experience of 1756. He seems to have been initially unconcerned by the change of the calendar, making light reference to it in the *Hilliad* of 1753. Despite Fielding's advocacy of the merits of Glastonbury Water, as we have seen, Smart, published an item in the *Midwife* unsupportive of the Glastonbury claims. In the *Jubilate Agno* and related poems, however, Smart adopts, as Blake was later to do, a stance critical of Newtonian scientific certainties and the whole 'enlightenment' agenda.

It is Smart's relationship to Blake which is a nexus of the present

---

414 One specimen, in a large garden directly below the Tor, has now developed the pagan habit of flowering for a third time, around Hallowe'en. On the history of the Thorn, see now, conveniently, Vickery, 1995, pp. 182-7 & refs..
415 Ed. Rev. Gerard Smith, 1874.

enquiry. While Smart's politics were royalist and imperialist, whereas
Blake's were radical, and sympathetic to the American and (initially
at least) French revolutions, neither doubted the elect status of Britain
herself. Blake's pictures of *The spiritual form of Nelson guiding
Leviathan* and *of Pitt guiding Behemoth*, included alongside *The
Ancient Britons* in the exhibition of 1809, are not simplistically
patriotic, although he wished he could execute them 'on a scale that is
suitable to the grandeur of the nation who is the parent of his heroes.'
They show the human admiral and politician from a perspective of
eternity as angelic figures fulfilling the prophecies of *Revelation*.[416]
'All things Begin & End in Albion's Ancient Druid Rocky Shore,' as
he elsewhere expressed it. Both shared an intense love of nature and
a sense of Christ's imminence in the natural world. Smart, subsequent
to his breakdown, shared with Blake a visionary sensibility intensified
by isolation and alienation from a world which could not share their
vision and therefore deemed them mad. It would not be entirely
surprising, therefore, if both came to react as poets in a similar way
to the Arimathean legends and to see them as a touchstone to their
own private vision of Christ as tangibly present in England's 'green
and pleasant land.'

We must ask, however, firstly whether Smart's statements
concerning Christ's presence in Britain are wholly the product of his
own eccentric imagination, or if he is, in fact, our oldest surviving
witness to specific traditions which existed outside of his own writing,
and, secondly, whether he himself could have been a direct influence
on Blake and his lines in *Milton*. Does Smart represent any kind of
missing link?

Unlike Blake, who, as we have seen, has no interest in Somerset
tradition as such, Smart specifically places Christ 'in the body' at
both Glastonbury and Bristol. Moreover, whereas Blake's family
connections to Somerset are illusory, Smart potentially had direct
access to Glastonbury oral tradition *via* Fielding, who grew up there

416 K 564-6; Bindman, 1977, pp. 160-1, 163-4. Both pictures are now at the
Tate.

and had both a personal and commercial stake in that tradition through the promotion of the Glastonbury Waters. The ailing Fielding revisited the town in the summer of 1751 to investigate the efficacy of its waters for himself.[417] The exact degree of Smart's intimacy with Fielding is uncertain, and he apparently remained sceptical about the Glastonbury claims until after the latter's death in 1754. However, the possibility cannot be excluded that he heard some early version of the voyage story, whether in earnest or in jest, from Fielding in the Bedford Coffee House, from whence Smart dated his *Hilliad* on 16 January 1753, and where the 'Shakespeare Club,' to which he belonged, held its meetings. The Bedford was a haunt of Fielding, as well as of David Garrick, William Hogarth and Thomas Arne.[418]

In such an early version, the Bristol Avon might have filled the role of Berrow Bay in the chapbooks, and Uphill on the Axe in the 1930s, as the putative landing-place of Arimathean Joseph, thus offering a 'rational' explanation for Smart's surprising localisation. We should be wary of such prosaic analysis, however. As with Blake, Smart's vision was a poetic one, and he could also write in *Jubilate Agno* that 'the Lord is the builder of the wall of CHINA -- REJOICE' (B1). John Jackson, in a lengthy digression in his journal in which he sets down with some erudition the antiquarian version of Glastonbury's foundation, gives no hint of having heard anything like the voyage story during his stay in 1755-6.

Any possibility of Smart's direct influence on Blake is likewise problematical. As we have seen, *Jubilate Agno* was unpublished in Smart's lifetime, and the manuscript remained unknown until 1938. However, as with Fielding and Glastonbury tradition, a potential personal link existed in the person of William Hayley, Blake's patron at the time *Milton* was begun. The story of William Stead's rediscovery of Smart's lost master-work is best told in his own words:

Colonel Carwardine Probert, a man of letters, a scholar, and an

417 Battestin, 1980, p. 204.
418 Sherbo, 1967, p. 107.

early member of the Keats-Shelley Memorial Association (of which for a few years I have been Secretary), invited me to visit him at his home in Suffolk to look over some of his inherited treasures. He showed me old stained glass from a ruined priory; ancient monastic deeds and charters; documents relating to the Elizabethan Earl of Oxford; letters from William Hayley, the friend and biographer of Cowper, written to Colonel Probert's great-grandfather, the Reverend Thomas Carwardine (who flourished from 1734 to 1824); family portraits by Romney whom this ancestor, along with Hayley, had taken out to Italy, and sketches by the great masters which they collected on their Italian tour one hundred and fifty years ago. But it was the sixteen folio pages closely written on both sides in the handwriting of Christopher Smart (the manuscript printed in the following pages) to which my attention kept returning. Colonel Probert is not sure how these papers came into the possession of his family, but he believes they were left with the Reverend Thomas Carwardine at Colne Priory by William Hayley, when these two friends were discussing what could be done for Cowper in one of his attacks of madness, the subject of much of their correspondence. Apparently they regarded this manuscript by the demented Smart as a fair specimen of the nature of poetic insanity, and therefore of some value when they were dealing with Cowper, who had been attacked by the same disease. Hayley, by the way, visited William Collins's sister to inquire into the case of Collins; he was also the friend and patron of Blake, and thus became acquainted with various examples (four in all) of mad poets.

Colonel Probert is the soul of courtesy and consideration, as becomes one who for many years was a courtier in the best meaning of the word. Being skilled in fine points of honour, he was at first a little troubled about the propriety of printing a manuscript, the manifest absurdities of which might expose the writer to ridicule. But poor Smart has been dead for a long time now, and everyone who knows anything about him knows that he was insane. I confess that I am amused, and that I see no reason why one should not be amused, when, after mentioning a fish named dentex, the poet hastily adds, 'Blessed be the name Jesus for my teeth'. But one's amusement is tempered by a consciousness that the poor fellow was suffering. Here is a fine intellect, a highly aspiring spirit, all crumpled up and wrecked by some weakness in the body or will. If the result in places is grotesque enough to provoke our laughter, yet the whole is far more of a tragedy than of a comedy, and when we survey the whole, our laughter will be subdued by sympathy and regret. That, I feel sure, is the way this strange work will be received.

Many will value it as supplying a bridge over the gulf between a splendid poem [A Song to David] and an unhappy author. No claim need be made for it as literature, except that there are several passages and a number of individual lines which should appeal to those who appreciate the romantic and mystical. Students of poetry will value its revelation of the vast accumulation of poetic resources which Smart had to draw upon when writing *A Song to David*.[419]

It would be easy to leap to the conclusion that Blake must have read the manuscript of *Jubilate Agno* in the Turret library of William Hayley, and been moved by it to include Smart's vision in his own *Milton*. Once again, however, matters are not so simple. Although it is admittedly plausible, there is no proof that the courtly Colonel Probert's speculation was correct, and that it was through Hayley that the manuscript came into his ancestral library, nor any indication of the exact date at which it might have done so. Nor is it clear how Hayley himself might have acquired this intensely personal and presumably precious product of Smart's pen. Hayley was 23 years Smart's junior and was still at Eton College during Smart's indisposition, when it was written, going up to Trinity Hall, Cambridge in the year of his release, 1763. He failed to secure a degree, and despite entering the

419 Stead, 1939, pp.14-16.

Middle Temple in 1766, he neither resided nor practised there. His attempt to launch a career as a playwright was equally unsuccessful, a tragedy he had written being rejected by David Garrick in 1771 (the year of Smart's death). Although he did live in London after he came down from Cambridge, his family home was at Eartham House, near Chichester, and in 1769 he married the daughter of the Dean of Chichester in the cathedral there. He moved back to Eartham in 1774. He was apparently not introduced to Romney until 1776, and did not meet Cowper until 1792. Cowper died in April 1800, the year in which Hayley moved to Felpham, and so, by Probert's logic, the pages from *Jubilate Agno* should have come into the Rev. Carwardine's possession between 1792 and early 1800, before Blake himself came to Felpham to reside near Hayley in September 1800. Hayley died in 1820, and his extensive library was auctioned off over 13 days in 1821. Rev. Thomas Carwardine himself lived, as we have seen, until 1824.

It is estimated that only about a third of the original manuscript of *Jubilate Agno* survives, and we have no idea what might have been in the missing portion, which, theoretically, Hayley might have retained for Blake to examine. Even without the manuscript, it may well be supposed that, had he known of them, Hayley would have found Smart's statements about Christ's presence in Britain sufficiently memorable to share them verbally with Blake with whom, as we have seen, he was in almost daily contact, and who showed him portions of the 'epic' which he was composing which may represent drafts of what became *Vala, or the Four Zoas*, *Milton* and *Jerusalem*.[420] Enticing as the Smart-Hayley-Blake hypothesis might seem, however, it remains too tentative and speculative to form the basis of any firm conclusions. It is safer to suppose that Smart and Blake, both viewing themselves as prophets in their generation, and both grounded in the same widely-held antiquarian Protestant assumptions and millenarian expectations, gave tangible form to Christ's special election of Britain

420 *Milton* is in part a fantasy dramatising Blake's difficulties with Hayley. Bindman, 1977, offers a helpful synopsis, pp. 172-176.

in similar poetic language. We must also recognise that Smart gives no more support to the voyage-story as such than does Blake.

We may be more assured of Smart's influence on that other 'mad poet' who became a *protégé* of Hayley, Cowper. His patriotic *Boadicea, an Ode*, beginning 'When the British warrior queen...,' was published in 1780 against the background (perhaps rather incongruously) of the American rebellion. It has clear affinity with Thomas Gray's *The Bard*, published in 1754, with the figure of 'the Druid, hoary chief' taking the place of Gray's bard.

Its most famous lines, however, echo Smart's lines in *Hymns and Spiritual Songs* of 1765 which we have already noted:

> Where neither Philip's son was sped,
> Nor Roman eagles flew,
> The English standard rears its head,
> To storm and to subdue.

Cowper's Druid assures Boudica, before her last fatal battle and seeming defeat, that:

> Regions Cæsar never knew
> Thy posterity shall sway;
> Where his eagles never flew,
> None invincible as they.

Both poems find their echo in Tennyson's *Boadicea* (1860), a favourite of the author's. When the sculptor Thomas Thornycroft's monumental bronze group of Boudica and her daughters, first begun at the suggestion of Prince Albert in the 1860s, was finally placed on the Thames Embankment beneath the tower of Big Ben in 1902 as a memorial to that other great queen whose name in Latin, *Victoria*, is the synonym of the British *Boudica*, on the plinth were - and are - set Cowper's words: 'Regions Cæsar never knew thy posterity shall sway.' The bronze casting, from the plaster-cast of the long-dead

Thornycroft, was undertaken in the Somerset town of Frome.[421] I do not know if the bronze contained British tin.

Whether or not Smart inspired Blake, could he have influenced the genesis of the voyage-story more directly? However the manuscript of *Jubilate Agno* eventually found its way to Suffolk, who else besides Hayley might have seen it? Obvious candidates are Charles and Fanny Burney, who looked after Smart's welfare in the last phase of his life. Might Fanny have chattered about Smart's strange notion of Christ at Bristol when working on *Evelina* (1778), with its Bristol Hotwells setting? Her vast written output gives the impression of a voluble and opinionated scatter-brain who doubtless greatly enjoyed the exchange of witty anecdote.

She visited Glastonbury on Friday 19 August 1791, recording in her diary that 'A chapel of Joseph of Arimathea has the outworks nearly entire, and I was quite bewitched by the antique beauty.' She was also impressed by the great ruin of the tower-arches, mistaking them for the West Front. It was clearly not an occasion for profound enquiry, however. 'What strange inventions and superstitions even the ruins of what had belonged to St Dunstan can yet engender! The Glastonbury thorn we forgot to ask for.'[422]

She had already addressed a Glastonbury-related theme in 1790, with her verse tragedy *Edwy and Elgiva*. Her father opposed her writing for the public theatre and this was the only one of some eight plays written by her which saw public performance, being produced at Drury Lane on 21 March, 1795. Unfortunately, it was not well received and closed after the first night's performance. The story concerned the young Saxon king Edwy, who came to the throne aged about sixteen in 956. Absenting himself from his coronation feast, he was discovered by Dunstan, the powerful abbot of Glastonbury,

421 By the firm of John Singer and Sons, who still trade in the town. They also cast 'Justice' for the Old Bailey, Trafalgar Square's Lions, and many other famous statues. Thornycroft had died in 1885.
422 *Diary and Letters* vol. V, 1789-1793 (ed. by her daughter), London, 1842, pp. 246-8. Marson, 1909, p. 78., gives the date incorrectly as April 1790.

who had been nominated by his Council to recall him, in bed with a woman, Athelgifu, and her daughter, Alfgifu - the 'Elgiva' of the play. Edwy subsequently married the daughter, and Dunstan was driven into exile for a time. Burney adopts the traditional Protestant hostility to Dunstan's memory, which cast him as a Popish schemer, making him the villain of her play. She wrote of Glastonbury in 1791: 'If this monastery was built by the famous old, cruel hypocrite Dunstan, I shall grieve so much taste was bestowed on such a wretch.' Marson comments 'Thus they learned history in Fanny's century!' After a period in France (she had married a Frenchman named d'Arblay in 1793), Fanny eventually settled in Somerset after 1815, at Bath, where she reached the age of 87, dying as late as 1840.

The chapbooks had already augmented medieval tradition by bringing Joseph of Arimathea to Wells, where a sighting of the Wandering Jew was to be reported early in the nineteenth century, one of the last in England. Priddy, where the voyage story was first noted in Somerset, lies but three miles to the west of the high-road which connected Bristol with Wells before running on to Glastonbury (the modern A39). Could the amusing story of the 'mad poet's' fancies have circulated among those who took the waters, moving between the spas of Bath, Bristol Hotwells and Glastonbury (which continued as a minor health-resort into the nineteenth century), to be picked up by some local parson or antiquary familiar with the finding of Roman lead ingots in the Mendips and who did a little 'rationalising' of his own? The apocryphal idea that Christ had bathed up to his hips in mud, and which the Rev. Charlie Bennett, vicar of Pilton, was sure related to Bath and was told originated in an Icelandic saga, might perhaps have begun in reality as an anecdote related of Bristol, for the drawback of the original Hotwell as a resort was that it rose from the mud below the high-water mark of the tidal river Avon. A role for Fanny Burney as an intermediary is yet another intriguing possibility, and there is scope for further investigation of the part which she and Smart may have played.

Fig 58. Allenby's entry into Jerusalem seen as a culmination of the Crusades, and juxtaposed with a painting of Crusaders with the reliquary of the True Cross, 1917.

18

IN ENGLAND'S GREEN AND PLEASANT LAND

In its heyday as a belief, the story of the visit of Jesus may be seen as a myth appropriate to Britain's era of complacency in the 1920s and 1930s. God Himself might not be an Englishman, but what more natural than that He should want His only begotten Son to have the opportunity to see the Motherland and perhaps, even, like the heir of some native ruler of the *Raj*, to spend a term or two at a British public school, run by the kindly and tolerant druids, and there acquire a grounding in those values which the Church of England and the British Empire would, in the fullness of time, share with the wider world?

The accession of Palestine, and the actual Holy Places of Christendom, to the Empire as a mandate, and the problems which they brought in their wake, led, as the initial euphoria began to wane, to a certain disillusionment. This was already evident in the reaction of some of the Somerset men who served with Allenby in 1917. Captain Boyle, M.C., of the West Somerset Yeomanry wrote:

> Permission was now obtainable for visits to JERUSALEM, and many of us took advantage of the opportunity. It is to be hoped that the town came up to their expectations or that they did not expect too much. Probably many now share the opinion that it is one of the many spots which are more magnificent in the imagination than in the reality. In reality it is for the most part, dirty, cramped, foul, undrained and unilluminated - a typical Eastern town, with a dirty and cosmopolitan population. There

is, too, so little that is convincing in the answers which are given to enquiries on the one subject to which one's thoughts naturally turn in connection with JERUSALEM. You may make your choice between the rival Calvaries and, according as you decide, the inscriptions on the walls of the Via Dolorosa are true or false. ... Many mysteries of the Bible story are explained by a visit to the Holy Land - the ease with which a man may take up his bed and walk - the lack of effort necessary to let a man down through the roof of a house - and the habit of living among tombs; the frequent recourse to stoning, too, admits of easy explanation, such a superabundance of the necessary missile being always at hand asking to be thrown.[423]

With a little imagination, however, a less inappropriate Holy Land could be discovered much nearer to home, one more suited, as Henry Lewis thought, to quiet contemplation. Alas! it is to be feared that the English Jerusalem has gone the way of its archetype. Captain Boyle might now find a weary familiarity in the sight of the shops piled high with assorted spiritual knickknacks, and the unwashed beggars and their dogs lurking in every High Street doorway, if not in the disconsolate huddles on back-street corners, awaiting the arrival of the heroin-dealer's boy on his bicycle. To our more cynical eyes, the reveries of Henry Lewis and Cyril Dobson now take on a somewhat comic tinge. One may imagine the anti-hero of the controversial 1978 'Monty Python' film *The Life of Brian* practising his messianic donkey-riding skills on Weston sands.

This was not, however, the atmosphere of the story in its earliest phase. It was not originally presented as a religious belief, for whose dubious historicity desperate arguments must be produced, but as an echo of a distant Celtic folklore. The argument now concerns the genuineness of that folk-tradition, and for that, it must be said, with the possible exception of the Breton legend of St Anne, itself

423 Boyle, n.d., pp. 128-129.

recorded late and uncertainly attested, there is but little evidence. I have suggested above that the story may, perhaps, have had a kind of pre-history in radical London dissenting circles influenced by Blake, or among the more genteel aficionados of the West of England's fashionable spas, who might have heard rumour of the madness of Kit Smart. These speculations, also, are lacking in evidence. The 'tradition' of the voyage of the boy Jesus with Joseph of Arimathea, therefore, apparently emerges fully formed in 1895 in the pages of *Black's Guide to the Duchy of Cornwall*, and in a hesitant note in *Somerset and Dorset Notes and Queries*. The first notice depended, as we have seen, on Henry Jenner, and the second partially so.

It remains to reconsider the role of Jenner. The possibility has been alluded to that the story might have begun as a kind of after-dinner joke which he took seriously. This fails to convince as an explanation because, as its enthusiasts between the wars pointed out, the story does indeed seem to fit remarkably well with the gaps of scripture and with Old Testament prophecy, with little-known Glastonbury texts and with Blake, perhaps with fragments of Cornish and Breton folklore, and with archaeology as understood at the time. It is startlingly audacious, and incapable of proof, and yet neither is it susceptible to refutation, being, in Jenner's version, free from the obvious absurdities into which Lionell Smithett Lewis, Henry Lewis and Cyril Dobson fell in their well-meaning attempts to improve upon it. It 'naturally fits together' perhaps a little *too* well to be the product of casual whimsy. Yet it cannot be 'true', either as historical fact, or as a genuine tradition of any very great antiquity, not because of its inherent implausibility, but because the preservation of such a deeply significant history or tradition would involve a chain of transmission throughout the centuries of which we, with all the resources of modern scholarship, simply find no trace, and which is wholly unlikely to have been more accessible to late-nineteenth-century London foremen.

An alternative explanation to that of light-hearted, jocular, invention is that the story as we have it has been carefully crafted by one with real scholarly ability in some very obscure and difficult fields, and with enough cunning not to identify all the ingredients from which it had been made, leaving the analogies to be gradually discovered by others; that it represents, in fact, a kind of scholarly hoax somewhat after the manner of the near-contemporary Piltdown Skull 'discovery' of 1912.[424] If this possibility is admitted, then the obvious suspect is Jenner himself. As George Hallam, the dinner-party host, was still alive when Jenner published his first account in 1916, in which he need not have mentioned that gentleman by name, we must assume that some anecdote concerning a visit to the organ-maker's by the inventive Mr. James Baillie Hamilton did, indeed, plant the seed, but this visit may have taken place as much as ten years earlier, and the original form of Hamilton's story is irrecoverable. The story as known is that of Jenner alone. Jenner was, as we have seen, an antiquary of 'encyclopaedic' mind, with the resources of the British Museum's library at his disposal, that rare creature in his day, a genuine Celtic scholar, fluent in Cornish and Breton, a collector of Cornish folk-tradition, familiar also with Gaelic lore, and sympathetic to Hebridean and Breton popular religion. His writings on the Civil War, and on the Jacobite cause, show that he was not a man to take a dispassionate view of history.

Jenner was also a liturgiologist, and his researches in this field made him familiar with aspects of Eastern Christianity, on which he published several articles. In 1919 he even contributed a translation of a hymn from the Coptic to the journal *Pax*, in which he had first given his version of the voyage-story. He would certainly have known of the considerable body of hagiography and folklore which surrounds the travels of the Holy Family and the Christ Child in Egypt, where

---

424 Although not exact, this parallel is none the less instructive. Here, personal vanity and scholarly ambition seem to have motivated the actual forger, Dawson; but his imposture was uncritically accepted by his colleague, Woodward, because the skull seemed to conform to the appearance then expected for a theoretical 'missing link.' Local patriotism, in this case for Sussex, played a part. So too, undoubtedly, in a climate of fast-deteriorating relations with Germany, did a desire to see an 'English' rival for the ancient 'Heidelberg Man,' discovered in 1907. See Walsh, 1996.

St Matthew's Gospel (2:13-20) records that they fled from Herod, quoting the prophet Hosea (11:1): 'Out of Egypt have I called my Son,' and which forms a compelling parallel to the voyage-story as it developed in Britain.

With his interest in the folk-religion and folklore of Brittany, Jenner was also likely to have read the first, French, edition of Anatole Le Braz's *Land of Pardons*, with its story of *Sainte Anne de la Palude*, which, perhaps very significantly, was published in 1894, just a year before Hope Moncrieff, on Jenner's information, published the first version in print of the voyage-story in the 16th edition of *Black's Guide to the Duchy of Cornwall* of 1895.

For Jenner did not himself immediately publish his 'discovery', but planted it instead with this editor of Cornwall's most popular tourist guide, and with Baring-Gould, the leading contemporary populariser of folklore, who, of course, could not resist putting such a gem to use in his own way. Only twenty years later, when the acclaim which greeted Parry's *Jerusalem* directed attention to Blake, did Jenner break cover to give the 'legend' a kind of pedigree. When the story took on renewed life at the hands of Smithett Lewis and in the popular press, far from backing off in embarrassment, as might a lesser man, Jenner reiterated his claim to it, and seems to have encouraged Henry Lewis in his 'quest.' Such scholar's hoaxes are not usually perpetrated for pure mischief or amusement but to underline some serious point in which their author genuinely believes. Jenner also had a motive. He was struggling, in the 1890s, to secure Cornwall's recognition, not as merely a backward English county, sparsely inhabited by smallholders, fishermen and rowdy miners, but as a genuine Celtic nation in its own right. Lady Wilde, W. B. Yeats, and many others, had popularised the notion of Ireland as a mystic land of timeless, other-worldly, enchantment. From 1894 William Sharp, a lowland Scot, began to give the same kind of literary prominence to Gaelic Scotland in his feminine 'alter ego' as the Highland writer 'Fionna Macleod', whose popular spiritual stories based themselves on traditions of the Isles of the kind to which Jenner was to refer in 1916. Little Celtic Cornwall could produce few popular writers, intellectuals and scholars to plead its cause - except for Jenner. His struggle was crowned with success in 1904, when at his instigation, and on a majority vote, Cornwall was accepted as a nation into the Pan-Celtic Congress.

In his paper read on that occasion, *Cornwall a Celtic Nation*, Jenner allows us an insight into his own religious musings in the years before he finally committed his soul to Rome:

> Not long ago I was talking to a Scottish minister of the name of Macgregor, who told me something that reminded me of the Cornish. He said that his clan until about a century ago had had a religion of their own. He could not tell me any details, for it was just out of reach. 'What sort of thing was it?' I asked. 'Were they Catholics or Protestants?' 'No,' he answered, 'they were neither Catholics nor Protestants. They were just Macgregors.' And we may say the same sort of thing of the Cornish. They are British subjects, no doubt, and loyal ones at that, but they are neither Englishmen, Welshmen, Irishmen, nor Scotsmen, they are just Cornishmen.[425]

A little later in his paper, he returned to the theme:

> As for Celtic characteristics, who can deny them to the Cornish? The imaginative temperament, the poetic mind, the superstitions, if you like to call them so, the religious fervour, the generosity of heart, the kindly hospitality, the passionate nature, the absolute honesty, the thirst for knowledge, the clan spirit, the homing instinct, all these are there. Like the Macgregors whom I have mentioned, the Celt may be a Catholic or a Protestant in the outward form of his religion, but below and beyond the outward form he is just a Celt, and the Wesleyanism of Cornwall and its offshoots, when you get below the surface and the mere outward

425 Jenner, 1905, p. 237.

expression, is nearer akin by far to that most beautiful of religions, Breton Catholicism, than the former is to English Protestantism or the latter to English Catholicism.[426]

His personal view of the relationship of parable to literal truth is perhaps illuminated by his conclusion to his paper on *The Legend of the Holy Cross in Cornwall* of 1918:

> The mental attitude of mediaeval people to legends such as this is not very easy to state. ... The ideas of the period regarding fact and fiction, history and romance, were perhaps different from ours, and in telling a story, edifying or otherwise, its literal truth was beside the question. ... They were useful to point a moral, or to illustrate a doctrine, and an allegory was true for its purpose. As for the unlearned and credulous, then, as now, they would believe anything, however fantastic.[427]

Is this, then, why Jenner went to such pains to popularise the Jesus-voyage story? Was it for him a ploy - an allegory if one likes - to help gain Cornwall's place, not so much in the sun, as in the Celtic Twilight? I hope that those who value Jenner's services to the cause of the Cornish language, and to Cornwall, and any surviving family, take no offence at the suggestion. I venture to believe that Henry Jenner himself might not. When, around 1933, Henry Lewis asked Jenner, at the end of his long life, where Blake might have got the legend, 'his reply was, "Where, indeed?"' May we believe that when he spoke those enigmatic words, there was a twinkle in his old eyes, and a faint smile playing about his lips?

So, at least, I had come to think as my researches appeared to be reaching a conclusion. Then, late in the day, I stumbled by accident upon something which suggested that Jenner's own assessment of his part in the story - 'I think, though I am not quite sure, that I am

426 Jenner, 1905, p. 238.
427 Jenner, 1918, p. 306.

answerable for the first publication in print of the curious legend' - may perhaps have been just a little inflated. I refer to the enigmatic letter of Σ. It is probably true that he wrote in response to the appearance of the 'legend' in *Black's Guide*. His concern, however, was not with Cornwall at all, but with the heartland of medieval and post-medieval Arimathean belief, Glastonbury - and, by a curious extension, with the mining region of the High Mendip. This fact, his passing allusion to a belief that 'the place where they sojourned near Glastonbury is called Paradise', and his variant form of the charm - 'Joseph was a tinman', suggest that the story might indeed have had a currency which did not depend entirely upon Jenner alone. Jenner was clear enough about *his* form of the charm to complain at Baring-Gould's suggested emendation; but Henry Lewis seemingly came upon Σ's version quite independently in the Cornwall of the 1930s. We do not hear of Paradise again until a similar date. It played no part in Jenner's version of the story, in which, although Jenner accepted that it was possibly 'a Cornish pendant' to the 'Glastonbury and Grail' stories, Glastonbury itself is quite marginalised. We are left, therefore, with traces, faint but not easily to be dismissed, of a popular or craft tradition which might be found towards the end of the nineteenth century in Somerset and London, perhaps also, although the evidence is later and less clear, in Cornwall. The final word on the mystery of its emergence, however, still remains to be written.

Fig 59. The original Holy Thorn in the Abbey's Wirrall deer park. Nineteenth century, provenance unknown.

BIBLIOGRAPHY

Abbreviations:

CSG Central Somerset Gazette

PSANHS Proceedings of the Somerset Archaeological and Natural History
Society

SDNQ Somerset & Dorset Notes & Queries.

Abrams, Lesley, & Carley, James P., (eds.), 1991, The Archaeology and History
of Glastonbury Abbey, Boydell, Woodbridge.

Ackroyd, Peter, 1995, Blake, London.

Anon., 1719, 1770 *etc.*, The History of that Holy Disciple Joseph of Arimathea
& varients (chapbook).

Anon., 1906, Butleigh Revel, (programme).

Anon., 1988, A Walk Though Pilton's Past, Pilton Village History Group.

Anon., n.d., 199., St. Just-in-Roseland Church - the Parish Church of St. Just and
St. Mawes, des. & print. Beric Tempest & Co., St. Ives, Cornwall.

Anon., 1775, Britannica curiosa: or a description.., &c..., London.

Dumville, David, 1973, Biblical Apocrypha and the Early Irish Church, in Proc.
Roy. Ir. Acad., Vol. 73, Sect. C, pp. 299-338.

Anson, P., 1958, Abbot Extraordinary, The Faith Press, London.

Ashe, Geoffrey, 1957, King Arthur's Avalon, The Story of Glastonbury, Collins,
London.

1971, Camelot and the Vision of Albion, Heineman, London.

1982, Avalonian Quest, 1982, Methuen, London.

Ashdown, P., 2003, Glastonbury and the Shroud of Christ, in *The Downside
Review*, no. 424, July 2003, Downside, Bath, pp. 171-196.

2004, King Lucius and the Evangelisation of Britain, in *The Glastonbury*

Review, Vol. xii, no.111, December 2004, pp. 94-100.

2005, How Old is Chalice Well?, in *The Glastonbury Review*, Vol. xii, no.112, July 2005, pp. 152-157.

2009, Some Coptic Parallels to Glastonbury Legend, in *The Glastonbury Review*, Vol. xiv, no.117, June 2009, pp. 79-117.

Baker, H. Kendra, 1930, Glastonbury Traditions Concerning Josepnh of Arimathea, Being a translation from the Latin .. of the second chapter of *Britannicarum Ecclesiarum Antiquitates* of James Usher, Archbishop of Ardmagh & Primate of All Ireland, published at Dublin, 1639, with the original footnotes, Covenant Publishing Co. Ltd, 6, Buckingham Gate, London.

Ball, T. Hopkinson, 2004, Alice Buckton, 1867-1944, A Brief Introduction, in *Glastonbury Past & Present*, Programe, Strode Theatre, Street, pp. 5-8.

2007, The Rediscovery of Glastonbury, Sutton, Stroud.

Baring-Gould, Sabine, 1897, Guavas the Tinner, Methuen, London.

1899 A Book of the West, an Introduction to Devon and Cornwall (2 vols, vol. i, Devon, vol. 2, Cornwall), Methuen, London.

Barrett, C.R.B., 1894, Somersetshire: Highways, Byways and Waterways, Bliss, Sands and Foster, London.

Battestin, M. C., 1980, Fielding and the Glastonbury Waters, in The Yearbook of English Studies, vol. 10, pp. 204-209.

Benham, Patrick, 1993, The Avalonians, Gothic Image Publications, Glastonbury.

Bennett, C.W., 191., Joseph of Arimathea as the Founder of Pilton Church, The History of "Our Race". Pilton Church Fund, Pilton.

Beresford Ellis, P., n.d. The Story of the Cornish Language, Tor Mark Press, Truro.

Biggs, C.R. Davey, 1933, Ictis and Avalon: Why Joseph of Arimathea Chose Glastonbury for his Home.

Bindman, David, 1977, Blake as an Artist, Phaidon, Oxford.

Birley, Anthony, 1979, The People of Roman Britain, Batsford, London.

Bishop, Morchard, 1951, Blake's Hayley, London.

Blake, William, *see Keynes, Geoffrey*.

Bond, F.B., 1918, The Gate of Remembrance, Blackwell, Oxford.

1919, The Hill of Vision, Constable, London.

1938, The Mystery of Glaston and her Immortal Traditions, Glastonbury Publications, 30, Homefield Rd., S.W.19, London

Bond, W.H., 1954, Christopher Smart, Jubilate Agno, re-edited from the original manuscript with an introduction and notes, London.

Boyle, Captn. R. C., n.d. (1920s), A Record of the West Somerset Yeomanry, 1914-

1919, London.

Braz, Anatole le, 1894, *Au Pays des Pardons*, (Eng. trans. as The Land of Pardons, by Frances M. Gostling, Methuen, London, 1906).

Buchedd Collen, in *Y Greal* 7, 1807, pp. 337-41.

Butlin, Martin, 1990, William Blake 1757-1827, Tate Gallery Collections Vol. 5, London.

Caine, Mary, 1969(?), The Glastonbury Giants, 2 vols., privately printed.
1977, The Glastonbury Giants or Zodiac, in Glastonbury, Ancient Avalon, New Jerusalem, edited by Anthony Roberts, Rider, London, pp. 32-62.
1978, The Glastonbury Zodiac, Grael Communications, Torquay.

Capt, E. Raymond, 1983, The Traditions of Glastonbury, Artisan Sales, California.

Carley, James P., 1981, Melkin the Bard and Esoteric Tradition at Glastonbury Abbey, in *Downside Review*, 99, pp. 1-17.

Carley, James P., ed., 1985, The Chronicle of Glastonbury Abbey; an edition, translation and study of John of Glastonbury's *Cronica sive Antiquitates Glastoniensis Ecclesie*, trans. by David Townsend, Boydell, Woodbridge.

Carpenter, Rhys, 1966, Beyond the Pillars of Hercules, The Classical World Seen Through the Eyes of its Discoverers, UK ed. Tandem, London, 1973.

Chambers, E. K., 1927, Sidgwick & Jackson, London (pbk. rep. 1966).

Chant, Arthur Guy, 1948, The Legend of Glastonbury, Epworth Press, London.

Clapp, Louise, 2000, Baltonsborough, the past Behind the Present, Baltonsborough.

Clark, John, 1848, The Avalonian Guide to the Town of Glastonbury and its Environs, 9th ed., Glastonbury & London.

Clements, Pauline, & Robertson, James, 1982, The Somerset Book, Nutshell Series, Clover Press, Brompton Regis, Somerset.

Cole, Norah, (n.d., *c*.1975), The Truth Before the World.

Cunliffe, Barry, 2001, Facing the Ocean: The Atlantic and its Peoples, 8000 BC-AD 1500, Oxford.

Damon, Foster S., 1965, A Blake Dictionary; The Ideas and Symbols of William Blake, orig, pub. Brown Univ. Press, rep. in UK with index, Thames & Hudson, London, 1979.

Day, Joan, 1973, Bristol Brass: The History of the Industry, Newton Abbot.

Dibble, Jeremy, 1992, C. Hubert H. Parry: His Life and Music, (2nd. ed. with corrections, 1998) Clarendon Press, Oxford.

Ditmas, Edith M. R., 1979, Traditions and Legends of Glastonbury, West Country

Folklore No. 14, Toucan Press, Guernsey.

Doble, Canon G.H., 1937, Saint Budoc, Cornish Saints Series, no. 3, (2nd ed.).

Dobson, Cyril Comyn, 1936, (April), Did Our Lord visit Britain as they say in Cornwall and Somerset?, Glastonbury (2nd. ed., rev., Sept. 1936;.3rd. ed., rev., 1938; 4th. ed., rev., 1940; 5th ed. rev., 1947; 6th ed., 'slightly' rev., 1949; 7th ed., rev., 1954, Covenant Pub., London).

1936 A Tradition Dear to Somerset and Cornish Hearts, in *Central Somerset Gazette*, 12 June, 1936.

n.d., 194., The Boyhood and Early Manhood of Jesus, Privately printed, Hastings.

Dumville, David, 1973, Biblical Apocrypha and the Early Irish Church, in Proc. Roy. Ir. Acad., Vol. 73, Sect. C, pp. 299-338.

Dunning, R., 1975, Christianity in Somerset, Somerset County Council, Taunton.

Dunstan, Victor, 1985, Did the Virgin Mary Live and Die in England?, Megiddo Press, Cardiff.

Elder, Isabel Hill, n.d., ?194., *Joseph of Arimathea, The Story of Glastonbury, Truth Never Dies* (all printed in Bangor, Co. Down).

Evans, Sebastian, 1898, The High History of the Holy Graal, Temple Classics, J.M. Dent, London.

Firth, Violet, 1934, Avalon of the Heart, F. Muller, London, (rep. as Fortune, Dion, Glastonbury: Avalon of the Heart, Aquarian Press, Wellingborough,1986).

Fisher, Peter F., 1959, Blake and the Druids, in *The Journal of English and Germanic Philology*, LVIII, pp. 589-612; rep. in Frye, Nortrhrop, ed., 1966, Blake: A Collection of Critical Essays, Prentice Hall, New Jersey, pp. 156-178.

Fowles (ed.), 1980, Monumenta Britannica, A Miscellany of British Antiquities by John Aubrey; annotated by Rodney Legg, (2 vols.) Toronto.

French, Peter, 1994, Younghusband, London.

Frye, Northrop, 1957, Blake's Introduction to Experience, *Huntingdon Library Quarterly*, XXI, pp. 57-67; rep. in Frye, Nortrhrop, ed., 1966, Blake: A Collection of Critical Essays, Prentice Hall, New Jersey, pp. 23-31.

Gray, H. St George, 1943, Glastonbury Water, *PSANHS*, lxxxix, pp. 54-58.

Graves, Charles L., 1926, Hubert Parry, His Life and Works, London.

Graves, Robert, 1958, The Glass Castle and the Grail, in Men and Books, *Time and Tide*, 11 January, 1958, pp. 45-46.

H., 1893, The Abbot of Glastonbury's Waterways, in *SDNQ*, Vol. III, Part xxiv, December1893, pp. 298-301.

Hamilton, James Baillie, 1883?, The new musical instrument, the vocalion, A. S. Mallett, London.

Harding, J. A., 1999, The Diocese of Clifton 1850-2000, A Celebratory History of Events & Personalities, Clifton Catholic Diocesan Trustees, Bristol.

Harris, P. R., 1998, A History of the British Museum Library, 1753-1973, London.

Hodge, F. Vere, 1991, Glastonbury Gleanings, The Canterbury Press, Norwich.

Horne, Ethelbert, 1922, Idylls of Mendip, Somerset Folk Press. 1924, St Joseph of Arimathea, A Legend of Glastonbury, in *The Somerset Yearbook*, 1924, pp. 93-95.

    1938, Somerset Folk.

    1948, West Country Folk.

Hunt, Robert, 1865, Popular Romances of the West of England, or, The Drolls, Traditions, and Superstitions of Old Cornwall, London.

Jacob, Margaret C., 1976, The Newtonians and the English Revolution 1689-1720, The Harvesster Press, Hassocks, Sussex.

James, M.R., 1924, The Apocryphal New Testament, Oxford.

Jenner, Henry, 1905, Cornwall a Celtic Nation, in *The Celtic Review*, Vol. 1, 1904-5, pp. 234-246.

    1916, St. Joseph of Arimathea as the Apostle of Britain, in *Pax*, The Journal of the Benedictines of Cladey Island, Summer, 1916, pp.125-141.

    1918, The Legend of the Holy Cross in Cornwall, in *Journal of the Royal Institution of Cornwall*, Vol.XX, parts 3&4, 1917-18, pp. 295-306.

    1919, A Hymn in the Bohairic Dialect of Lower Egypt, (trans.) in *Pax*, The Journal of the Benedictines of Cladey Island, Spring, 1916.

    1933, Was Christ in Cornwall? in *The Western Morning News*, 6 April, 1933, Plymouth, p. 6.

Johnson, Mary Lynn, 2003, *Milton* and its contexts, in The Cambridge Companion to William Blake, ed. Harris Eaves.

Jowett, George F., 1961, The Drama of the Lost Disciples, Covenant Pub. Co., London.

Keynes, Geoffrey, ed., 1966,1979, Blake, Complete Writings, Oxford Univ. Press, Oxford.

Lagorio, Valerie M., 1971, The Evolving Legend of St Joseph of Glastonbury, in *Speculum*, vol. xlvi, no. 2, April 1971, pp. 209-231.

    1975, Joseph of Arimathea: The Vita of a Grail Saint, in *Zeitschrift fur Romanische Philologie*, Band 91, Max Niemeyer Verlag, Tubingen, pp. 54-68.

Lawrence, Berta, 1973, Somerset Legends, David Charles, Newton Abbot, Devon.

Lewis, Glyn S., 2008, Did Jesus Come to Britain? Clairview Books, East Sussex.

Lewis, Henry Arden, 1934, The Child Christ at Llammana, a Legend of Looe and Talland. (2nd. ed. 1938).

    1936, "*Ab Antiquo*": The Story of Lammana (Looe Island), (rep. 1946).

    1939, Christ in Cornwall? Legends of St Just-in-Roseland and Other Parts,

J.H. Lake, Falmouth.

1946, Christ in Cornwall? And Glastonbury the Holy Land of Britain. (2nd. ed. of (1939), above; 3rd. ed. 1948).

Lewis, Lionel Smithett, 1922, St Joseph of Arimathea at Glastonbury or The Apostolic Church of Britain, A.R. Mowbray, London & Oxford. (2nd. ed., 1923; 3rd. ed., 1924; 4th ed., 1927; 5th ed., 1931; 6th ed. 1937; 7th ed., 1955, James Clark & Co., London.)

1925, Glastonbury, "The Mother of Saints."- Her Saints, A.D.37-1539, St Stephen's Press, Bristol. (2nd. ed., 1927, Mowbray, London & Oxford, rep. 1985, R.I.L.K.O., Thorson's Pub. Group, Wellingborough).

Lonely Planet: Britain, 1999, (3rd ed.), ed. B. Thomas, T. Smallman, P. Yale, Melbourne, London etc..

Marson, C.L., 1909, Glastonbury: The Historic Guide to the "English Jerusalem", Bath and London.

Maxwell, Donald, 1927, Unknown Somerset, John Lane, The Bodley Head, London.

Moncrieff, Ascot R. Hope, ed., 1895, Black's Guide to the Duchy of Cornwall, 16th ed., London.

Morgan, R. W., 1861, St Paul in Britain; or, The Origin of British as opposed to Papal Christianity, (quotations from 4th ed., Marshall Bros., London & Edinburgh, 1922).

Morris, Joseph Ernest., ed., 1927, Black's Guide to the Duchy of Cornwall, 25th ed., London.

Munby, A.N.L., 1971, Sales Catalogues of Eminent Persons, vol. II, Sotheby-Parke-Bernet, London.

O'Gorman, Richard, 1995, Robert de Boron, Joseph d'Arimathie, A Critical Edition of the Verse and Prose Versions, Toronto.

Padel, O.J., 1991, Glastonbury's Cornish Connections, in Abrams & Carley, 1991, pp.253-6.

Parsons, Kirsten, 1965, Reflections on Glastonbury, Covenant Pub. Co. Ltd. London.

Patten, R., 1977, Avon & Somerset Legends & Folklore, James Pike Ltd., St Ives, Cornwall.

Phelps, Rev. W., 1836, The History and Antiquities of Somersetshire.

Piggott, Stuart, 1968, The Druids, London.

Plot, Dr. Robert, 1677, The Natural History of Oxfordshire, being an essay towards the natural history of England, The Theatre, Oxford.

Powell, J.U., 1906, South Wilts. in Romano-British Times, in Wilts. Arch. Mag.,

Vol. XXXIV, 1905-6, pp.281-8.

Proceedings of the Musical Association, 1883, The Vocalion, in *Proc. of the Mus. Assoc.*, ix, (1882-3), Stanley Lucas, Weber & Co., London, pp. 59-69.

Raeburn, M., Voronikhina, L., & Nurnberg, A., eds, 1995, The Green Frog Service, Cracklegoose Press, London, in assoc. with the State Hermitage, St Petersburg.

Raine, Kathleen, 1970, William Blake, The World of Art Library, Thames & Hudson, London.

Reaney, P.H., 1960, The Origin of English Place-Names, (3rd. impr., rev., 1964), London.

Reid, Christopher, 2000, Sacramental time: John Jackson, Christopher Smart, and the reform of the calendar, in *Eighteenth Century, Theory and Interpretation*, September, vol. 41, i3, pp. 205-21.

Riddy, Felicity, 1991, Glastonbury, Joseph of Arimathea and the Grail in John Hardyng's Chronicle, in The Archaeology and History of Glastonbury Abbey, ed. L. Abrams & J. Carley, Boydell, Woodbridge, pp. 317-331.

Robinson, J. Armitage, 1921, Somerset Historical Essays, Oxford.

1923, The Times of St Dunstan, Ford Lectures, Oxford.

1926, Two Glastonbury Legends, Cambridge.

Σ, 1895, Glastonbury Tradition, in *SDNQ*, Vol. IV, Sherborne, 1895, ed. F. W. Weaver & C. H. Mayo, pp. 312-313.

Schuchard, Marsha Keith, 2006, Why Mrs Blake Cried, William Blake and the Sexual Basis of Spiritual Vision, Century, London.

Scott, John, ed., 1981, The Early History of Glastonbury, An Edition, Translation and Study of William of Malmesbury's *De Antiquitate Glastonie Ecclesie*, Boydell, Woodbridge.

Sherbo, Arthur, 1967, Christopher Smart: Scholar of the University, State University Press, Michigan.

Sherlock, Helen Travers, 1930, St Joseph and the Saintes-Maries, Sunset Essays, No. 5., Heffer & Sons Ltd, Cambridge.

Skeat, Walter W., (ed)., 1871, Joseph of Arimathie, EETS, London, (rep. 1996, Llanerch, Felinfach).

Smith, A.W., 1989, 'And Did those Feet …?': the 'Legend' of Christ's Visit to Britain, in *Folklore*, vol. 100:1, pp. 63-83.

Smith. Gerard (ed.), 1874, Diary of a Journey to Glastonbury Thorn, in *The Reliquary*, 1st series, Vol. 15, 1874, pp. 45-51, 73-80, 140-144, 201-206; Vol. 16, 1875, pp. 19-27.

Smith, Malcolm (ed.), 1977, The Triads of Britain compiled by Iolo Morganwg, trans. by W. Probert, with an int. & glossary by Malcolm Smith, Wildwood House, London.

Snell, F.J., 1926, King Arthur's Country, Dent & Sons.

Stead, William Force, 1938, A Christopher Smart Manuscript: Anticipations of 'A Song to David,' in *The Times Literary Supplement*, 5 March, 1938, p. 152. 1939, (ed.), Rejoice in the Lamb - A Song from Bedlam by Christopher Smart, with int. & notes, Cape, London.

Stephenson, Joseph, 1854, Malmesbury's History of the Kings, Seely's The Church Historians of England, London; rep. as William of Malmesbury (Vol. 1) The Kings Before the Norman Conquest, Llanerch, Felinfach, 1989.

Stevenson, W.H., (ed.), 1989, Blake: The Complete Poems (2nd. ed.), Longmans, London.

Stillingfleet, Edward, 1685, Orignes Brtannicae, or the Antiquities of the British Churches, London.

Stout, Adam, 2007, The Thorn and the Waters: Miraculous Glastonbury in the Eighteenth Century, Library of Avalon, Glastonbury.

Stubbs, W., ed. 1874, Memorials of St Dunstan, Rolls Series 63, London.

Swinburne, A.C., 1868, William Blake: A Critical Essay, London (rpt. NY, 1967).

Tara, Lord Brabazon of, 1963, Glastonbury: A Legend, Heineman, London.

Taylor, John W., 1906, The Coming of the Saints, Methuen, London.
1910, The Doorkeeper & Other Poems, with a Memoir by his Wife [Pauline], London.

Taylor, T.F., 1991, J. Armitage Robinson, James Clarke & Co., Cambridge.

Tennyson, Hallam, 1906, Alfred Lord Tennyson, A Memoir by his Son, 1897, one-volume ed. 1906, Macmillan, London.

Thomas, Alan, 1989, The Story of Priddy, Ina Rex Books, Wells.

Thompson, A. Hamilton, 1913, English Monasteries, Cambridge.

Thompson, Beatrice Hamilton, 1939, Glastonbury, Truth and Fiction, Mowbray, London & Oxford..

Thurston, Herbert, 1931, The English Legend of Joseph of Arimathea, in *The Month*, vol. clviii, July-Dec. 1931, no. 805, July, Longman Green, London.

Tongue, R.L., 1965, Somerset Folklore, County Folklore VIII, Folklore Soc., (rep. Llanerch, Felinfach, 1995).

Vickery, Roy, 1995, A Dictionary of Plant Lore, Oxford.

Walsh, John Evangelist, 1996, Unravelling Piltdown, Random House Inc., New York.

Warner, Richard, 1826, An History of the Abbey of Glaston; and of the Town of

Glastonbury, Richard Critwell, Bath.

Watkin, Aelred, 1973, The Story of Glastonbury, Catholic Truth Society, London.

Watson, Sally, 1991, Secret Underground Bristol, Bristol Junior Chamber, Bristol.

Webb, Albert E., 1929, Glastonbury Ynyswytryn (Isle of Avalon), Its Story from Celtic Days to the Twentieth Century, Avalon Press, 'at the Office of the "Central Somerset Gazette,"' Glastonbury.

Who's Who in Somerset?, 1934, No. 88, Ltd. ed., Wilson & Philips, Hereford.

Williams, Gwyn A., 1979, Madoc, The Legend of the Welsh Discovery of America, Oxford.

1994, Excalibur: The Search for Arthur.

Williams, H.V., n.d., 197., Cornwall's Old Mines, Tor Mark Press, Truro.

Williamson, Karina, 1980, ed., The Poetical Works of Christopher Smart, Vol. I, Jubilate Agno, Oxford.

Williamson, Karina, & Walsh, Marcus, eds., 1983, The Poetical Works of Christopher Smart, Vol. II, Religious Poetry 1763-1771, Oxford.

Williamson, Karina, 2..., Christopher Smart (1722 - 1771), (essay on The Poetry Foundation website, www.poetryfoundation.org/archive/poet/html?id=6348).

Wilson, Mona, 1927; 1971, The Life of William Blake (new ed. ed. G. Keynes, 1971).

Wilson, F. P.(revisor) , 1970, The Oxford Dictionary of English Proverbs, 3rd. ed., Oxford.

Wright, G.W., 1887, The Chalice Well, or Blood Spring, and its traditions, in Glastonbury Antiquarian Society Proceedings, 1886, Goodall, printer, Glastonbury, pp. 20-36.

Wood, Juliette, 2001, Nibbling Pilgrims and the Nanteos Cup: A Cardiganshire Legend, in Nanteos, A Welsh House and its Families, ed. Gerald Morgan, Gomer, Llandysul, pp 219-253.

Wood, Michael, 1999, In Search of England, Viking, Harmondsworth.

Yeats, W.B., ed., 1893, The Poems of William Blake, Muses' Library, London.

INDEX

336